CW01572404

Palgrave Studies in European Union Politics

Series Editors
Michelle Egan
American University
Washington, USA

Neill Nugent
Manchester Metropolitan University
Manchester, UK

William E. Paterson
Aston University
Birmingham, UK

Following on the sustained success of the acclaimed European Union Series, which essentially publishes research-based textbooks, Palgrave Studies in European Union Politics publishes cutting edge research-driven monographs. The remit of the series is broadly defined, both in terms of subject and academic discipline. All topics of significance concerning the nature and operation of the European Union potentially fall within the scope of the series. The series is multidisciplinary to reflect the growing importance of the EU as a political, economic and social phenomenon.

More information about this series at
http://www.palgrave.com/gp/series/14629

Pierre Georges Van Wolleghem

The EU's Policy on the Integration of Migrants

A Case of Soft-Europeanization?

Pierre Georges Van Wolleghem
Fondazione ISMU and University of Milan
Milan, Italy

Palgrave Studies in European Union Politics
ISBN 978-3-319-97681-5   ISBN 978-3-319-97682-2   (eBook)
https://doi.org/10.1007/978-3-319-97682-2

Library of Congress Control Number: 2018950498

© The Editor(s) (if applicable) and The Author(s) 2019
This work is subject to copyright. All rights are solely and exclusively licensed by the Publisher, whether the whole or part of the material is concerned, specifically the rights of translation, reprinting, reuse of illustrations, recitation, broadcasting, reproduction on microfilms or in any other physical way, and transmission or information storage and retrieval, electronic adaptation, computer software, or by similar or dissimilar methodology now known or hereafter developed.
The use of general descriptive names, registered names, trademarks, service marks, etc. in this publication does not imply, even in the absence of a specific statement, that such names are exempt from the relevant protective laws and regulations and therefore free for general use.
The publisher, the authors and the editors are safe to assume that the advice and information in this book are believed to be true and accurate at the date of publication. Neither the publisher nor the authors or the editors give a warranty, express or implied, with respect to the material contained herein or for any errors or omissions that may have been made. The publisher remains neutral with regard to jurisdictional claims in published maps and institutional affiliations.

Cover credit: Sami Sert/Getty Images

This Palgrave Macmillan imprint is published by the registered company Springer Nature Switzerland AG
The registered company address is: Gewerbestrasse 11, 6330 Cham, Switzerland

ACKNOWLEDGEMENTS

Writing a book is a long and lonely road, punctuated with decisive moments of sharing and discussion. I wish to thank all those who in one way or another have helped me with their invaluable input. I wish to thank particularly, Professor Fabio Franchino, University of Milan, for his precious advice and the time he spent reading my work or discussing it. Many thanks also to Professor Claudio Radaelli, University of Exeter, for everything he has done for me. I also wish to thank Professor. Jenny Phillimore, University of Birmingham, Professor Sabine Saurugger, Sciences Po Grenoble, Professor Federiga Bindi, University of Rome Tor Vergata, and Dr. Marcello Carammia, University of Malta and European Asylum Support Office, for their input. Finally, I must thank the Network for the Advancement of Social and Political Studies and Fondazione Cariplo for having funded three years of research. This book would never have been written without their support.

CONTENTS

ABBREVIATIONS

AFSJ	Area of Freedom, Security and Justice
AMIF	Asylum, Migration and Integration Fund
AMPI	Athens Migration Policy Initiative
AP	Annual Programme
CBPs	Common Basic Principles on Integration
CHES	Chapel Hill Expert Survey
CSOs	Civil Society Organisation(s)
DG	Directorate General
EIF	European Integration Fund
ESF	European Social Fund
EU	European Union
EU15	Designates the 15 member states before the 2004 enlargement
EU+12	Designates the 12 member states that joined between 2004 and 2007
EU27	Designates the EU without Croatia, with the United Kingdom
i.i.d.	Independent and identically distributed
JHA	Justice and Home Affairs
LOWESS	Locally Weighted Scatterplot Smoothing
MAP	Multi Annual Programme
ML	Maximum Likelihood
MPI	Migration Policy Institute
NCPI	National Contact Points on Integration
OECD	Organisation of Economic Cooperation and Development
OMC	Open Method of Coordination
QMV	Qualified Majority Voting
RAI	Regional Authority Index

REML	Residual Maximum Likelihood
SCIFA	Strategic Committee on Immigration Frontiers and Asylum
TEC	Treaty on the European Communities
TEU	Treaty on the European Union

LIST OF EU MEMBER STATES
AND ABBREVIATIONS

AT	Austria
BE	Belgium
BG	Bulgaria
CY	Cyprus
CZ	Czech Republic
DE	Germany
DK	Denmark
EE	Estonia
EL	Greece
ES	Spain
FI	Finland
FR	France
HU	Hungary
IE	Ireland
IT	Italy
LT	Lithuania
LU	Luxemburg
LV	Latvia
MT	Malta
NL	The Netherlands
PL	Poland
PT	Portugal
RO	Romania
SE	Sweden

SI   Slovenia
SK   Slovakia
UK   The United Kingdom

LIST OF FIGURES

LIST OF TABLES

CHAPTER 1

Introduction

Immigration is very fashionable in scholarship these days. Overcrowded reception centres, repeated tragedies in the Mediterranean Sea, populist parties in government and anti-immigrant marches across Europe, in addition to constant media coverage, have put the issue at the forefront of academic production. However, one element is frequently overlooked in political science: the policies for the integration of immigrants. Yet, integration is what (inexorably) comes next.

Immigration to European countries has drastically increased over the last decades. More than one million immigrants come to the European Union (EU) each year, more than to any other OECD country.[1] In an ageing Europe, migration presents indubitable positive economic effects. By feeding the workforce, it alleviates the old-age dependency ratio (the number of workers compared to that of pensioners) and the risks looming over the European population's ability to sustain its economy.[2] But immigration also poses considerable socio-economic challenges to receiving societies. Firstly because migrants' contribution to the EU labour market and its economy in general is by no means immediate. Coming from different cultural, linguistic and institutional backgrounds, migrants need to adapt to a reasonable extent to the pre-existing structures of

---

[1] For a comprehensive analysis on immigration to the EU as well as integration outcomes, see OECD (2016).

[2] So argues the EU Commission, see European Commission (2011), for more on this.

© The Author(s) 2019
P. G. Van Wolleghem, *The EU's Policy on the Integration of Migrants*, Palgrave Studies in European Union Politics, https://doi.org/10.1007/978-3-319-97682-2_1

their receiving societies. They need to acquire some command of the language, a basic understanding of how institutions work and, ideally, they also need to have their skills and qualifications recognised. As a matter of fact, language is often a barrier to employment and, at present, migrants are overrepresented amongst the unemployed and are often overqualified for their job. In addition, the increasing diversity within societies nurtures tensions between natives and new- (and old-) comers and thus threatens social cohesion.[3] Social cohesion may also be in peril due to unequal opportunities induced by the presence of foreigners less acquainted to the ways of doing things in their receiving society.[4] Therefore, if EU member states want to make the most of the potential migration holds, as constantly repeated in EU documents,[5] integration is a key issue.

Aware of the advantages of migration but conscious of the challenges it poses, EU member states seized the opportunity of the creation of an EU competence on immigration in 1999 to call for a "more vigorous integration policy" (European Council 1999). But integration, in 1999 as in 2018, is by no means a competence of the EU; it pertains to the dominion of the state. The first reference to it in EU primary law came with the treaty of Lisbon that accorded the EU a role, even though limited to supporting national initiatives and excluding by the same token any legal harmonisation in this respect.

Yet, from 1999 to 2018, an EU integration policy unfolded, uncovering a series of puzzles that can be summarised in a single question: can there be Europeanization without an EU competence, and therefore without binding acts? This is a question little addressed by EU scholars and one that this book shall aim to address. True, the integration of third country nationals, just like immigration, inevitably has transnational features justifying the Union's action in the policy realm. Failure to integrate may have adverse consequences for other member

---

[3] Many studies have looked into this issue, see TNS Qual+ (2011), for qualitative data within the EU.

[4] The challenges immigration poses are plentiful, they range from discrimination on the labour market to spatial and residential segregation, racism, etc. (see inter alia Castles et al. 2013). It is not my purpose to treat these challenges. I will therefore not go further on this point.

[5] Realising the potential of migration has been a recurring theme of the EU integration policy from 2003 onwards; see notably COM (2003) 336 final.

states and the EU as a whole. But was this sufficient to spur the creation of a common policy? As best summarised in the Conclusions of the Council in 2004, immigration is a permanent feature of European society from which member states may reap benefits if it is orderly and well managed. The effective management of immigration is in the interest of all member states and, in order to be effective, such management must ensure successful integration. Failure of an individual member state to develop and implement a successful integration policy likely has consequences on European economies and labour markets, on social cohesion and security.[6] Such a standpoint was already recognised by EU member states in the post-Amsterdam era, when they committed to addressing unequal treatment as a priority of the Community (see European Council 1999; see also Kostakopoulou 2002a). However, the objective existence of a common interest was by no means sufficient for the creation of an EU competence. Acknowledging the transnational nature of migration and the relevance of integration for the Union, member states and EU institutions started formal collaboration on the matter in an unprecedented manner. Beginning without even an adequate or explicit legal basis in the domain, collaboration transformed into a policy with potentially significant effects on member states and migrant integration.[7] If the Tampere Programme—the first programme ever adopted for the implementation of the Area of Freedom Security and Justice (AFSJ) further to the adoption of the Treaty of Amsterdam in 1999—announced the need for a more vigorous policy at EU level, no legal basis explicitly referred to integration until the adoption of the treaty of Lisbon. Even attempts to launch an Open Method of Coordination[8] (OMC) touching upon integration failed. And yet, the policy developed during the 2000s, as a patchwork of soft instruments forming a fragmented, yet consistent, policy. Putting together a common acceptation of integration, benchmarks, networks of high ranking officials and systematic funding opportunities, this ensemble of instruments formed a sort of "quasi-Open Method of Coordination"

[6] See Council of the European Union 14776/04 (2004); recitals 4–8.

[7] In its report produced by the European Court of Auditors, the latter recognised the positive effect of the policy on the integration of migrants; see European Court of Auditors (2012).

[8] See Chapter 2 for more on the OMC and its failed attempt at immigration-related matters.

(Carrera 2008). Despite the softness of the policy, or perhaps because of it, this ensemble has had hard-to-fathom impacts, so much as they may range from far-reaching to inexistent according to what we look at and how we look at it. For instance, the EU integration policy has had a non-negligible impact on Central and Eastern member states little acquainted with immigration at the time, even less so with integration of migrants. The advent of the European Integration Fund in 2007, because it provided funding opportunities, required that national programmes be drafted and implemented. It therefore had a tremendous effect as it induced the creation of a systematic integration policy at national level. Conversely, the elaboration of a common set of principles supposed to guide member states' policies, principles highly praised by civil society actors and scholars in the domain, has had no effect whatsoever on member states' policies (Mulcahy 2011).

The emergence of an EU integration policy highlights many legitimate and worthwhile research themes such as normative considerations as to the legitimacy of a role for the EU in this field, or sociological approaches to the process of integration from migrants' perspective, or else the impact of the policy on the actual integration of migrants. But the way the policy unfolded sheds considerable light on the EU integration policy as an (odd) instance of Europeanization. To put it differently, the emergence of an ad hoc competence in a highly sovereign policy field was unlikely, and the manner in which this policy made its way through is inevitably puzzling. Hence the question at the core of this research: can there be Europeanization in the absence of an EU competence?

Throughout this book, I consider that the way a policy field emerges at EU level affects the outputs adopted thereafter throughout the policy cycle. I thus propose an investigation into the development of the integration policy at EU level, how and why it unfolded in spite of the absence of a clear mandate, in order to explain the passage of a sensitive policy onto the EU agenda. The way the policy develops, I argue, has consequences on policy-making rules and patterns, and therefore on the outputs adopted thereafter. This, in turn, likely affects the contents, both procedural and substantive, and the implementation of EU outputs. Accordingly, I examine the most significant policy device adopted in this field, the European Integration Fund, throughout its policy cycle. The five chapters to come are guided by the question: is there

Europeanization of integration policies through soft law? The answer to this, without keeping you in suspense any longer, is: it depends.[9] That said, the question as I have posed it raises a series of other questions as to integration and Europeanization that the remainder of this introduction is aimed at answering. I thus provide a general frame intended to help the understanding of the five chapters that follow. Firstly, I draw the reader's attention to integration-related matters such as: Why integrate? Who is integrating? How to integrate? Who has the competence to integrate? And integrating into what? Secondly, I shift to the nexus integration-Europeanization. I propose a selective review of the existing literature on integration policies at EU level, followed by a specification of what is meant by soft-Europeanization and a refinement of this book's purposes. I then briefly introduce the methodology used and conclude the section with a plan of the book.

INTEGRATING MIGRANTS: WHY? WHO? HOW? BY WHOM? INTO WHAT?

Integrating Migrants: A Normative Imperative

There is little doubt nowadays that immigration has become a permanent feature of European societies. Recognised in political discourse,[10] it is confirmed by the figures, which show a steady increase in the 2000s (OECD 2016: 83), or by the projections for the decades to come (Lanzieri 2010). In 2008, 15% of the population in the European Union was foreign-born or had at least one foreign-born parent (Lanzieri 2010). Considering only non-EU-born migrants, the OECD estimates the share of foreigners to be 6% for the EU27 (8% in the EU15; 2% in the EU + 12) in 2010–2011 (OECD 2016).

In an ageing Europe, immigration helps alleviate the old-age dependency ratio (people aged 65 or above compared to those aged 15–64) and the risks looming over the European population's ability to sustain its economy (European Commission 2011). For several years, it has been the main driver of population growth in an ageing Europe (Lanzieri 2010). But the ageing Europe issue cannot be solved by immigration

---

[9]For an interesting approach to the "it depends" answer, see Tilly and Goodin (2011).

[10]See above; or see Council of the European Union 14776/04 (2004).

alone; as much as immigration cannot only serve as a way to sustain member states' labour markets and social policies. It is nowadays little debatable that migrants should be entitled to certain rights; even though it has not always been the case. From a normative standpoint, the idea of liberal democracy and denial of rights can hardly be reconciled. Exclusionist models of interpreting the role of foreigners are no longer sustainable.[11] As a matter of fact, the heyday of utilitarian immigration philosophies, such as that underlying the *Gastarbeiter* policy (or guest worker policy; see Chapter 3), is long gone. After World War II, many European democracies resorted to guest worker policies: importing a workforce for a period of time and expecting them to leave once the job was done. The idea behind the guest worker policy is best summarised by Walzer (1983: 58): "They can quit their jobs, buy train or airline tickets, and go home; they are citizens elsewhere". Whatever their working or living conditions were, the state had no duty towards them. As free men, they had made the choice to leave their countries and it was for them to decide whether to accept the conditions offered or leave. That said, fleeing poor economic conditions and leaving in hope of a better life is a legitimate goal that does not only rely on free will but also on the scarcity of resources at the world scale, and their unequal and random distribution at birth (Carens 2000; Shachar and Hirschl 2007). The premise of a choice holds true even less when the second and third generations of migrants live in the territory. Oftentimes, the only country they know is that to which their parents or grandparents immigrated.

From a liberal egalitarian perspective, maintaining unequal opportunities between natives and foreigners is hardly justifiable when the state grants a permits to stay within its territory (see inter alia Miller 2008). As EU member states recognized when they adopted the Tampere Programme in 1999. They declared:

> The European Union must ensure fair treatment of third country nationals who reside legally on the territory of its Member States. A more vigorous integration policy should aim at granting them rights and obligations comparable to those of EU citizens. It should also enhance non-discrimination in economic, social and cultural life and develop measures against racism and xenophobia. (European Council 1999)

---

[11] See inter alia Castles (1995), and Kostakopoulou (2002a), on this point.

Aiming for comparable rights between natives and foreigners is morally laudable. It however begs more questions than it answers. Who is it that EU member states should integrate? What does integrating foreigners mean? Into what should they be integrated? And who has the competence and capacity to do that? These questions shall be addressed in turn.

Who Is a Migrant in the EU? A Legal Definition

At the time of writing, the EU officially counts 28 members; unofficially 27. The United Kingdom (UK) recently held a referendum to leave the Union after a long campaign marked by hostility to immigration and immigrants. Such hostility, however, pointed at EU nationals and non-EU citizens indistinctly. Since the Maastricht treaty, there exists an EU citizenship, a citizenship subsidiary to that of the member states, which grants rights to EU citizens across EU member states, notably that of going and staying in another member state freely. Are EU-citizens migrants, as the Brexit campaign suggested?

At the time of writing, the EU is also undergoing a critical time as regards asylum and international protection policies. Political instability in Northern Africa (the Arab Spring) and the Middle East (the ongoing war in Syria) since the mid-2000s spurs thousands of people to leave their country of birth in search of protection or a better life, many of them hoping to enter the EU. Are asylum seekers and refugees migrants?

In common parlance, EU citizens living in a country they are not native of and international protection seekers surely are migrants. For the purpose of scientific research, this is debatable as who is considered a migrant differs according to who is speaking (Anderson and Blinder 2015). Integrating migrants implies a clear distinction be made between who is a migrant and who is not. This exercise necessarily occurs through the categorization of the "migrant" (Mügge and van der Haar 2016). Such categories are indeed constructs that do not necessarily reflect the objective needs for integration of specific groups.[12] They are potentially normatively loaded and may consequently create inequalities (Anderson and Blinder 2015). They are however crucial for policy formulation. For the purposes of an EU integration policy, a legal definition needs to be

---

[12] In fact, a Spanish worker in Germany may need German courses; or a member of the Roma community may need to attend integration practices in the country she or he is a citizen of.

found so that the policy has a clear target. The term "migrants" in this instance considers third country nationals legally resident in any of the EU member states. Such definition *de jure* excludes EU citizens from its scope; including them would be inconsistent with the idea of an effective European citizenship. It also excludes irregularly staying migrants; including them would be practically sensible but theoretically inconsistent with the principle of Rule of Law. Finally, such a definition also excludes asylum seekers and those who have been granted refugee status; they fall under a different category ruled by the EU asylum policy. I shall endorse the same definition.

In summary, to the question "who is it that should be integrated?", the appropriate answer for the purpose of this study is: (i) people who are not nationals of any EU member state; (ii) who hold a legal resident permit; and (iii) and such a residence permit is not a refugee status permit.[13] Over the pages that follow, I will indifferently refer to migrants, foreigners, third country nationals and so forth, without ever departing from this definition.

What Definition of Integration for the EU?

The concept of integration has been widely discussed in specialized literature, resulting in innumerable definitions. Generally, the concept refers to the way a migrant becomes part of a society (Castles et al. 2013). Becoming part of a society may, however, imply very different understandings of where the process should lead: removal or acceptance of differences? The term integration commonly ranges from the most assimilationist to the most multicultural acceptations.[14] In order to set the boundaries of the concept, let us define assimilation as a one-sided process of adaptation whereby migrants are to be incorporated into the host society (see inter alia Brubaker 2001). At the other end of the continuum, one can define multiculturalism as the acceptance and (sometimes) promotion of long-term cultural differences (Kymlicka 1995).

---

[13]The refugee status stems from the 1951 Geneva Convention. There exist other protection permits granted by member states that do not fall under the Geneva Convention. These are permits defined under national law and thus fall within the definition of migrant endorsed here.

[14]See Kostakopoulou (2002a), for a typology of models and their respective goals.

Beyond scholarly definitions, political systems tend to have different conceptions of integration, mirrored in their legal framework and policies.[15] Such conceptions are not fixed; they may change over time or across policies. Despite the fact that the EU has no legal competence on integration,[16] a similar logic is applicable to it through the policies it adopts.[17] In 2004, the EU was equipped with a more coherent, yet loose, framework, within which policies in this domain would be inserted. This framework is formed by the Common Basic Principles on Integration (CBPs), a set of 11 short-worded non-binding principles intended to guide policy-making (see Box 3.2 for a complete list). These CBPs echo the definition of integration advanced in the integration scholarship by Penninx (2013) who simply defines it as the process of becoming an accepted part of society. Such a definition places at the core of the process the interaction between two sorts of actors: the migrants themselves, and the receiving society (Penninx et al. 2014). In these terms, it precisely matches CBP 1, defining integration as "a dynamic, two-way process of mutual accommodation by all immigrants and residents of Member States". From this point on, integration refers to the latter acceptation.

Integration of Migrants into What?

Murphy (2009) raises a question (without, however, answering it) quite interesting in the case of an EU integration policy. Integrating migrants, yes, but integrating them into what? There are at least two ways to understand the question and consequently two ways to answer it: one belongs to the physical world whilst the other is more conceptual.

Reasoning at the physical world level, an EU integration policy would suggest migrants are to be integrated into an "EU society"; so to speak, and would therefore amount to considering the EU as an entity (or society) in its own right, independent of the member states. CBP 2,

---

[15] See, for instance Carrera (2006), Murphy (2009), Schain (2010), Castles et al. (2013), but see also Schain (2010), and Kundnani (2012) on how conceptions change over time.

[16] A role was eventually granted with the Treaty of Lisbon but the policy evolved without a legal basis, notably from 2002 to 2007 (date of the adoption of the European Integration Fund).

[17] Some interesting examples may be found in Kostakopoulou (2002a), Groenendijk (2004), Murphy (2009).

reading "integration implies respect for the basic values of the European Union",[18] would corroborate such an acceptation. Nonetheless, at least three factors prevent such understanding: (i) true, the EU is endowed with a basic set of values, shared by the member states, but this does not prevent individual member states from having their own, refined, system of values to which migrants must abide by to obtain a right to residence or citizenship[19]; (ii) in a similar fashion, the competence on integration remains mainly that of the member states, so that there cannot be integration into the EU without having, first, integration into the member state; and (iii) finally, and perhaps most importantly, there is no absolute and automatic right for third country nationals to move and stay in a member state that has not issued the residence permit in the first place. Entry remains a competence of the state; it must therefore agree to the residence of a third country national in its territory, regardless of the latter's lawful residence in another member state. If the Union is a (somewhat) unified area for EU citizens, it is not so for third country nationals, even when they hold a legal residence permit.[20]

The foregoing summarises the most obvious understanding of the integrating-into-what issue. The second way to interpret it is more conceptual (even though it is somewhat linked to the first approach) and requires distinguishing between three spheres of migration-related policies: entry, settlement, and citizenship.[21] Only one of these three is related to integration. Entry is indubitably connected to immigration policy: the member state (and not the EU) grants or refuses the right to enter the territory. The distinction is subtler when it comes to distinguishing settlement and citizenship. Settlement concerns the rights and obligations of those that have been granted a right to stay in the territory. By the granting of civil and social rights, the foreigner is integrated into the *physical community*. This situation corresponds to "denizenship", as coined by Hammar in the 1990s to describe the status of long-term residents (Hammar 1990). Policies in this respect are what are generally referred to as policy for the integration of third country

---

[18] See Box 3.2.

[19] The existence of national criteria to be fulfilled to be granted a legal residence permit bears witness to that.

[20] This is also the case for the long-term residence permit.

[21] This distinction between three spheres is largely shared in specialised literature. See notably Hammar 1990; Helbling 2013; Helbling et al. 2013; de Haas and Czaika 2013.

nationals in that they aim to ease the presence of the foreigner and her/ his interaction with the receiving society, but do not provide for her/ his integration into the *political community*, which falls under citizenship policies. Integration into the political community refers to political rights, to the right to participate in the collective definition of the future of a society.[22]

In definitive, 'integrating migrants' means integrating them into a community of rights and obligations, but not into a political community. This has consequences on the definition of the authorities that may undertake integration policies. Whereas the physical community may be governed by a series of policy making levels, the definition of the political community rests with the state alone.

Integration in a Multilevel System: Who Has Competence Over What?

From a number of perspectives, studying the EU policy for the integration of third country nationals necessarily emphasizes the role of the states: (i) historically, integration is strongly related to nationally specific models of identity and belonging (Castles et al. 2013; Scholten and Penninx 2016); (ii) member states, as the primary subject of EU law, vote EU law outputs and are legally responsible for their implementation within the frontiers of their territory (see Chapters 5 and 6); (iii) the EU has no formal competence on the matter so that integration at EU level is vested with the member states and displays intergovernmental features (see Chapter 3); (iv) when a stretched competence at EU level is found on immigration (until 2004; see Chapter 2) or integration (until 2010; see Chapters 3 and 4), any decision has to be taken by the unanimity of the member states; and (v) integration funding is mostly decided and coordinated at national level, and then reaches subnational bodies (Collett 2011). It is evident, therefore, that the interaction between the EU and its member states is the driver of policy development at EU level.

Integration is nevertheless a policy field counting a variety of actors located at different levels of policy making. Since I am concerned with policy making, I disregard private organisations and focus on policy making actors, namely cities and regions (Penninx 2009; Penninx et al. 2014).

---

[22] See Van Wolleghem (2014), for a discussion.

Firstly, cities have been primary policy actors since at least the 1990s if one considers the wealth of research in this domain at the time (Penninx et al. 2014). At the forefront of the daily challenges of integration, the city is where migrants work, send their children to school, access services and so forth. The role cities play is constantly expanding. The most diverse cities such as London, Berlin, Barcelona and Rotterdam are now developing their own philosophy of integration, sometimes departing from national philosophies, thereby generating a decoupling of the two levels (Scholten and Penninx 2016). Poppelaars and Scholten (2008) showed that, in the Netherlands, the national level and the local level are "two worlds apart" when it comes to integration policies. Whereas the issue is politicized at the national level, it appears to be more of a pragmatic, problem-solving approach at the local level (see also Keating 2009).

Secondly, regional authorities may also have a say in the matter, if not the exclusive competence of integrating foreign citizens. For instance, Italian *Regioni*, German *Länder*, Spanish *Comunidades Autonomas* and Belgian *Communautés* all have a legal competence, either shared with national authorities or exclusive, on integration (Hepburn 2010; Thränhardt 2014). Regional authorities may also be deprived of such competence in cases of a strong centralist tradition (Scholten and Penninx 2016).

In light of the foregoing, integration is indeed inserted in a multilevel policy making system; but when it comes to the EU integration policy, the answer to the question "who decides what?" is rather straightforward: the member states shape the EU policy, not subnational authorities (see Chapters 3 and 4 for a detailed analysis). However this does not mean that the role of subnational bodies should be underestimated. Member states have their particular administrative organization and their consultation procedures, and these must be accounted for; but at the end of the day, the final word is that of the central administration; hence the focus on member states here.

Integration at EU Level: Defining Soft-Europeanization

Integration at EU Level: A Review of Existing Literature

The policy on the integration of third country nationals at EU level has had a short existence as of yet, most of which has been disseminated across policy fields, Commission's DGs, EU programmes and so on.

This may be why little attention has been granted to it in scholarship. In an interesting report, Kate and Niessen (2007) propose to map the measures relating to integration within the machinery of the Commission. Endorsing a wider definition of the term 'migrant' than that of this research (e.g. including refugees), they list the policy instruments in place that (de facto) favour third country national integration. They notably count anti-discrimination measures, employment and education funding opportunities under the European Social Fund, the European integration fund and other instruments that have fostered integration in one way or another. Alternatively, most of the existing literature on the European integration policy has concentrated on a narrower extent, focusing on policies that have integration of third country nationals as a primary goal rather than on policies that may have an impact on integration (see Chapter 2). In doing so, scholarship aimed to analyse more visible and potentially more controversial policy outputs.[23] I shall do the same.

The birth of an immigration policy touching upon legal migration and containing integration measures sparked vivid interest among law scholars, notably because the creation of an EU competence stressed the possibility of conflicts between EU and national legal orders, and posed the question of what integration model the EU was implicitly carrying (Kostakopoulou 2002a; Groenendijk 2004; Murphy 2009; Handoll 2012; see also Acosta Arcarazo 2014). In the same vein, a significant amount of articles pertaining to social sciences at large looked into the effects or consequences of the provisions contained in EU secondary law, touching therefore in some ways on integration. These primarily focused on the Family Reunification Directive (Oosterom-Staples 2007; Groenendijk et al. 2007; Hailbronner 2010), the long-term residence Directive (Halleskov 2005; Kostakopoulou 2002b), and the couple of Directives relating to the fight against discrimination (although only indirectly linked to integration; Geddes 2004; Bribosia 2012; but see also Guiraudon 2003; Murphy 2009).

Other law scholars paid attention to the EU integration policy when, considering the hindrances every single piece of binding legislation would face, this very policy took on the shape of the recently created Open Method of Coordination (OMC; see Chapter 3, but see also

---

[23] See notably Gunningham and Sinclair (1998), on visibility and controversy.

Caviedes 2004; Szyszczak 2006; Velluti 2007). Conversely, and despite the failure of the OMC in this domain, little importance has been given to the development of a soft European policy on integration, and its instruments have often been treated analytically or as secondary elements to be taken notice of. Geddes and Achtnich (2015) analyse research-policy dialogues through the exchange of experience and knowledge in the ambit of networks of member states officials; they list soft govern-ance instruments without, however, going into much depth. Scholten and Penninx (2016) propose an analysis of migration and integration multilevel governance in which they underline the expansive importance of local authorities in policy-making as far as integration is concerned. Attention to EU soft instruments is there limited to a list of instruments. Rosenow (2009) takes a different stance and provides elements as to the creation of a European policy on integration in a paper that remains, however, largely analytical. Other works emanate from EU and national officers that took part in the policy making process over the 2000s and provide interesting factual elements, although without placing them in a wider theoretical perspective (Urth 2005; Pratt 2015; Hauschild 2008).

The lack of attention granted to these soft instruments may find a reason in the presumed lack of consistency of the EU integration pol-icy. As Handoll (2012: 15) put it: "this activity [on integration] is rather fragmented and is not sufficient for the EU to be said to have its own 'integration policy', though it undoubtedly has a 'policy on integra-tion'". The successive adoption of soft instruments, however, devel-oped into a consistent ensemble resembling an OMC, and sometimes called a "quasi-OMC" (Carrera 2008; see Chapter 3). With a definition of an approach to integration, the existence of networks of officials to exchange expertise, and the presence of common goals supported by financial means, the limit between "integration policy" and "policy on integration", to take on Handoll's phrasing, may well be fading away. This may also be the reason why some scholars have dedicated more of their work to the EU integration policy. Carrera, notably, has writ-ten a significant number of papers and reports, and a book on the topic (see inter alia Carrera 2006, 2008, 2009; Carrera and Wiesbrock 2009; Carrera and Faure Atger 2011). His work is often descriptive and analyt-ical, defining the EU approach to integration or pointing to the contra-dictions between ends and means. A final study is worth mentioning in this introduction, that of Mulcahy (2011). She dedicated a book to the subject, that is, to my knowledge, the most comprehensive opus dealing with the policy at EU level. She aims to provide a comparative analysis of the impact of the EU on the politics and policies of immigrant integration in EU member states. Her book, she argues, is situated in a framework of "interactive Europeanization". The analysis takes the Common Basic Principles on integration as a starting point and looks into their implementation at national level. More explicitly, the question Mulcahy poses is whether integration policies across Europe are converging and, if so, whether the EU has a role in that. She posits the diffusion of EU norms as a mechanism driving the implementation of these principles but finds no evidence in support of the hypothesis. On the contrary, she concludes that the EU has been "almost irrelevant to immigrant integration policymaking in Europe" (2011: 181). Mulcahy's is not the only study to have placed the emphasis on the CBPs.[24] Most studies touching upon the EU policy for the integration of third country nationals have considered the Common Basic Principles as the cornerstone of the integration policy at EU level. True, they form together a first conceptualisation of what integration means, a first common understanding of a European concept which lends itself particularly well to analytical approaches. That said, the CBPs remain *principles* and are therefore necessarily loose (Carrera 2006). Looking into whether they have had an impact or not is indeed an interesting, yet uncertain, exercise. The approach to Europeanization of integration policies I propose is different in several regards; from the acceptation of Europeanization to its empirical manifestation (see next sections).

A Soft-Europeanization Approach to Integration and Policy Cycle

The question at the core of this research is indeed whether or not we can speak of a Europeanization of integration policies. Considering the institutional setting established by the treaty of Amsterdam (see Chapter 2), there is little doubt that if there is Europeanization, it is necessarily soft-Europeanization; i.e. Europeanization via soft law. According to a henceforth classic definition, soft law refers to the "rules of conduct which in principle have no legal force but which nevertheless may have

---

[24] This is also the case in Carrera (2006), Carrera and Faure Atger (2011), Murphy (2009), Gilardoni et al. (2015), and Pratt (2015).

practical effects" (Snyder 1993: 198). Such a definition is rather straight-forward. Instead, defining Europeanization is a whole-new kettle of fish.

Simply put, "Europeanization is like one of those bumblebees that seem to defy the laws of aerodynamics, yet they fly" (Exadaktylos and Radaelli 2012: 17). Although the term punctuates research on the EU, none of its many definitions earns unanimity in scholarship.[25] Some authors even use the term in opposite senses (as Caporaso 2007: 27 admits). Definitions of Europeanization can nevertheless be classified in three distinct categories. The first two either insist on a top-down or a bottom-up model, the former being most frequently used. The top-down approach generally considers the effect of EU outputs on member states (as that of Mulcahy 2011, for the EU integration policy). Such an approach encompasses, but is not limited to, the implementation of EU outputs, as we shall see below (but see also Treib 2014). In a minimal acceptation, Featherstone (2003) suggests that Europeanization involves a response to EU policy. Differently, the bottom-up approach concentrates on the transfer of the policy locus to the EU, or, as Richardson puts it (2012: 5), "the processes by which the key decisions about public policies are gradually transferred to the European level (or for new policy areas, emerge at the European level)". Yet other models of Europeanization, more comprehensive, make up the third category. They consider that Europeanization is a process encompassing both bottom-up and top-down conceptions as two sides of the same coin. Radaelli (2003b), for instance, defines Europeanization as a circular process of co-construction of norms that goes up to the EU sphere before coming back down to domestic environment, discourses, identities and policies. Based on the construction of shared beliefs, such acceptation necessarily implies processes of diffusion and learning are at play. In a similar, yet different manner, Börzel (2002) posits that, in order to reduce the costs of implementation of EU outputs, member states are incentivised to *upload* their domestic policies to the EU level. In doing so, they reduce the adaptation effort to be produced at a later stage. Member states thus compete (however with different resources, different strategies, and different chances of success) to have their policies adopted at EU level.

[25] Many are the authors agreeing on this point. See inter alia (Bache 2005; Caporaso 2007; Richardson 2012; Exadaktylos and Radaelli 2012; see also Chapter 3).

Considering the foregoing, it becomes obvious that the way Europeanization is defined can introduce conceptual opacity in that the term may overlap with other concepts such as EU integration, convergence, or else harmonisation (Radaelli 2003b). The top-down approach may encompass harmonisation whilst the bottom-up approach may encroach on integration. Since "what is badly defined is likely to be badly measured" (Nardo et al. 2005: 12), a suitable definition ought to be found. Note, in addition, that, since the process in the case at issue is necessarily based on soft law, the definition of an operational concept of Europeanization is further complicated. So how do we recognize soft-Europeanization when we see it?

If the concept of Europeanization has acquired compelling relevance in specialised literature, soft-Europeanization, on the other hand, has seldom been mentioned, conceptualized or empirically analysed.[26] In the ambit of this book, I endorse a definition inspired from that of Börzel (2002). Börzel's definition has to do with hard law, stringent sets of provisions that member states must comply with. The pressure to upload policy preferences is indeed higher where the duty to implement is more constraining. Similarly, the lower the obligation to implement, the more difficult the empirical observation of implementation becomes. Since her definition does not consider soft law provisions, a definition suitable for my purposes must necessarily be softer. I consider that the way a policy takes shape at EU level conditions, to some extent, the way it will be implemented afterwards. More precisely, the way interactions are structured (see Chapter 2), the way the policy field emerges as an EU competence (see Chapter 3), and the stakes of a given policy instrument (see Chapter 4) lead to certain policy options that will in turn determine how implementation will be played out and what the effects of the policy will be (see Chapters 5 and 6). The two sides of the coin; bottom-up and top-down logics, shall therefore be included in a unified framework and applied throughout the policy cycle (see Fig. 1.1).

Soft-Europeanization in the ambit of this book therefore draws from both bottom-up and top-down models, regarded as two different phases of the same process. Following Richardson, the bottom-up phase consists in the process by which the policy emerges as an EU policy and its implication for policy-making. Following Featherstone, the

---

[26]Notable exceptions are, for example, Thielemann (2001) and López-Santana (2007).

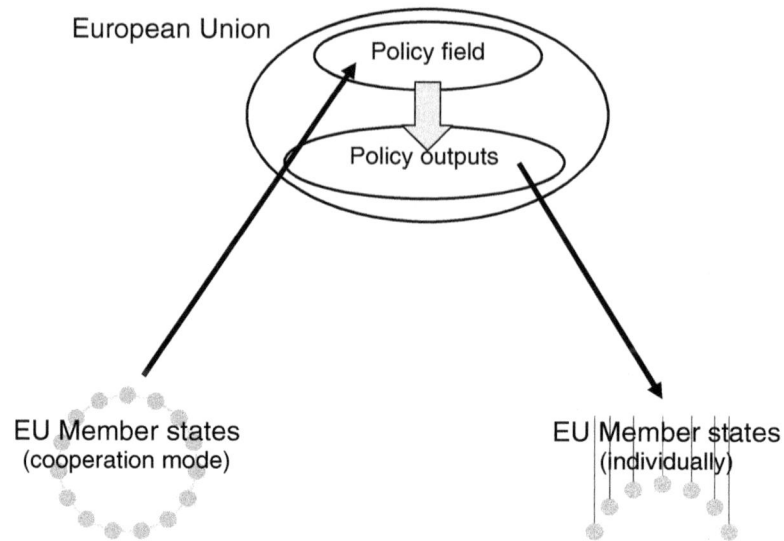

Fig. 1.1   The process of soft-Europeanization

top-down phase looks into member states' response to EU soft outputs, or else their effects on member states via implementation (see Fig. 1.1). In other words, I consider that the way through which the policy emerges at EU level, and the modes through which EU outputs are subsequently adopted, determines the level of discretion left to the state and the likely implementation of the very same outputs.

In the case of soft law though, implementation of EU outputs is not driven by EU legislation but by national initiatives, carried out by national governments. Consequently, soft law fundamentally puts the burden of the decision on national governments, working in national contexts with national actors (Bercusson 2009). The study of a soft Europeanization process at play necessarily accounts for such a feature.

This acceptation of Europeanization is significantly different from the interactive Europeanization advanced in Mulcahy (2011: 10). The question she poses is the following: "[a]re immigrant integration policies in Europe converging and if so, has the EU anything to do with it?" She is interested in whether ideas (the CBPs) diffuse in the EU sphere through repeated interactions, and she aims at assessing the extent to which this leads to convergence at national level in the implementation of national policies. Alternatively, I am interested in explaining whether and how such a policy field becomes an EU policy, and what member states' response to it is. I do not seek to assess the level of convergence between member states' respective policies; rather, I explore the response they individually produce in reaction to an instrument.[27] Consequently, the mechanism I am interested in is not diffusion but: (i) uploading preferences and bargaining in the bottom-up phase; (ii) implementation of EU outputs in the top-down phase.

One caveat is in order. The contribution this research brings to the concept of Europeanization itself is fairly limited. More than providing a new definition or a new approach to it, I propose to look into an instance of odd Europeanization whilst trying to avoid the degreeism trap according to which "'a certain degree of Europeanization' may be found everywhere" (Radaelli 2003b: 32). The question arising now is thus: where do I draw the line between Europeanization and non-Europeanization? Very simply, I assess Europeanization in the light of two questions that mirror the split between bottom-up and top-down approaches. Is there a passage from member states to the EU? Do member states respond to EU outputs?

Whereas Mulcahy seeks to assess Europeanization through the diffusion of the Common Basic Principles, I apply the abovementioned conception of Europeanization to another policy instrument that has been largely overlooked in existing literature: the European Integration Fund (EIF; an exception is Carrera and Faure Atger 2011, who link the CBPs to the EIF). As already said, the CBPs are widely worded and therefore construable, so that observing their true empirical manifestation is a difficult undertaking. Conversely, the European Integration Fund is a systematic instrument. It concerns all member states[28] and requires implementation at national level via the preparation of national annual programmes and reporting activities. Consequently, despite its soft law

---

[27] As just stated, in the case of soft law, the burden is placed on national governments evolving in national contexts with national actors; hence a focus on member states' individual response instead of diffusion-like mechanisms. Note in addition that this is one of the conclusions reached by Mulcahy (2011): no cross-country diffusion but rather national dynamics.

[28] Except Denmark that does not participate in AFSJ policies and Croatia that was not a member state at the time.

character (Trimikliniotis 2012), its implementation implies a tangible interaction between the EU and the member states. The EIF will be analysed throughout its policy cycle, from adoption to implementation, in a Europeanization key.

Elements of Methodology

As the purposes of this book become clearer, some elements of method ought to be outlined. Needless to say, there is not a best method; there is a suitable way to go about a specific research question. Bearing that in mind, it is evident that, given the ambition set out in the previous pages, methodological diversity is in order: mixing methods is surely the best way to fit the empirical reality of the puzzle at hand. More precisely, for the purpose of this research, Europeanization is defined as a comprehensive process that encompasses both bottom-up and top-down phases. Given how each of these phases are defined in the previous pages, they may hardly be empirically approached in the same manner. Whilst the former phase requires a process be reconstructed (i.e. case-based approach), the latter implies we observe the response of 26 member states at once (i.e. comparative or cross-section approach; see Keman 2011 on the different approaches to research design). For this reason, this book mixes methods and implements, on the one hand, a qualitative approach aimed at identifying causal mechanisms and, on the other hand, quantitative methods to compare a set of countries on issues of interest.

Process tracing[29] and case-studies methods are used to document the bottom-up phase and highlight the mechanisms at play (Chapters 3 and 4). Invoking process tracing implies a thorough description of contextual elements shedding light on the phenomenon under study. It is a within-case analysis that aims to establish the causal mechanism that best explain a given outcome.[30] Process tracing relies on qualitative data that may be obtained in different ways. For this research, different data

---

[29] Process tracing is a commonly used qualitative method; a detailed description is therefore not necessary here. Some references are provided to the reader interested in learning more about it in the appendices.

[30] For more on process tracing, see Checkel (2005), Vennesson (2008), Mahoney (2010), and Collier (2011).

stream were used: official documents[31] (Bowen 2009) and elite interviews with EU and national officials (Harvey 2011).

Quantitative methods are employed to study the top-down phase in
a comparative manner whilst retaining EU instruments (the EIF in this
instance) as the unit of analysis (Chapters 5 and 6; see inter alia Keman
2011). More specifically, I use multilevel regressions to test hypotheses
regarding the determinants of member states' responses to the EIF over
time (Beck 2006).

The reader interested in knowing more about the technicalities of this
research may find useful information within each chapter as well as in the
appendices which provide details regarding methods, data and models.

Plan of the Book

This research is presented in five distinct chapters. Chapter 2 sets the
scene and defines the lens through which the policy is looked at in
Chapters 3–6. I start by painting a picture of the gradual construction
of an immigration policy at EU level since the adoption of the Schengen
agreement in the 1980s and show that member states were eager to
keep a firm grip on the policy despite the growing objective need of a
common policy induced by the creation of an inner space without borders. Considering the dynamics at play in this process, I infer that the
most suitable approach to explore immigration-related policies is that of
actor-centred institutionalism as developed by Scharpf (1990, 1997). In
a nutshell, I consider that actors make choices in accordance with their
preferences and resources, within an institutional framework, with different chances of success. Chapter 3 departs from immigration to focus
the analysis on the integration of third country nationals. Drawing from
case studies and process-tracing methods, I show that the emergence of
an integration policy at EU level results from the combination of three
conditions in a political context sensitized to the issue. Firstly, a policy at
EU level was possible because a policy in this domain had to be of a soft
law nature. Upon this necessary condition, a condition sufficient to the
emergence of the EU policy rests on the occurrence of three Presidencies
of the Council with rather similar preferences within a relatively short

---

[31] Such documents are of different sorts, they range from unpublicised minutes of expert
committees to public pieces of information available on EU websites. See appendices for
more on the data collected.

time span. Finally, the third condition, rather an intervening factor, lies with the Commission that, whilst executing the wishes of the Council, proved capable of developing a policy within the margins of acceptability of the Council, exploiting them to flesh out a sounder policy. In parallel, the Commission also proved capable of carving out a role for itself on integration, notably through the creation of funding opportunities that would eventually give rise to the European Integration Fund (EIF), the first systematic EU instrument in this field, and arguably also the most important one. Whilst the end of Chapter 3 starts the analysis of the EIF policy cycle with a focus on policy formulation, Chapter 4 goes through the successive steps that led to the adoption of the fund. Mostly using document analysis and interviews, I show that the absence of a sound competence at EU level and the permanence of unanimity voting in the Council resulted in the creation of a fund that would grant great discretion to member states as to its spending. In other words, the decision making process emptied the fund of its most constraining clauses. By looking at the most disputed provision, I also show that most of the debate revolved around the classic "who gets what" question. Chapters 5 and 6 shift the focus to another step in the policy cycle, the implementation of the fund, the top-down Europeanization phase referred to above. In order to study the implementation of the EIF, I draw an analogy between the implementation of the fund and the implementation of Directives. According to Börzel (2001) and Treib (2014), the implementation of Directives comprises three components that are transposition, application and enforcement. For the implementation of the fund, I study two components: (i) programming, that corresponds in a way to transposition in that the member states state the way they implement; (ii) engagement of the sums, that somewhat corresponds to the application phase in that it concerns the use of the EU outputs at national level. Accordingly, I consider member states' response to the EIF in these terms. In Chapter 5, I argue that the way the fund was adopted had consequences on its programming at the national level. Using quantitative methods, time-series cross-section regression to be precise, I propose to look into member states' response to the EIF and the determinants of the implementation of its provisions. I notably answer the question "why do member states implement EU outputs if they have no legal obligation to do so?", and show that when there is no oversight from above (i.e. the Commission), soft law provisions have little effect. I also show that government preferences and the constraint exercised by public opinion and organized civil society matter. Chapter 6 leaves the EIF programming phase to look at the actual implementation of the fund; i.e. the spending of the amounts allocated. Again using time-series cross-section regression, I explain why member states do not use the funds placed at their disposal via the EIF and show that, whereas the programming phase is a matter of preferences, the engagement of the funds is rather dependant on member states' capacity to implement.

Last but not least, I conclude this book with an analysis of the facts and an answer to the question asked in the first pages above: a case of soft-Europeanization? I answer in the negative, basing the appraisal on the five chapters of this research and the features of the new Asylum, Migration and Integration Fund (AMIF) for the period 2014–2020.

REFERENCES

SCHOLARSHIP AND EXPERT REFERENCES

Acosta Arcarazo, D. (2014). *EU Integration Policy: Between Soft Law and Hard Law* (Fondazione ISMU, KING Project, Desk Research Paper, No. 1).

Anderson, B., & Blinder, S. (2015). Who Counts as a Migrant? Definitions and Their Consequences. *The Migration Observatory*. Available at http://www.migrationobservatory.ox.ac.uk/resources/briefings/who-counts-as-a-migrant-definitions-and-their-consequences/. Last Consulted November 12, 2016.

Bache, I. (2005). *Europeanization and Britain: Towards Multi-level Governance?* Paper prepared for the EUSA 9th Biennial Conference in Austin, Texas, March 31–April 2.

Beck, N. (2006). *Time-Series–Cross-Section Methods*. No. draft as of June 5.

Bercusson, B. (2009). *European Labour Law* (2nd ed.). Cambridge: Cambridge University Press.

Börzel, T. A. (2001). Non-compliance in the European Union: Pathology or Statistical Artefact? *Journal of European Public Policy, 8*(5), 803–824.

Börzel, T. A. (2002). Pace-Setting, Foot-Dragging, and Fence-Sitting: Member State Responses to Europeanization. *JCMS. Journal of Common Market Studies, 40*(2), 193–214.

Bowen, G. A. (2009). Document Analysis as a Qualitative Research Method. *Qualitative Research Journal, 9*(2), 27–40.

Bribosia, E. (2012). Les Politiques D'intégration de l'Union Européenne et Des Etats Membres à L'épreuve Du Principe de Non-Discrimination. In Y. Pascouau & T. Strik (Eds.), *Which Integration Policies for Migrants? Interaction Between the EU and its Member States* (pp. 51–82). Nijmegen: Wolf Legal Publishers.

Brubaker, R. (2001). The Return of Assimilation? Changing Perspectives on Immigration and Its Sequels in France, Germany, and the United States. *Ethnic and Racial Studies, 24*(4), 531–548.

Caporaso, J. (2007). The Three Worlds of Integration Theory. In P. R. Graziano (Ed.), *Europeanization: New Research Agendas* (pp. 23–34). Basingstoke: Palgrave Macmillan.

Carens, J. H. (2000). *Culture, Citizenship, and Community a Contextual Exploration of Justice as Evenhandedness.* Oxford: Oxford University Press.

Carrera, S. (2006). *A Comparison of Integration Programmes in the EU. Trends and Weaknesses.* (Centre for European Policy Studies, Challenge, No. 1).

Carrera, S. (2008). *Benchmarking Integration in the EU: Analyzing the Debate on Integration Indicators and Moving It Forward.* Gütersloh: Bertelsmann Foundation.

Carrera, S. (2009). *In Search of the Perfect Citizen? The Intersection Between Integration, Immigration and Nationality in the EU.* Leiden: Martinus Nijhoff Publishers.

Carrera, S., & Faure Atger, A. (2011). *Integration as a Two-Way Process in the EU? Assessing the Relationship Between the European Integration Fund and the Common Basic Principles.* Brussels: Centre for European Policy Studies.

Carrera, S., & Wiesbrock, A. (2009). *Civic Integration of Third-Country Nationals Nationalism versus Europeanization in the Common EU Immigration Policy.* Brussels: Centre for European Policy Studies.

Castles, S. (1995). How Nation-States Respond to Immigration and Ethnic Diversity. *Journal of Ethnic and Migration Studies, 21*(3), 293–308.

Castles, S., de Haas, H., & Miller, M. J. (2013). *The Age of Migration. International Population Movements in the Modern World* (5th ed.). Basingstoke: Palgrave Macmillan.

Caviedes, A. (2004). The Open Method of Co-ordination in Immigration Policy: A Tool for Prying Open Fortress Europe? *Journal of European Public Policy, 11*(2), 289–310.

Checkel, J. T. (2005). *It's the Process Stupid! Process Tracing in the Study of European and International Politics* (ARENA Centre for European Studies Working Papers No. 26), University of Oslo.

Collett, E. (2011). Immigrant Integration in Europe in a Time of Austerity. *Migration Policy Institute.* Available at http://www.migrationpolicy.org/research/TCM-immigrant-integration-europe-time-austerity. Last Consulted November 12, 2016.

Collier, D. (2011). Understanding Process Tracing. *PS: Political Science & Politics, 44*(4), 823–830.

de Haas, H., & Czaika, M. (2013). Measuring Migration Policies: Some Conceptual and Methodological Reflections. *Migration and Citizenship, 1*(2), 40–47.

European Commission. (2011). *The 2012 Ageing Report: Underlying Assumptions and Projection Methodologies*. Brussels: European Commission.

Exadaktylos, T., & Radaelli, C. M. (2012). Looking for Causality in the Literature on Europeanization. In T. Exadaktylos & C. M. Radaelli (Eds.), *Research Design in European Studies: Establishing Causality in Europeanization*. Basingstoke: Palgrave Macmillan.

Featherstone, K. (2003). Introduction: In the Name of "Europe". In K. Featherstone & C. M. Radaelli (Eds.), *The Politics of Europeanization* (pp. 3–26). New York: Oxford University Press.

Geddes, A. (2004). Britain, France, and EU Anti-discrimination Policy: The Emergence of an EU Policy Paradigm. *West European Politics, 27*(2), 334–353.

Geddes, A., & Achtnich, M. (2015). Research-Policy Dialogues in the European Union. In P. Scholten, H. Entzinger, R. Penninx, & S. Verbeek (Eds.), *Integrating Immigrants in Europe. Research-Policy Dialogues* (pp. 293–314). Amsterdam: IMISCOE Research Series.

Gilardoni, G., D'odorico, M., & Carrillo, D. (2015). *KING Knowledge for Integration Governance Evidence on Migrants' Integration in Europe*. Milan: Fondazione ISMU.

Groenendijk, K. (2004). Legal Concepts of Integration in EU Migration Law. *European Journal of Migration and Law, 6*(2), 111–126.

Groenendijk, K., Fernhout, R., van Dam, D., van Oers, R., & Strik, T. (2007). *The Family Reunification Directive in EU Member States: The First Year of Implementation*. Nijmegen: Centre for Migration Law.

Guiraudon, V. (2003). The Constitution of a European Immigration Policy Domain: A Political Sociology Approach. *Journal of European Public Policy, 10*(2), 263–282.

Gunningham, N., & Sinclair, D. (1998). *Designing Smart Regulation*. OECD and International Energy Agency.

Hailbronner, K. (2010). *Implications of the EU Lisbon Treaty on EU Immigration Law*. Paper Prepared for the Transatlantic Exchange for Academics in Migration Studies, San Diego.

Halleskov, L. (2005). The Long-Term Residents Directive: A Fulfilment of the Tampere Objective of Near-Equality? *European Journal of Migration and Law, 7*(2), 181–202.

Hammar, T. (1990). *Democracy and the Nation State: Aliens, Denizens and Citizens in a World of International Migration*. Aldershot: Ashgate.

Handoll, J. (2012). Integration Policy in the European Union: The Question of Competence. In Y. Pascouau & T. Strik (Eds.), *Which Integration Policies for Migrants? Interaction Between the EU and Its Member States* (pp. 15–50). Nijmegen: Wolf Legal Publishers.

Harvey, W. S. (2011). Strategies for Conducting Elite Interviews. *Qualitative Research, 11*(4), 431–441.

Hauschild, C. (2008). Die Integration von Zuwanderern. Ein Neues Politikfeld Für Die Europäische Union. In S. Magiera, K.-P. Sommermann, & J. Ziller (Eds.), *Verwaltungswissenschaft und Verwaltungspraxis in nationaler und transnationaler Perspektive* (pp. 59–74). Berlin: Duncker & Humbliot.

Helbling, M. (2013). Validating Integration and Citizenship Policy Indices. *Comparative European Politics, 11*(5), 555–576.

Helbling, M., Bjerre, L., Römer, F., & Zobel, M. (2013). The Immigration Policies in Comparison (IMPIC) Index: The Importance of a Sound Conceptualization. *Migration and Citizenship, 1*(2), 8–14.

Hepburn, E. (2010). "Citizens of the Region": Party Conceptions of Regional Citizenship and Immigrant Integration. *European Journal of Political Research, 50*(4), 504–529.

Kate, M.-A., & Niessen, J. (2007). *Locating Immigrant Integration Policy Measures in the Machinery of the European Commission.* European Programme for Integration and Migration.

Keating, M. (2009). Social Citizenship, Devolution and Policy Divergence. In S. L. Greer (Ed.), *Devolution and Social Citizenship in the UK* (pp. 97–116). Bristol: Policy Press.

Keman, H. (2011). Comparative Research Methods. In D. Caramani (Ed.), *Comparative Politics* (2nd ed., pp. 50–64). Oxford: Oxford University Press.

Kostakopoulou, T. (2002a). "Integrating" Non-EU Migrants in the European Union: Ambivalent Legacies and Mutating Paradigms. *Columbia Journal of European Law, 8*(2), 181–201.

Kostakopoulou, T. (2002b). Long-Term Resident Third-Country Nationals in the European Union: Normative Expectations and Institutional Openings. *Journal of Ethnic and Migration Studies, 28*(3), 443–462.

Kundnani, A. (2012). Multiculturalism and Its Discontents: Left, Right and Liberal. *European Journal of Cultural Studies, 15*(2), 155–166.

Kymlicka, W. (1995). *Multicultural Citizenship: A Liberal Theory of Minority Rights.* New York: Oxford University Press.

Lanzieri, G. (2010). *Fewer, Older and Multicultural? A Projection of the Populations of the European Union Member States by Foreign/National Background.* (Eurostat Statistical Working Paper).

López-Santana, M. (2007). *Soft Europeanization? How the Soft Pressure from Above Affects the Bottom (Differently): The Belgian, Spanish and Swedish Experiences.* (EUI Working Papers, Vol. 10).

Mahoney, J. (2010). After KKV: The New Methodology of Qualitative Research. *World Politics, 62*(1), 120–147.

Miller, D. (2008). Immigrants, Nations, and Citizenship. *Journal of Political Philosophy, 16*(4), 371–390.

Mügge, L., & van der Haar, M. (2016). Who Is an Immigrant and Who Requires Integration? Categorizing in European Policies. In B. Garcés-Mascareñas & R. Penninx (Eds.), *Integration Processes and Policies in Europe.*

Contexts, Levels and Actors. (pp. 77–90). Amsterdam: IMISCOE Research Series.

Mulcahy, S. (2011). *Europe's Migrant Policies: Illusions of Integration.* Basingstoke: Palgrave Macmillan.

Murphy, C. (2009). Immigration, Integration and Citizenship in European Union Law: The Position of Third Country Nationals. *Hibernian Law Journal, 8,* 155–177.

Nardo, M., Saisana, M., Saltelli, A., Tarantola, S., Hoffman, A., & Giovannini, E. (2005). *Handbook on Constructing Composite Indicators: Methodology and User Guide.* Paris: Organization for Economic Co-operation and Development (OECD).

OECD. (2016). *Recruiting Immigrant Workers: Europe.* Paris: OECD Publishing.

Oosterom-Staples, H. (2007). The Family Reunification Directive: A Tool Preserving Member State Interest or Conducive to Family Unity? In A. Baldaccini, H. Toner, & P. E. Guild (Eds.), *Whose Freedom, Security and Justice? EU Immigration and Asylum Law and Policy* (pp. 451–488). Oxford: Hart Publishing.

Penninx, R. (2009). *Decentralising Integration Policies. Managing Integration in Cities, Regions and Localities.* (Policy Network Paper).

Penninx, R. (2013). *Research on Migration and Integration in Europe: Achievements and Lessons.* Amsterdam: Vossiuspers UvA.

Penninx, M., Garcés-Mascareñas, B., Protasiewicz, P. M., Schwarz, H., & Caponio, T. (2014). *European Cities and Their Migrant Integration Policies A State of the Art Study for the Knowledge for Integration Governance (KING) Project.* (Fondazione ISMU, KING Project, Overview Paper No. 5).

Poppelaars, C., & Scholten, P. (2008). Two Worlds Apart: The Divergence of National and Local Immigrant Integration Policies in the Netherlands. *Administration & Society, 40*(4), 335–357.

Pratt, S. (2015). EU Policymaking and Research: Case Studies of the Communication on a Community Immigration Policy and the Common Basic Principles for Integration. In P. Scholten, H. Entzinger, R. Penninx, & S. Verbeek (Eds.), *Integrating Immigrants in Europe: Research-Policy Dialogues* (pp. 117–131). Amsterdam: IMISCOE Research Series.

Radaelli, C. (2003). The Europeanization of Public Policy. In K. Featherstone & C. M. Radaelli (Eds.), *The politics of Europeanization* (pp. 27–56). New York: Oxford University Press.

Richardson, J. (2012). Supranational State Building in the European Union. In J. Richardson (Ed.), *Constructing a Policy-Making State? Policy Dynamics in the EU.* Oxford: Oxford University Press.

Rosenow, K. (2009). The Europeanization of Integration Policies. *International Migration, 47*(1), 133–159.

Schain, M. (2010). Managing Difference: Immigrant Integration Policy in France, Britain, and the United States. *Social Research: An International Quarterly, 77*(1), 205–236.

Scharpf, F. W. (1990). Games Real Actors Could Play: The Problem of Mutual Predictability. *Rationality and Society, 2*(4), 471–494.

Scharpf, F. W. (1997). *Games Real Actors Play: Actor-Centered Institutionalism in Policy Research.* Boulder: Westview Press.

Scholten, P., & Penninx, R. (2016). The Multilevel Governance of Migration and Integration'. In *Integration Processes and Policies in Europe. Contexts, Levels and Actors* (pp. 91–108). Amsterdam: IMISCOE Research Series.

Shachar, A., & Hirschl, R. (2007). Citizenship as Inherited Property. *Political Theory, 35*(3), 253–287.

Snyder, F. (1993). Soft Law and Institutional Practice in the European Community. In S. Martin (Ed.), *The Construction of Europe: Essays in Honour of Emile Noel* (pp. 197–225). Boston: Kluwer Academic Publishers.

Szyszczak, E. (2006). Experimental Governance: The Open Method of Coordination. *European Law Journal, 12*(4), 486–502.

Thielemann, E. (2001). *The "Soft" Europeanization of Migration Policy: European Integration and Domestic Policy Change.* Paper Presented at the ECSA Seventh Biennial International Conference.

Thränhardt, D. (2014). *The State of European Integration Governance: A Comparative Evaluation.* (Fondazione ISMU, KING Project, Desk Research Paper, No. 7).

Tilly, C., & Goodin, R. E. (2011). Overview of Contextual Political Analysis It Depends. In R. E. Goodin (Ed.), *The Oxford Handbook of Political Science.* Oxford: Oxford University Press.

TNS Qual+. (2011). *Migrant Integration.* European Commission: Qualitative Eurobarometer.

Treib, O. (2014). Implementing and Complying with EU Governance Outputs. *Living Reviews in European Governance, 9*, 5–47.

Trimikliniotis, N. (2012). The Instrumentalisation of EU Integration Policy: Reflecting on the Dignified Efficient and Undeclared Policy Aspects. In Y. Pascouau & T. Strik (Eds.), *Which Integration Policies for Migrants? Interaction Between the EU and Its Member States* (pp. 109–128). Nijmegen: Wolf Legal Publishers.

Urth, H. (2005). Building a Momentum for the Integration of Third-Country Nationals in the European Union. *European Journal of Migration and Law, 7*(2), 163–180.

Van Wolleghem, P. G. (2014). Inclusive Political Community: The Challenge of Liberal Polities. In E. Codini & M. D'Odorico (Eds.), *Democracy and Citizenship in the 21st Century: Critical Issues and Perspectives* (pp. 23–38). Milan: McGraw-Hill Education.

Velluti, S. (2007). What European Union Strategy for Integrating Migrants? The Role of OMC Soft Mechanisms in the Development of an EU Immigration Policy. *European Journal of Migration and Law, 9*(1), 53–82.

Vennesson, P. (2008). Case Studies and Process Tracing Theories and Practices. In D. Della Porta & M. Keating (Eds.), *Approaches and Methodologies in the Social Sciences: A Pluralist Perspective* (4th ed., pp. 223–239). Cambridge, NY: Cambridge University Press.

Walzer, M. (1983). *Spheres of Justice: A Defense of Pluralism and Equality*. New York: Basic Books.

EU Acts and Other Official Documents

COM. (2003). 336 Final—European Commission (2003). *Communication from the Commission on Immigration, Integration and Employment.*

Council of the European Union 14776/04. (2004). *Note.*

European Council. (1999). *Tampere European Council 15 And 16 October 1999, Presidency Conclusions.*

European Court of Auditors. (2012). Do the European Integration Fund and European Refugee Fund Contribute Effectively to the Integration of Third-Country Nationals? (Luxembourg).

CHAPTER 2

Setting the Scene: History of a Competence and Analytical Framework

As simple and trivial as it may sound, the EU is not a state. Nor is it an international institution comparable to any other. It is this "*objet politique non-identifié*" that Jacques Delors (1985)—then president of the European Commission—talked about; a political body of a *sui generis* nature, devoid of the competence of its own competence. "Less than a federation" but "more than a regime" (Wallace 1983), the foundation of its power rests upon a set of intertwined principles such as conferral, subsidiarity and proportionality. If defining what the EU precisely is remains challenging, there is little doubt nowadays that the EU is a 'political system': it features institutional stability, it receives political demands from a complex network of public and private groups, and the decisions it takes are highly significant (Hix 2005). Beyond the outdated debate between intergovernmentalism and neo-functionalism, history has it that the EU was not built in a day but that its construction followed a gradual and intermittent transfer of competences. Initially limited to the management of the coal and steel industry, atomic energy, and tariffs, its scope gradually extended to the creation of a single market and started to touch upon policy domains that would have transnational stakes; e.g. transport, environments, fisheries, and immigration, to name but a few.

In an area within which people can move without being controlled at the borders of one or another member state, immigration inevitably features transnational stakes. The transfer of the competence at EU level was however not to be taken for granted; on the contrary, there were

© The Author(s) 2019
P. G. Van Wolleghem, *The EU's Policy on the Integration of Migrants*, Palgrave Studies in European Union Politics,
https://doi.org/10.1007/978-3-319-97682-2_2

many bumps on that road, one of them being sovereignty (or national interest). Integration, as a subset of the immigration policy, is characterized by similar features. This chapter describes the development of the immigration policy and the failed competence of the EU when it comes to the integration of third country nationals (first part). Acknowledging the delicate nature of this policy realm as well as the prevalent role of actors and their diverging preferences in the making of an EU policy, I build upon Scharpf's actor-centred institutionalism to provide an analytical framework suitable to the intents and purposes of this research (second part). After defining the key concepts of Scharpf's approach, I propose a theoretical framework (to be applied within the analytical framework) that starts from the mode of interaction ruling actors' behaviours; namely, unanimity (third part). I conclude by presenting the main expectable consequences of it: least common denominator decisions and discretion granted to the member states in the implementation phase.

THE WINDING ROAD TOWARDS AN EU COMPETENCE

A Common Immigration Policy

Until the mid-1990s, immigration was the safe haven of national sovereignties; the policy realm appeared amongst the least likely to be communitarised (Faist and Ette 2007). Not that diverging national policies would not have negative externalities over a country's neighbour (Borràs and Jacobsson 2004; Velluti 2007); but rather that, to the European Communities, member states preferred an intergovernmental framework that would better fit their purposes and sovereignty concerns. To date, the EU has acquired significant competence in immigration matters, to the point that it is often referred to as a "common immigration policy". However, the story of its construction is more tumultuous than linear.

Following Geddes (2003), four periods in the development of a European immigration policy can be distinguished. The first period covers the years 1957–1986 and consists of policies firmly anchored in national authorities' hands. It is the era of "minimal policy involvement" (Geddes 2003: 130). Immigration was dealt with within the Trevi group, a network of national officials from ministries of home affairs and justice established in the mid-1970s, allegedly named after its foundation meeting in Rome where the Trevi fountain is located (Guiraudon 2003). Cooperation was then informal and mainly revolved around trans-border police cooperation. The topic fell under a more formal, but still intergovernmental, framework on 14 June 1985, when five member states of the European Communities (EC) signed the Schengen Convention, although outside the framework constituted by EC law. The objective was to abolish border controls between Belgium, France, Germany, Luxembourg and the Netherlands. An implementation convention was then adopted in 1990, and entered into force some five years after. The Schengen convention allowed free circulation between signatory states and comprised common rules on security, crossing of external borders[1] and a common system of visa.[2] Membership to the convention gradually expanded including more and more states. By 1997, all EU member states but the UK and Ireland, and also non-EU member states such as Norway and Iceland, were part of the free movement area. Schengen was eventually integrated into the EU *acquis* in a protocol attached to the Treaty of Amsterdam.

A second phase consists of "informal inter-governmentalism" (1986–1993; Geddes 2003: 132). With the growing commitment towards the creation of an area without frontiers, as laid down in the Single European Act, the issues of immigration and asylum gained importance. But member states were reluctant to delegate competence in this area and therefore opted for the addition of a declaration attached to the Single European Act stating that they would cooperate on immigration but that such cooperation should not affect member states' ability to control their borders. Consequently, in 1986, the member states established yet another intergovernmental and informal framework, with loose participation of the Commission and the exclusion of other EC institutions. This group was called the Ad hoc Working Group on Immigration (AWGI) and was to deal with issues such as visas, asylum, expulsions and border controls. The implementation of measures agreed in this framework would need to go through the international law channel, which, unlike EU secondary law,[3] would require ratification further to adoption,

---

[1] See Title II; Chapter 2 Crossing External Borders. Convention implementing the Schengen agreement of 14 June 1985 between the Governments of the States of the Benelux Economic Union, the Federal Republic of Germany and the French Republic on the gradual abolition of checks at their common borders, 19 June 1990.

[2] Convention implementing the Schengen Agreement. Article 9.1 and 10.1 notably.

[3] The effectiveness of EU secondary law rests upon the principles of direct effect and precedence as respectively established by the famous Van Gen den Loos (1963) and Costa vs. Enel (1964) cases. Together, these two principles allow citizens to invoke EU provisions before national and European courts and have these provisions supersede national ones.

with all the problems it comprises: the Dublin convention on Asylum, adopted in 1990, was not ratified until 1997; and the External Frontiers Convention of 1991 was never signed by Spain and the UK due to their (still ongoing) dispute over Gibraltar.

With the fall of the Berlin Wall and the outbreak of the Yugoslavian war in 1991, a sudden increase of asylum applications[4] aroused fears of massive influxes from the East and precipitated the search for a more efficient solution than intergovernmental cooperation. And then started the third period: "formal intergovernmental cooperation" (1993–1999; Geddes 2003: 134). Although it was clear that the functioning of previous international law agreements was not suitable, no agreement existed on what the solution was. More precisely, if the idea of a greater involvement of EU institutions was looming, a change in the treaties would have required unanimity, which was the least likely scenario given the positions of the UK and Denmark on that matter at the time. The solution opted for was the pillarisation of the European Communities' institutional structure with the creation of the Justice and Home Affairs pillar and the Common Foreign and Security Policy pillar with the Treaty of Maastricht. The newly created European Union would have a Community pillar (first pillar), for the most integrated issues, and two intergovernmental pillars for sensitive affairs. The third pillar integrated the work of the AWGI within the EU framework (Hix 2005). Article K.1 TEU, under its title VI (Provisions on cooperation in the fields of justice and home affairs) stipulated that asylum policy, rules on the crossing of external borders and more widely, policies related to immigration were "matters of common interest"; meaning not common policies (Geddes 2003). This institutional change did not significantly alter the intergovernmental logic in effect hitherto: decisions would be taken by unanimity, the Commission had no right of initiative, and the European Parliament and European Court of Justice had no role in the process.

A leap forward was taken with the adoption of the Treaty of Amsterdam which aimed, inter alia, at the creation of an Area of Freedom Security and Justice (AFSJ). It is the starting point of Geddes's "Communitarisation" period (from 1999 onwards; Geddes 2003: 136). At the time, a common immigration policy was essentially conceived as a corollary to the construction of the single market (Guild 1998; Ziller 2009).

---

[4] See Eurostat (1996), for more information on the number of applications.

The free movement of persons, which had been a pillar of the European construction from the very outset, has had a scope reduced to EU nationals. But in a rather open economic space, member states had become highly interdependent. Independently designed immigration regimes may have implied competitive policy-making that would have entailed externalities for the others (Borràs and Jacobsson 2004). More restrictive policies in a member state could have, for instance, re-oriented influxes towards the others as much as a more generous welfare state could have attracted more foreigners. The creation of a common free circulation area called for a common immigration policy that would reduce the externalities national rules could have had over other countries (Borràs and Jacobsson 2004; Velluti 2007). What the treaty of Amsterdam did was actually integrate the bulky Schengen legacy into EU primary law via a protocol, and introduce a Title IV TEC on "Visas, asylum, immigration and other policies related to free movement of persons". Consequently, policies in this realm were transferred from the third to the first pillar, thereby shifting decision-making rules from unanimity to qualified majority voting (QMV). This bold gesture however shied of sound integration. Article 68 TEC provided for a series of derogations that would undermine a true EU competence. Firstly, the reference for preliminary ruling to the European Court of Justice could only be done by a national court of last instance. Secondly, the European Court of Justice would have no jurisdiction over measures regarding the crossing of internal borders without checks on persons in the instance that a member state would invoke public order and internal security. Thirdly and most importantly, article 61 TEU provided for a five-year transition period, thereby postponing the shift to QMV to April 2004. At the end of this period, the Council was to decide, with the unanimity of its members, what parts of Title IV should pass to QMV. On 22 December 2004, the Council unanimously adopted Decision 2004/927/EC, thus extending QMV to the entire title IV, save for those issues relating to legal immigration, excluding by the same token the integration of migrants from QMV.

Opting for a transition period that would postpone the actual integration under the first pillar of immigration policy can be read as a divergence of member states' preferences. As a matter of fact, the negotiations on the treaty of Amsterdam saw the Netherlands, Belgium, Italy and Spain supporting the creation of a truly integrated Community immigration policy (Hix and Niessen 1996). They were however opposed by the French and the Germans who, having a stronger position within the Schengen circle, had little interest in pooling their competence. Concessions were made in favour of these two countries to reach an agreement. The Germans obtained unanimous voting in the Council of Ministers, and the French the limited role of the European Court of Justice (Guiraudon 2003). Opposition also came from Denmark, Ireland and the United Kingdom, along with the remaining member states (Hix and Niessen 1996). The UK and Ireland opted out from title IV with the possibility to opt into individual proposals, whereas Denmark opted out with no such possibility.

No Competence on Migrant Integration Policy

The institution of the AFSJ with the treaty of Amsterdam, conferred the EU a say on circulation, entry and stay of third country nationals within the territory of the Union (Guild 1998). As a consequence, the Justice and Home Affairs (JHA) task force was replaced by a Directorate General for JHA to face expanded responsibilities. Endowed with new means, the Commission was given mandate to develop the immigration policy in accordance with the guidelines set by the European Council gathered in Tampere in October 1999. In the five-year Tampere Programme, the European Council laid down milestones that encompassed a section on the "fair treatment of third country nationals". Member states established that third country nationals should enjoy "comparable rights and obligations" to those of nationals of the member state in which they live, and called for "a more vigorous integration policy".[5] Bolstered by such an impetus, the Commission started its work on legal acts for the establishment of standards and procedures. As Commission official Helene Urth[6] explains (Urth 2005: 164),[7]

> The approach proposed by the Commission to implement the provisions in the Amsterdam treaty related to asylum and immigration was initially a two-step one. On the one hand, establishing by May 2004 a basic legislative framework of European directives which set minimum standards

[5] European Council (1999).

[6] Helene Urth is referred to as Commission Official but was actually a Danish national expert detached to the European Commission from 2002 to 2005 and was responsible for developing the Commission's policy for the integration of third country nationals.

[7] But see also COM (2000) 757 final.

and establishes common procedures for legal admission and, on the other hand, an open coordination mechanism to encourage discussion of migration issues so as to promote the progressive convergence of national policies and practices and - in the longer term - the development of common objectives and standards.

The first step launched by the Commission was something of a failure. Against all expectations, negotiations turned out to be long and difficult. Initially, the Commission proposed a text on family reunion. Given the strong assertions made at Tampere and given the unanimous agreement on the fact that family is, in itself, a factor of integration, a Directive on family reunion was thought little controversial. And yet, it took nearly four years and a second proposal by the Commission to reach an agreement in February 2003. Following a very similar pattern, the Directive on the status of long-term residents, relating to comparability of rights, took about three years of negotiation before being adopted in June 2003. A third example lies with the proposal for a Directive on the conditions of entry and stay of migrants for the purpose of paid employment and self-employed activities, dismissed after a first reading in the Council for reaching too far.

Even though some pieces of legislation were eventually adopted, achievements fell short of their announced ambition. The permanence of unanimity voting and the fact that immigration inevitably touches on delicate sovereignty features led to legal acts of a rather limited reach. By looking at the measures regarding immigration at large, and adopted after the entry into force of the Treaty of Amsterdam, grey areas and derogations are plentiful.[8] Altogether, the legal framework only provides basic rights that can, most of the time, be summarised by the race-to-the-bottom logic, following the "lowest common denominator approach to convergence" (Velluti 2007: 62). This is most likely related to member states diverging preferences (Caviedes 2004) in such sensitive matters and the resulting voting rule in the Council.

---

[8] These grey areas and derogations were dealt with at length in legal and political scholarships. Some underline the little binding power of such a legal framework (Mazeron 2008; de Bruycker 2005; Luedtke 2011). To give two examples: Hailbronner (2010) underscores the derogations to the family reunion and blue card Directives; de Bruycker (2005) counted about 50 derogations out of 40 articles to Directive 2005/85/EC on minimum standards on procedures in Member States for granting and withdrawing refugee status.

As a matter of fact, the second step of the Commission's approach also ended up being a failure. As a second step in the announced programme, the Commission put forth a proposal for an Open Method of Coordination[9] (OMC). Originally, the Open Method of Coordination is rooted in the European Monetary Union that foresaw convergence criteria in the shape of common goals for macroeconomic performance without, however, specifying the policy means to be employed (de la Porte 2002). It first came into being on the occasion of the 1997 European Council of Luxembourg on employment. In this instance, the Council was to set guidelines as to the number of unemployed people who would receive assistance, without, however, fixing precise targets for unemployment rates. According to Caviedes (2004: 295), "This illustrates a key frustration in European policy-making: agreement in principle that fails to blossom into obligation". This approach officially became OMC on the occasion of the 2000 European Council of Lisbon and, even though it was to take different forms according to the policy field (Radaelli 2003a), would consist in: (i) establishing guidelines and timetables; (ii) establishing indicators to compare and benchmark policies and progress; and (iii) periodic monitoring and evaluation through peer-review. The idea behind the OMC is to reduce intergovernmental decision-making, very much dependent on "great moments", and "achieve incremental change along a policy-learning continuum where the issues can be de-politicized" (Caviedes 2004: 297). The OMC has thus been approached as a new mode of governance (Scott and Trubeck 2002), a soft law mechanism that, through widened involvement of actors, would develop a new form of input legitimacy that would then translate into more efficient policies. In principle its low political costs made it a favoured option in delicate policy fields but, in fact, its soft-law features weakened its incentive power and its enforcement altogether. More flexible, the OMC was supposed to better suit sovereignty concerns than the Community method but its actual effects were uncertain.

Further to its development as a policy method, research on the topic blossomed and tried to capture the mechanisms at play when it comes to reaching the goals set through the OMC. Two main strands in the existing literature are discernible, although not mutually exclusive. One insists on a peer-pressure driver that, through name-and-shame logics,

---

[9]COM (2001) 387 final.

would put member states under pressure to reach the benchmarks, to conform to the objectives defined at EU level and recommendations flowing therefrom (de la Porte 2002; Borràs and Jacobsson 2004). The mechanism at play here is some sort of soft compliance: despite the absence of formal modes of coercion, member states lend themselves to competition and attempt to meet the objectives set. As de la Porte (2002: 43) put it:

> Recommendations are made to member states in view of their performance, which is based on their position with regard to the European guidelines and benchmarks, and the member states claim to be very uncomfortable with this 'finger-pointing session'.

The other strand stresses the learning potential of such open coordination. The introduction of a coordination venue may alter cognitive frames and initiate ideational change (Knill and Lehmkuhl 2002; Radaelli 2003a). Exposure to new information and new ways of looking at things paves the way for a series of mechanisms: socialisation and learning through contact; reflexivity about one's own policies and institutions; and diffusion of ideas.

Analytical contributions are rich and plentiful but empirical findings are still few and causal linkages remain weak (de la Porte and Pochet 2012). What remains of great interest is the way in which the Commission, through the OMC, carved out a role for itself in fields in which it had little competence. Dehousse (2005) contends that the OMC can be seen as a foot-in-the-door strategy: the OMC may not be the best option available, but the instrument is adopted because member states cannot agree on objectives or because they want to avoid substantive decisions. In other words, the instrument used is not the most suitable to do the job but rather the one that is politically acceptable.[10]

Moulded on the basis of the European Employment Strategy, the OMC for an immigration policy was conceived of as an iterative process to foster policy learning and innovation (Velluti 2007). As the proposal read[11]:

[10] In this regard, see also Kassim and Le Galès (2010) and Tholoniat (2010).
[11] COM (2001) 387 final, paragraph 3.

The key element of the open co-ordination method is the approval by the Council of multiannual guidelines for the Union accompanied by specific timetables for achieving the goals which they set in the short, medium and long term. These guidelines will then be translated into national policy by the setting of specific targets, which take into account national and regional differences.

In total, six guidelines were drafted, one of which would address the integration of third country nationals. The latter aimed at the creation of a comprehensive policy framework that would inter alia "ensure the involvement of local and regional actors, the social partners, civil society and the migrants themselves in developing and implementing the national strategy".[12] The OMC would be implemented through the elaboration of National Action Plans for the six years foreseen, with annual revisions and adaptations. These plans would comprise two parts. The first part would provide an overview of the actions carried out in the previous year in relation to the guidelines, whilst in the second one, the member state would detail the measures it envisages to implement the guidelines for the years to come. The whole process would take place under the supervision of the Commission.

The OMC on immigration was however never put forth by the Council. From its adoption by the Commission under the lead of Commissioner Vitorino in July 2001, it was then sent to the European Parliament, the Economic and Social Committee, the Committee of Regions and the Council, but never made it to a vote. Caviedes's diagnosis is that this is:

> a testament to the perceived discursive power of the OMC process. Being forced to compare and evaluate immigration policy in an open forum together with civil societal and international actors, whose views on immigration are often quite liberal, involves a risk of losing control over the agenda-setting process. (Caviedes 2004: 306)

It appears however that the time was not right for an OMC on immigration matters.[13] Back in 2001, member states had faced a Commission

---

[12] COM (2001) 387 final, paragraph 3.4.

[13] See for instance Bourdrez (2010). This point was corroborated by the interviews conducted with Commission staff.

eager to use the OMC to significantly increase its competence. This had left a bad taste in member states' mouths and led them to discard the idea of an OMC in this policy area without much debate. Some six years later, propelled by pivotal member states and the support of the Commission, the policy on integration developed via a range of soft law instruments that together would look like a "quasi-OMC" (Carrera 2008; see Chapter 3 of this book for a full analysis).

In Search of an Analytical Framework

Getting the Framework Right

A framework is not a theory, nor is it a model. "A framework identifies a set of general variables and relationships that should be studied in order to understand a particular phenomenon, but assigns no values to the variables and does not specify the direction of relationships between them" (Schuyler House and Araral 2013: 116). It is therefore necessarily broad and flexible so that it can be applied to different empirical realities. Most importantly, it ought to provide conceptual tools to organise and discipline the search for explanations, it helps find the questions that are worth asking (Scharpf 1997: 29). But it does not provide answers; these remain to be found with the support of theories (that provide a more coherent set of assumptions) and models (representations of a more specific situation). This precision as to what a framework is is important since it is under this framework that theories and models will be applied and tested. The framework is a conceptual umbrella under which a series of assumptions drawn from different strands in the existing literature will be placed.

Even though the member states committed to the development of a common immigration policy, the two-step approach envisaged by the Commission failed. It is evident from the succession of events reported in the previous pages that the solutions envisaged at each step of the policy development are not the outcome of a result-driven approach to decision-making. To put it differently, the formal intergovernmental cooperation mentioned above and set up with the Treaty of Maastricht was not the best way to handle borders that would very soon be under strain; rather, considering divergences amongst member states, and notably the most likely veto of Denmark and the UK, this was the most acceptable solution. In the same fashion, the creation of the Area of

Freedom, Security and Justice (AFSJ) with the Treaty of Amsterdam, hampered by a transition period, does not seem to be the most desirable outcome but rather the most feasible one. Other examples could be listed, they would support, as the scholarship does, the fact that member states' diverging preferences govern outcomes more than the EU's eagerness to tackle a problem. To use yet a different phrasing: we are not in a situation where the policy-maker is engaged in a "game against nature" but rather in a "constellation" of players engaged "in purposeful action under conditions in which the outcomes are a joint product of their separate choices" (Scharpf 1997: 5). Actors do not play into the void but within sets of rules. Indeed, it would be erroneous to ignore institutions. Institutions, understood as "the rules of the game of a society, or, more formally, the humanly devised constraints that structure human interaction" (North 1990: 3), constrain actors' behaviour and orientate the strategies they wish to implement. The implementation of such strategies eventually defines the outcomes. Hinich and Munger summarise this under the "fundamental equation of politics" (Hinich and Munger 1997: 17):

Preferences + institutions = outcomes

When it comes to considering the immigration policy (until 2004) and its subset policy on integration of third country nationals (until the Lisbon treaty), actors' preferences are expressed in a unanimity decision-making framework, thereby reinforcing the importance of the states compared to that of the European institutions. The Commission is present and has somewhat of an agenda-setting power that is however limited by the possibility member states have to amend Commission proposals in the same way they have to adopt the final text.[14] The Commission has therefore no hold on the legislation being eventually passed. Effectively, if the Commission wants the text to be adopted, its proposal needs to be agreeable to all member states. Formally at least, member states are plunged into a game in which each one of them can block any legislation. Informal rules are likely to weigh, too; they may

---

[14] Tsebelis (2013: 17); but see also Franchino (2007) posits the "conditional agenda setting" power of the Commission under qualified majority voting given the fact the Commission proposes a text to the Council that is more difficult to amend than to accept: the Council vote at qualified majority but may only amend the Commission's proposal with unanimity.

even be more important than formal ones. Ostrom (2007: 23) suggests that "rules-in-use" are often more influential than "rules-in-form". This may particularly be the case in unanimity situations: who wants to be the one that breaks the consensus-seeking approach? The risk of being finger-pointed is high, especially in so-called repeated games; i.e. when the interaction between partners is repeated over time. A good example is that of Aus's analysis of the adoption of the Dublin II Regulation in February 2003 (Aus 2008): the Regulation was clearly making losers given the way asylum claims were to be processed. Yet, nobody was ready to take the blame for standing in the way of adoption. Clearly, member states are not equal when bargaining; be that in terms of economic power or in terms of capacity to build up alliances (Cross 2012). Each member state nonetheless has the possibility to stop the passage of a piece of legislation.

Bearing the foregoing in mind, I consider that the interaction between member states, more than the search for objective solutions to tackle problems, is the driver of decision-making. Who the actors are and what their strengths are remain to be seen. But it is clear that member states are placed in a bargaining situation in which they will try to have their interests prevail. I therefore start from an umbrella analytical framework that builds on Scharpf's actor-centred institutionalism (1997). I borrow from other strands in literature in order to come closer to the specifics of the policy under scrutiny, but these are placed under the umbrella of actor-centred institutionalism.

Scharpf and Actor-Centred Institutionalism

Actor-centred institutionalism is a framework originally developed by Scharpf and Mayntz in the 1990s, based on their empirical research conducted since the 1970s. It was first formalised in an article titled "Games Real Actors Could Play" in *Rationality and Society* in 1990 (Scharpf 1990). The stance taken therein drew from game theory and its conceptualisation of interactions. It advocated the applicability of such framework to the empirical world. For that very reason, it received criticism from both sides: game theorists rejected the claim for empirical application; empiricists rejected game-theoretic assumptions for being unrealistic (perfect rationality, complete information and so on). In his book *Games Real Actors Play* (1997), Scharpf expands and underpins his approach within 200 pages of theory and practical examples. To sum up the argument, he considers that policy outcomes are not the mere calculations on the best solution to do the job, but rather the product of diversely constructed perceptions of the solution to a problem. These diversely constructed perceptions collide, coalesce and confront with each other. Policy outcomes are the product of interactions between different actors that have a different view of reality, and consequently different preferences, and different capacities to enforce their preferences. These actors are not free to use whatever means to reach their purposes but, on the contrary, are constrained by institutions. The lines that follow break down Scharpf's analytical framework into a set of concepts that will prove useful for the remainder of this research.

Why Institutions Matter

Like North (1990), Ostrom (2007), and Hinich and Munger (1997), Scharpf emphasises the role of institutions in shaping the courses of action envisaged by actors. Institutions place actors in a game in which interactions amongst players are organised. Actors therefore plan their sequence of moves and are given the possibility to anticipate other actors. What institution means, however, is always a thorny question: what are the rules? Should we consider only formal rules? Should we consider informal rules? What are those rules? A complete list of applicable rules would be impossible but also inefficient. The law of nature is indeed a factor that limits individuals' capabilities. Should they be accounted for? Listing the rules that apply to a particular situation could range from international law to national labour law for instance, not to mention the bulk of informal rules that are likely to apply in a given context. Ostrom (2007), for instance, considers a set of fixed institutions that weigh on actors' strategy. Scharpf opts for a more pragmatic definition of institutions. If he acknowledges the existence of formal and informal rules, he considers institutions as being the rules that are likely to produce causal effects in their concrete shape. As he puts it:

> In our framework, therefore, the concept of the "institutional setting" does not have the status of a theoretically defined set of variables that could be systematized and operationalized to serve as explanatory factors in empirical research. Rather, we use it as a shorthand term to describe the most important influences on those factors that in fact drive our explanations—namely, actors with their orientations and capabilities, actor constellations, and modes of interaction. (1997: 39)

The institutional setting is therefore those most important influences that reduce the range of potential behaviours, a 'common knowledge' that defines what is required from, prohibited to, and permitted to players. The added-value of including institutions in the game becomes clearer when the researcher considers handling collective actors. Whereas individuals act on their account, collective actors involved in policy-forming act on behalf of members, on behalf of a constituency, to say the least, but they are also institutionally constituted – they are "said to 'exist' only to the extent that the individuals acting within and for them are able to coordinate their choices within a common frame of reference that is constituted by institutional rules" (1997: 39). Institutions therefore constrain the range of possible strategies and outcomes; they define the relevant players and shape their appreciation of available outcomes. This has two main consequences: (i) it limits the pretention to generalisation of the results of a specific piece of research since there exists a wide range of possible combinations of rules; (ii) they considerably limit the choice for plausible explanatory mechanisms to be tested.

That being said, a caveat is in order. If institutions greatly influence the definition of relevant players, the array of options available, and actors' preferences, they do not determine choices and outcomes; actors do. Institutions may help the researcher to envisage the possible courses of action, but strategies to reach one's goal remain up to the intentional actor.

Actors, Constellations and Modes of Interaction
Within the framework established by the institutional setting, actors seek to enforce their preferred outcomes. Not everyone is an actor though. When it comes to policies, one can consider there exist distant and proximate actors, not all being of relevance in the determination of the outcome. Scharpf thus advises to look first at the set of interactions that produces policy outcomes in order to identify the actual players whose choices ultimately determine the outcome.

In Scharpf's terminology, "actors are characterised by their orientations (perceptions and preferences) and by their capabilities" (1997: 51). Actors are embedded in different contexts that shape their representations of policy problems and their idea of policy solutions. Out of these perceptions come preferences. In order to enforce their preferences, actors mobilise capabilities, resources of different natures that allow an actor to influence an outcome. Resultantly, I consider the actors

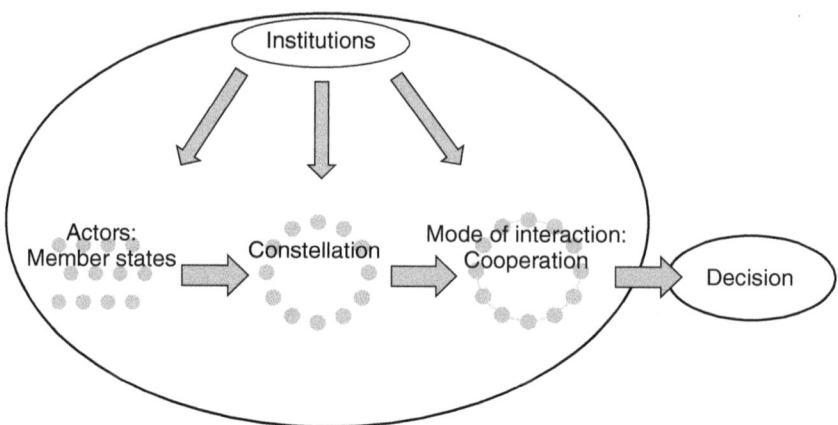

Fig. 2.1 Institutions in Scharpf's actor-centred institutionalism (*Source* Adapted from Fig. 2.1, "the domain of interaction-oriented policy research," from *Games Real Actors Play* by Fritz Scharpf, copyright © 1997. Adapted by permission of Westview Press, an imprint of Hachette Book Group, Inc.)

to be the relevant players who, within a venue formed by specific rules, express their preferences in a bargaining situation with variable chances of success, which depend on their capacity to enforce their preferences. Moreover, actors are not one-sidedly deciding the outcome they desire; they are inserted into a system of interaction in which other actors seek to enforce contrasting preferences, so that the outcome is far from being one's preferred result but is the joint product of individual choices. Only in rare occasions can a single actor get away with their preferred outcome remaining unaltered.

In order to understand the game actors play, two other concepts are necessary: the concept of constellation; and the concept of mode of interaction. 'Constellation' refers to an ensemble that encompasses "the players involved, their strategy options, the outcomes associated with strategy combinations, and the preferences of the players over these outcomes" (1997: 44). It is a static depiction of the interplay between the actors that matter for the policy outcomes under scrutiny. In a more dynamic fashion, actors in a constellation engage with one another in accordance with specific "modes of interaction". They may be unilateral actions, negotiated agreements, majority votes or hierarchical directions, to give some examples. These modes of interaction are indeed influenced by the institutional setting that, for instance, defines whether a decision is to be taken by unanimity or by qualified majority voting (see Fig. 2.1 for a depiction of the articulation between institutions, actors, constellations and modes of interaction). Now, it is evident that member states, if we go back to EU policy-making, do not behave in the same manner when unanimity prevails or when majority is in order. Unanimity triggers logics of consensus-seeking. Either member states compromise to make sure the bill passes; or their relative positions are too distant and one member state, irrespective of its material capabilities,[15] kills the bill.

These two concepts seem to depart from game-theoretic conventions but are actually further specifications for their application to the empirical world. Constellation, together with the mode of interaction, make up what game theory simply calls the "game". Non-cooperative games for instance are those in which the mode of interaction consists in unilateral actions, whereas a decision with unanimity translates into a negotiated agreement which is already what game theorists call cooperative games.

A Point on Composite Actors
The study of policy assumes that actors are intentional. This is little debatable in the sense that policy is a matter of choice to act that is little reconcilable with the idea of institutional permanence. Institutions do not undertake policies, actors do. The most obvious objection that comes to mind when considering the application of actor-centred institutionalism is that, ultimately, everything comes down to the individual actor. The individual actor is the subject of choice; not the European Commission, or the national government, but the people that make up these 'composite', 'aggregate' or 'collective' actors. Therefore, it seems difficult to attribute preferences to these actors or to hypothesise their behaviour without going down to the individual level. I ought to make a distinction between the one and the other, but for the sake of simplicity, I will stick to a distinction between two categories: aggregate actors and composite actors.

---

[15] As Scharpf argues, there are different kinds of capabilities, one of which flows directly from the institutional design. Institutional capabilities for a small member state, say Slovenia, are much greater under unanimity (in which it weighs as much as any other member states, at least formally), than under qualified majority (in which, at least until 2014, it has 4 votes out of 352). Differently, material capabilities may refer to items not directly related to the institutional design, such as GDP and the likes.

Aggregate actors are to be understood as aggregates of individuals or groups of individuals that do not feature structured coordination characteristics. Public opinion is an aggregate actor in the sense that the individuals that make it up are not coordinated in any way. Civil society organisations (CSOs) are another. If they necessarily display structured coordination *within*, they do not display it *between*: one organisation is internally organised and may speak with a single voice; considered together, these organisations are not coordinated. Nonetheless, one may speak of public opinion or CSOs because, irrespective of individual characteristics or preferences, their utility functions may be similar, they can be "modelled as responding in a predictable fashion to the moves of (individual or composite) actors that are capable of strategic action" (Scharpf 1997: 54).

As for composite actors, unlike aggregates, their action is supposed to be coordinated and the individuals that compose the whole aim at reaching a common position for a common purpose. It therefore makes sense to hypothesise a composite actor's intention. Indeed, the possibility of leaving a whole always exists, especially when we are dealing with governments and coalitions. It remains that concerted action is actively sought.

The Consequences of Unanimity Voting

After having acknowledged the role of the actors, the purpose of this section is to fathom the consequences of unanimity voting on policy design. I further assume that the output of the decision making process greatly determine implementation afterwards.

The Permanence of Unanimity Voting

Now that I have laid the framework for the overall understanding of this research, some further specifications are in order. Actors interact within a framework that is in a significant measure determined by institutions. Of particular interest here is the institutional setting inherited from the Treaty of Amsterdam that placed legal immigration (and in a way integration of third country nationals) under the unanimity rule. As established in the first part of this chapter, the shift towards majority voting, which should have taken place after the pillarisation of immigration policies and/or the adoption of the Council Decision that was supposed to bring unanimity to an end, did not occur.[16] Consequently, the mode of interaction that organises member states' interaction when it comes to integration measures is that of negotiated agreements. This, I argue, has dire consequences on the overall development of a policy domain (see notably Chapters 3 and 4). As Moravcsik (1998) argued, pooling sovereignty can be regarded as a way to increase the credibility of a commitment. Since member states entering into a contract (such as the treaties) may be incentivised to defect from their commitment, delegating powers to the EU by stipulating measures be adopted by qualified majority voting reinforces member states' commitment since they give away some of their sovereignty. Here, this shift did not occur. Since treaty delegation is weak, the implementing acts stemming therefrom are likely to leave great discretion to member states and little space to the Commission (Franchino 2004, 2007). I have established at the beginning of this chapter that it has been the case for the few Directives adopted in the first years following the entry into force of the treaty of Amsterdam. In this section, I argue that this likely affected the unfolding of the EU integration policy in the same manner. This section expands on this basic assumption, mobilising different theoretical frameworks.

Unanimity and Its Implications

Rational Choice Literature proves relevant in helping us to grasp the game at play. Early rational choice scholars such as Buchanan and Tullock (1958) held that, where transaction costs are negligible, unanimity voting is most desirable, since a change in the status quo would always be a Pareto improvement: any rational actor called to decide will assess the possible consequences of her/his actions and ensuing payoffs. In the event that the actor is called to cast a vote under unanimity rule, they have the full opportunity to voice their consent or disagreement, insofar as a dissident minority cannot be imposed an alternative that it does not accept, unlike under majority voting. The self-interested actor would not agree unless the expected payoff is more attractive than the costs entailed. In Tsebelis's words, all actors become veto-players, "actors whose agreement is necessary for a change of the status quo" (Tsebelis 2001: 36). Consequently, what matters is member states' respective preferences (and the distance between them) each time a vote is called for.

---

[16] At least not until the Treaty of Lisbon entered into force.

If the status quo is closer to any member state than the policy proposal, then the probability the text is rejected increases. In spite of diverging preferences, it is not rare to see the Council agreeing on a legislative piece that requires the unanimity of its members.

Consensus Through Imprecision

There exist different ways to reach consensus even where preferences are distant. One consists in moving the agreement towards the "least common denominator" (Tsebelis 2013: 14). Resultantly, entire policy areas may be left out of the final decision, or potential restrictions in the final decision may be loosened, or requirements may become more flexible, thus offering wide margins of interpretation. Imprecision results in an incomplete contract that, to use delegation theory terminology, the agent will have to 'fill in'.[17]

Another way to achieve consensus, although not exclusive of the first one, consists in overcoming distant *substantive* preferences through proximate *procedural* preferences, or, put differently, through the institutional design of the policy under consideration. Actors may not agree on goals, but they may more easily agree on methods (Kassim and Le Galès 2010). One way or another (or both combined), reaching consensus when the voting rule is unanimity is likely to have consequences on the effective delegation of competence.

Delegation Theory

Delegation literature looks into the relationship that connects a principal to an agent. The principal delegates some competence to the agent in order to decrease the transaction costs of permanent bargaining, information and expertise gathering, or else enforcing agreements.[18] Who the principal is and who the agent is changes throughout the policy phases: transferring further competence to the EU (treaty delegation) places member states in the shoes of the principal (see notably Moravcsik 1998; Pollack 1997), and the Commission in the agent's; transposition of Directives reverses the roles.[19] Delegation is no straightforward process

---

[17] See notably Kassim and Menon (2003), in this regard.

[18] See Kassim and Menon (2003), for an overview.

[19] See for instance executive delegation in Franchino (2007).

in that the agent may have its own preferences and find incentives to shirk from the task it was endowed with; or the agent may even be ill-selected.[20] For this reason, delegation is a matter of high stakes with, at its centre, the questions: whom to delegate power to? And how much power should be delegated?

Franchino (2007) proposes an interesting theory for the explanation of delegation that shall prove most relevant for the framing of the argument developed in this book, even though it is considerably simplified given the scope of the present research. If Franchino's model regards the delegation of executive powers via the design of EU laws, this book considers a single policy realm, ruled by a single mode of interaction: unanimity.[21] It remains that some of the assumptions made in Franchino's book are applicable here and help the understanding of my work. He considers that executive delegation through EU law operates a twofold choice: on the one hand the bill delegates implementation either to the Commission or to the national administration; on the other hand the very same bill grants more or less discretion to the chosen policy implementer. This delegation game is played through a series of factors, namely: (i) decision rules; (ii) conflict within the Council; (iii) conflict between the Commission and the pivotal government; and (iv) policy complexity. When it comes to unanimity voting, Franchino shows that the most likely outcome consists in delegation to national administration, with sizable discretion.

The Policy-Politics Nexus

It is beyond doubt that the policy-making process has a huge impact on the shape a policy is to take; to put it differently, politics determines policy. A very interesting point raised by Franchino (2007) regards the likely impact of decision-making rules on the policy design for further implementation, a point that has been partly explored by the literature on policy instruments. In a nutshell, the literature on policy instruments posits that policy design defines the actors that are going to matter in the implementation. As Salamon puts it (2000: 1627–1628),

---

[20]What Lupia (2003), calls the "perils" of delegation.

[21]The Treaty of Lisbon ended the unanimity voting rule. The scope of this research however does not cover policy outputs adopted after its entry into force.

the choice of tool is often a central part of the political battle that shapes public programs. What is at stake in these battles is not simply the most efficient way to solve a particular public problem, but also the relative influence that various affected interests will have in shaping the program's post-enactment evolution.

Kassim and Le Galès (2010) underpin the idea and hold that the choice for a tool is not guided by the best option to do the job but, rather, such choice disconnects policy instruments from political goals, upholding the principle whereby "actors find it easier to reach agreement on methods than goals" (2010: 8; see also Dehousse 2005). This is an extension of the thought introduced in early political science by Lowi that "policy determines politics" or that to each type of policy corresponds a diverse venue of power, a different network of actors, and a different decision-making process (Lowi 1964; see also Regonini 2001).

Since the tool chosen determines the actors that are going to be involved in the implementation, such choice is highly political. We thus observe a cycle that consists in the aphorism: politics determines policy that, in turn, determines politics; an aphorism mirrored in the definition of soft-Europeanization provided in the introduction of this book.[22] The tool opted for may associate a wider or narrower range of actors to the implementation process, bearing in mind that the association of actors place them in interdependence and as such, "no single actor, including the state, can enforce its will" (Salamon 2000: 1631). This point is of great relevance to Chapters 5 and 6 of this book.

CONCLUSION

The development of an EU immigration policy has been a long and winding road. From an intergovernmental framework marked by the development of the Schengen area, the competence fully fell within the EU framework some 15 years later with the adoption of the Treaty of Amsterdam. Going through the different steps of such a passage reveals that the main policy driver has never really been (at least not only) a response to a given problem, but rather the manifestation of diverging

---

[22]The first part of the aphorism, politics determines policy, corresponds to the bottom-up phase of Europeanization whilst the second part, policy determines politics, reflects the top-down phase.

preferences to answer a common issue, thereby emphasising the role of actors and reducing the importance of functionalist explanations. Accordingly, I establish that the most relevant analytical framework for this research is that of actor-centred institutionalism as developed by Scharpf (1997). It posits that actors are the subject of actions and actors undertake policies. Most often, however, actors do not decide alone when it comes to policies. They are placed in a constellation with other actors, who may have different preferences and different resources, but the same will to take action. Preferences may thus collide, rendering the outcome of a decision process uncertain. The expression of such preferences within a constellation of actors is not, however, free of rules. On the contrary, interactions are located within institutions, they are constrained by rules, ways of doing things that structure human interactions. For most of the timespan in which the EU integration policy unfolded, such rules have entrenched policy developments in unanimity voting. Unanimity voting places each concerned actor in the position to block the adoption of a bill. It is likely therefore that, in consensus-seeking logics, agreement be attained through less constraining provisions, which in turn may hamper implementation of the very same bill. This chapter develops this series of arguments in order to provide a framework, both analytical and theoretical, for the overall understanding of the four empirical chapters that follow, starting with the genesis of the policy at EU level (Chapter 3).

References

Scholarship and Expert References

Aus, J. P. (2008). The Mechanisms of Consensus: Coming to Agreement on Community Asylum Policy. In D. Naurin & H. Wallace (Eds.), *Unveiling the Council of the European Union: Games Governments Play in Brussels* (pp. 99–120). Basingstoke: Palgrave Macmillan.

Borràs, S., & Jacobsson, K. (2004). The Open Method of Co-ordination and New Governance Patterns in the EU. *Journal of European Public Policy, 11*(2), 185–208.

Bourdrez, L. (2010). *The EU Policy on the Integration of Third-Country Nationals. "A Two-Way Process?".* Master's thesis, University of Amsterdam.

Buchanan, J. M., & Tullock, G. (1958). *The Calculus of Consent: The Foundations of Constitutional Democracy.* Indiana: Liberty Fund. Available at http://www.econlib.org/library/Buchanan/buchCv3c7.html. Last Consulted November 12, 2016.

Carrera, S. (2008). *Benchmarking Integration in the EU: Analyzing the Debate on Integration Indicators and Moving It Forward.* Gütersloh: Bertelsmann Foundation.

Caviedes, A. (2004). The Open Method of Co-ordination in Immigration Policy: A Tool for Prying Open Fortress Europe? *Journal of European Public Policy, 11*(2), 289–310.

Cross, J. P. (2012). Everyone's a Winner (Almost): Bargaining Success in the Council of Ministers of the European Union. *European Union Politics, 14*(1), 70–94.

de Bruycker, P. (2005). Le Niveau D'harmonisation Legislative de La Politique Européenne D'immigration et D'asile. In Julien-Laferriere & Labayle (Eds.), *La politique européenne d'immigration et d'asile: bilan critique 5 ans après le traité d'Amsterdam.* Brussels: Bruylant.

Dehousse, R. (2005). La Méthode Ouverte de Coordination. Quand L'instrument Tient Lieu de Politique. In P. Lascoumes & P. Le Galès (Eds.), *Gouverner par les Instruments* (pp. 331–356). Paris: Presses de Sciences Po «Académique».

de la Porte, C. (2002). Is the Open Method of Coordination Appropriate for Organising Activities at European Level in Sensitive Policy Areas? *European Law Journal, 8*(1), 38–58.

de la Porte, C., & Pochet, P. (2012). Why and How (Still) Study the Open Method of Co-ordination (OMC)? *Journal of European Social Policy, 22*(3), 336–349.

Delors, J. (1985). *Intervention de Jacques Delors, Luxembourg, 9 septembre 1985,* Bulletin des Communautés européennes, Luxembourg: Office des publications officielles des Communautés européennes Septembre 1985, n° 9.

Eurostat. (1996). Asylum-Seekers in Europe 1985–1995. Statistics in Focus.

Faist, T., & Ette, A. (2007). The Europeanization of National Policies and Politics of Immigration: Research, Questions and Concepts. In T. Faist & A. Ette (Eds.), *The Europeanization of National Policies and Politics of Immigration: Between Autonomy and the European Union* (pp. 3–31). New York: Palgrave Macmillan.

Franchino, F. (2004). Delegating Powers in the European Community. *British Journal of Political Science, 34*(2), 269–293.

Franchino, F. (2007). *The Powers of the Union: Delegation in the EU.* Cambridge: Cambridge University Press.

Geddes, A. (2003). *The Politics of Migration and Immigration in Europe.* London: Sage.

Guild, E. (1998). Competence, Discretion and Third Country Nationals: The European Union's Legal Struggle with Migration. *Journal of Ethnic and Migration Studies, 24*(4), 613–625.

Guiraudon, V. (2003). The Constitution of a European Immigration Policy Domain: A Political Sociology Approach. *Journal of European Public Policy, 10*(2), 263–282.

Hailbronner, K. (2010). *Implications of the EU Lisbon Treaty on EU Immigration Law*. Paper prepared for the Transatlantic Exchange for Academics in Migration Studies, San Diego.

Hinich, H. J., & Munger, M. C. (1997). *Analytical Politics*. Cambridge: Cambridge University Press.

Hix, S. (2005). *The Political System of the European Union* (2nd ed.). Basingstoke: Palgrave Macmillan.

Hix, S., & Niessen, J. (1996). *Reconsidering European Migration Policies: The 1996 Intergovernmental Conference and the Reform of the Maastricht Treaty*. Brussels: Migration Policy Group.

Kassim, H., & Le Galès, P. (2010). Exploring Governance in a Multi-level Polity: A Policy Instruments Approach. *West European Politics, 33*(1), 1–21.

Kassim, H., & Menon, A. (2003). The Principal-Agent Approach and the Study of the European Union: Promise Unfulfilled? *Journal of European Public Policy, 10*(1), 121–139.

Knill, C., & Lehmkuhl, D. (2002). The National Impact of European Union Regulatory Policy: Three Europeanization Mechanisms. *European Journal of Political Research, 41*(2), 255–280.

Lowi, T. J. (1964). American Business, Public Policy, Case-Studies, and Political Theory. *World Politics, 16*(04), 677–715.

Luedtke, A. (2011). Uncovering European Union Immigration Legislation: Policy Dynamics and Outcomes. *International Migration, 49*(2), 1–27.

Lupia, A. (2003). Delegation and Its Perils. In K. Strom, W. C. Muller, & T. Bergman (Eds.), *Delegation and Accountability in Parliamentary Democracies*. New York: Oxford University Press.

Mazeron, F. (2008). Le Droit Communautaire de L'immigration et de L'asile à L'épreuve Du Droit International. In C. Bertrand (Ed.), *L'immigration dans l'Union Européenne: aspects actuels de droit interne et de droit européen*. Paris: L'Harmattan.

Moravcsik, A. (1998). *The Choice for Europe: Social Purpose and State Power from Messina to Maastricht*. Ithaca: Cornell University Press.

North, D. C. (1990). *Institutions, Institutional Change, and Economic Performance*. Cambridge: Cambridge University Press.

Ostrom, E. (2007). Institutional Rational Choice: An Assessment of the Institutional Analysis and Development Framework. In P. A. Sabatier (Ed.), *Theories of the Policy Process* (2nd ed., pp. 21–34). Boulder, CO: Westview Press.

Pollack, M. A. (1997). Delegation, Agency, and Agenda Setting in the European Community. *International Organization, 51*(1), 99–134.

Radaelli, C. (2003a). *The Open Method of Coordination: A New Governance Architecture for the European Union?* (Vol. 1). Stockholm: Swedish Institute for European Policy Studies.

Regonini, G. (2001). *Capire le politiche pubbliche.* Bologna: Il Mulino.

Salamon, L. M. (2000). The New Governance and the Tools of Public Action: An Introduction. *Fordham Urban Law Journal, 28*(5), 1611–1674.

Scharpf, F. W. (1990). Games Real Actors Could Play: The Problem of Mutual Predictability. *Rationality and Society, 2*(4), 471–494.

Scharpf, F. W. (1997). *Games Real Actors Play: Actor-Centered Institutionalism in Policy Research.* Boulder: Westview Press.

Schuyler House, R., & Araral, E. (2013). The Institutional Analysis and Development Framework. In E. Araral, S. Fritzen, M. Howlett, M. Ramesh, & X. Wu (Eds.), *Routledge Handbook of Public Policy* (pp. 115–125). New York: Taylor & Francis.

Scott, J., & Trubek, D. M. (2002). Mind the Gap: Law and New Approaches to Governance in the European Union. *European Law Journal, 8*(1), 1–18.

Tholoniat, L. (2010). The Career of the Open Method of Coordination: Lessons from a "Soft" EU Instrument. *West European Politics, 33*(1), 93–117.

Tsebelis, G. (2001). *Veto Players: How Political Institutions Work.* Princeton: Princeton University Press.

Tsebelis, G. (2013). Bridging Qualified Majority and Unanimity Decisionmaking in the EU. *Journal of European Public Policy, 20*(8), 1083–1103.

Urth, H. (2005). Building a Momentum for the Integration of Third-Country Nationals in the European Union. *European Journal of Migration and Law, 7*(2), 163–180.

Velluti, S. (2007). What European Union Strategy for Integrating Migrants? The Role of OMC Soft Mechanisms in the Development of an EU Immigration Policy. *European Journal of Migration and Law, 9*(1), 53–82.

Wallace, W. (1983). Less Than a Federation. More Than a Regime. The Community as a Political System. In H. Wallace & W. Wallace (Eds.), *Policy-Making in the European Community* (pp. 403–436). Oxford: Oxford University Press.

Ziller, J. (2009). Le Droit Au Séjour et à La Libre Circulation Dans l'Union Européenne, à La Lumière de La Jurisprudence et Du Traité de Lisbonne. In H. Bauer, P. Cruz Villalòn, & J. Iliopoulos-Strangas (Eds.), *The new Europeans—Migration and Integration in Europe.* Baden-Baden: Nomos Verlagsgesellschaft.

Eu Acts and Other Official Documents

COM (2000) 757 Final—European Commission. (2000). *Communication from the Commission to the Council and the European Parliament on a Community Immigration Policy.*

COM (2001) 387 Final—European Commission. (2001). *Communication from the Commission to the Council and the European Parliament on an Open Method of Coordination for the Community Immigration Policy.*

European Council. (1999). *Tampere European Council 15 and 16 October 1999, Presidency Conclusions.*

CHAPTER 3

Explaining the Genesis of a Policy

With the adoption of the Amsterdam treaty and the intent to build up an Area of Freedom, Security and Justice (AFSJ), immigration matters passed from the third pillar to the first. We saw in Chapter 2 that such a change lacked substantial meaning in the sense that policies would still be adopted under the unanimity rule. Nonetheless, important institutional changes occurred. The Commission, which formerly had a small Justice and Home Affairs unit, was henceforth provided with a Directorate General for Justice and Home Affairs[1] (DG JHA), a suitably staffed division that would be able to work out a European policy, make proposals and so forth. Integration was not the immediate focus, but, as new JHA Commissioner Vitorino joked about his height "I'm a little man and I take little steps forward" (*The Economist* 2001), the policy would start out small and develop with the passage of time.

The first steps were slow to be taken despite the early commitment made at Tampere[2] in 1999. The Commission first put forth a set of proposals responding to the Tampere milestones to the letter, and focused on Directives for an approximation of migrants' rights with that of European Union citizens. Proposals for family reunification, long-term resident status, and the fight against discrimination were submitted to

---

[1] The name of which has changed over the years.
[2] European Council (1999).

© The Author(s) 2019
P. G. Van Wolleghem, *The EU's Policy on the Integration of Migrants*, Palgrave Studies in European Union Politics, https://doi.org/10.1007/978-3-319-97682-2_3

Council scrutiny. The legal framework against discrimination did not take long to be adopted. The so-called Racial Directive was given the green light in 2000, in a particular conjuncture that saw Jorg Häider, then leader of the far-right Austrian Freedom Party, within a coalition government in Austria, encouraging the French and Germans to advocate the Directive's early adoption (Guiraudon 2003). In addition, this Directive revolved around racial discrimination and was not initially or formally designed for discrimination on nationality grounds. The two other Directives, more targeted and perhaps more visible, took up to four years of heated negotiations before being adopted (see Chapter 2). It ought to be mentioned that the main focus at the time, since the Trevi group and the Schengen agreements (see Chapter 2) was security- and border-oriented.[3] However, under the guise of the fight against social exclusion, integration of third country nationals would progressively make its way onto the EU agenda.

Taking note of the specific institutional structure in place in this policy realm (Scharpf 1997; Chapter 2), this chapter looks at actors' moves within the rules established; it uses process tracing[4] to reconstruct the process that led the policy onto the EU agenda and identifies the mechanism at play. I argue that the meeting of three elements allowed an EU integration policy to emerge. Firstly, beyond a mere legal requirement, proceeding through soft law was a necessary condition to joint action. Secondly, the issue reached the EU agenda thanks to three member states that held the Presidency of the Council and that, for one reason or another, were eager (and able) to build consensus and upload their preferences. Thirdly, the Commission played an essential role in developing the policy whilst remaining within the margins set by the member states. That said, the Commission displayed significant energy in carving out a role for itself in integration matters, confirming its role as a purposeful opportunist. These three elements together allowed for an embryo of a policy to exist and grow in breadth with time.

---

[3] In this regard, see inter alia Bigo (1996, 2002), Guiraudon (2003), and Duez (2008).

[4] Process tracing has been the object of many articles and books in existing literature (see notably Checkel 2005; Vennesson 2008; Mahoney 2010; Collier 2011). Here I follow Mahoney (2010) and rely on mechanism causal-process observations. See appendices for more detail on data.

This chapter first outlines the traits of a specific context, favourable to the creation of a European policy for the integration of third country nationals. Then, I formulate and formalise the causal mechanism that explains the passage of the policy to the EU. Finally, the third part of this chapter moves to the empirical evidence, designates the main actors and fleshes out the causal mechanism with facts. It also shows how the Commission gained momentum for the creation of a sounder integration policy, embodied by the adoption of the European Integration Fund.

THE OPENING OF A WINDOW OF OPPORTUNITY

Colliding Paradigms in Europe: Security vs. Inclusion

The Securitization of Migration

The common immigration policy was developed in a climate dominated by security concerns.[5] Immigration and migrants were socially constructed as a security question, "reifying migration as a force which endangers the good life in west European societies" (Huysmans 2000: 752). The establishment of an area of free movement under the EU framework and the prospect of a further enlargement to Eastern and Central Europe pushed for more formal police cooperation (reinforcement of Europol, implementation of Eurodac, development of the Schengen Information System II) and border control. Borders were especially important since the full inclusion of Eastern and Central European states would eventually push further the borders of the EU; it was therefore important for them, in order to join the Schengen area, to be able to secure their own (hence European) borders. From there, it becomes evident that more cooperation but also legal integration of a competence was in order. Even before the entry into force of the Treaty of Amsterdam, the Justice and Home Affairs Council fixed the priorities for the effective construction of the AFSJ.[6] The terrorist attacks on the Twin Towers on September 11, 2001, did not help shift the focus (Urth 2005; Heidbreder 2014). Despite the Commission's initiatives in the field, governments brought further transfer of competence to the

---

[5] There are many examples in existing literature on this point but see Bigo (1996, 2002), Guiraudon (2003), and Duez (2008).

[6] JHA Council (1999).

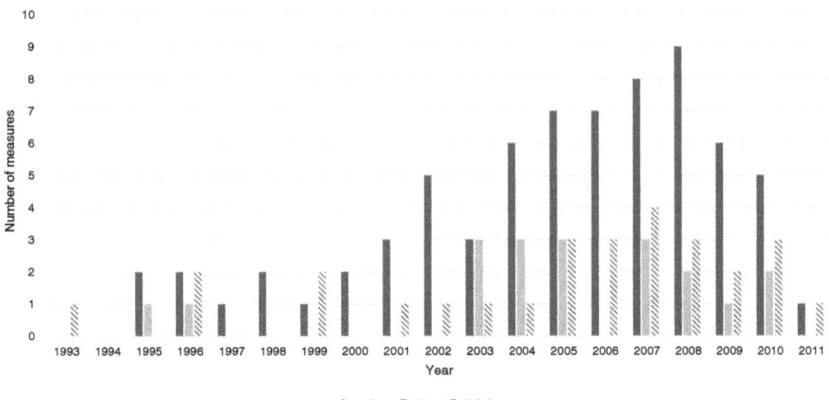

Fig. 3.1 Policy measures by policy types on migration over time (*Source* Adapted from Heidbreder, Copyright © 2014: 7. Adapted by permission of Fondazione ISMU)

EU to a halt: no follow-up to the Tampere milestones was carried out; the Laeken Council conclusions in December 2001 did not even mention integration,[7] and the proposal for an OMC in 2001 did not make it to the Council. Until 2003, the only clear achievement was the Racial Discrimination Directive that was not even directly linked to integration, nor did it belong to Title IV, TEC (i.e. immigration). Figure 3.1, adapted from Heidbreder (2014), shows the distribution over time of immigration-related measures according to three types[8]: security-oriented, rights-oriented and a catch-all category for the remainders.[9] These three categories account for respectively 60.3, 15.5, and 24.1% of the total number of measures.

The securitization of immigration is a phenomenon that dates back to the 1980s. Before that, western European states observed a rather permissive immigration policy in order to fill the gaps in their labour

[7] European Council (2001).

[8] The three types include all EU measures but especially: treaties, secondary law, and soft steering measures.

[9] Since the three categories encompass primary law, treaties are classified in the catch-all category for instance.

markets (see below). In the 1980s however, the phenomenon was increasingly framed in terms of protection of public order and preservation of domestic stability. As Huysmans (2000: 757) argues,

> [t]he development of security discourses and policies in the area of migration is often presented as an inevitable policy response to the challenges for public order and domestic stability (...). But this limited interpretation reflects how security practices actually affect social relations. They are also defining practices which turn an issue like migration into a security problem by mobilizing specific institutions and expectations.

To put it another way, the policy is not only a solution to a problem; it also creates or frames it. The link created between terrorism and immigration by the Convention Applying the Schengen Agreement contributes to framing the regulation of migration as a security matter (Bigo 1996). In the same fashion, member states' representatives in Council meetings were mostly ministers of the interior and the prevalent priority was securing the borders.

That being said, a European policy for the integration of third country nationals was brought to bear, slowly but surely. From nothing, it reached a consistent body of instruments that together formed a "quasi-OMC" (Carrera 2008: 6), despite the actual proposal for an OMC of 2001 having being rejected.

The Fight Against Social Exclusion

At the same time as, and perhaps even earlier than, the security paradigm, there existed the paradigm of social exclusion. As Murard (2002: 41) puts it:

> 'Exclusion' is not a concept rooted in the social sciences, but an empty box given by the French state to the social sciences in the late 1980s as a subject to study... The empty box has since been filled with a huge number of pages, treatises and pictures, in varying degrees academic, popular, original and valuable.

Appearing in France in the 1970s as a policy problem with Gaullist Minister René Lenoir, initially designating the victims of the economic crisis and increasing social inequalities, the concept of social exclusion grew to the point of becoming a European paradigm, embodied by the treaty of Amsterdam, article 137 TEC. The European enthusiasm for social exclusion was first manifested through the fight against poverty initiated with a first programme for the years 1975–1980 (Mathieson et al. 2008). If a second such programme took on the fight against poverty, the third observed somewhat of a shift in terminology towards social exclusion, despite it being nicknamed "Poverty III" (Vanhercke 2012; Mathieson et al. 2008). The succession of anti-poverty or social inclusion programmes created momentum for the introduction of article 137 TEC with the treaty of Amsterdam (Vanhercke 2012). The Commission,[10] and more specifically DG Employment and Social Affairs, seized the opportunity to include migrants within the category of populations at risk of exclusion, if not already excluded, and provided for action to be taken by NGOs via its 'Preparatory Measures to Combat Social Exclusion 1998'. Within the frame of this generally favourable context for social inclusion, member states' agendas unfolded in a compatible way that would end up on a European agenda for integration.

Integration Is in the Air: Developments at National Level

The first steps for a Europeanised integration policy took place at a time when there were 15 member states. At least half of them had a similar immigration history and were on the brink of designing systematic integration policies.[11] That said, from concerns to actual action-taking, these states moved at different paces, with Denmark[12] and the Netherlands ahead of the others.

After the Second World War, most western European[13] countries resorted to immigration to fill the gaps in their labour markets. Most

[10] European Commission (1998).

[11] Notably the United Kingdom, Germany, France (Schnapper 1994), Austria (Wischenbart 1994), Denmark (Mouritsen and Hovmark Jensen 2014), Belgium (Mandin 2014), and the Netherlands (Fischler 2014). In actual facts, almost all 15 member states had already taken action on integration by 2003. For more information see COM (2003) 336 final, Annex 1.

[12] It is interesting to note in this respect that the first person that ever worked on integration in the Commission's DG Justice and Home Affairs was not a Commission official but a national expert from a Danish Ministry detached to the Commission.

[13] Note that in some instances, most foreign workers came from the then European periphery: southern European states such as Italy, Greece, Spain, Portugal, Ireland, Finland, or else Turkey and Maghreb countries (Castles et al. 2013). These imports of workforce were mainly organised through bilateral agreements between single European

of them followed a model similar to the German's *Gastarbeiter* (guest worker) or to colonial workers: importing a workforce on a temporary basis to meet the countries' needs of the moment.[14] Throughout Western Europe, single males or males without their family were hired through institutional channels.[15] When the oil crisis hit in the 1970s, these states sought to stem influxes of workers and send their guests back through voluntary repatriation schemes. Contemplating a temporary phenomenon becoming permanent, and given the blatant failure of repatriation schemes, those states had to envisage legal devices to organize foreigners' stay, notably *de jure* family reunion, which would in turn mark the failure of attempts to stem influxes.[16] Soon, rising concerns as to immigration in the face of cultural diversity begged the questions of national identity and integration. Those started to gain public attention mostly in the 1980s and 1990s.[17]

The United Kingdom had been undergoing riots in the most multi-ethnic cities in the 1990s and particularly during summer 2001, prompting the debate on the creation of a sentiment of Englishness and common elements of nationhood (Cantle 2001). The terrorist attacks in the US in September 2001 further crystalized the issue around the presence of Islam and significantly increased its relevance on the New Labour political agenda (Kundnani 2012; Van Wolleghem 2016). From a debate framed in terms of race relations and the fight against discrimination, the UK started a policy turn towards more cultural integration from 2002 onward (Schain 2010).

In France, the issue has been on the agenda since the emergence of the debate on national identity in the 1980s (Schnapper 1994; Thiesse 2001), brought back into focus by President Sarkozy in 2007. Institutionally speaking, a High Council for Integration (*Haut Conseil à*

---

countries (Germany, Belgium, the United Kingdom, and the Netherlands) and the supplier countries (Guild 2001).

[14] On this point, see notably Rubio-Marín (2004), Castles et al. (2013), Hollifield (1992), and Penninx et al. (2014).

[15] See the German *Bundesanstalt für Arbeit* for instance or the French *Office National d'Immigration*.

[16] See Castles et al. (2013), for an overview.

[17] In this regard, see Schnapper (1994), Wischenbart (1994), Mouritsen and Hovmark Jensen (2014), Mandin (2014), and Fischler (2014); but see also Zincone et al. (2011).

l'Intégration) was created in 1989 and was vested with the task of advising the Government on integration issues. It actually contributed to the design of a French Republican Integration model. Immigration, integration and national identity were given a ministry under Sarkozy's presidency of the Republic in 2007. Notably, the ever louder voice of the National Front on the national scene from the 1980s onward contributed to the emergence and permanence of integration on the agenda, worded in terms of "integration crisis" (Favell 2001; Noiriel 2006). The unexpected rise of the National Front in the presidential election of 2002 politicized the already salient issues of immigration and integration, notably with regard to Muslims present in French territory.

Germany, quintessence of a *ius sanguinis* tradition, saw in 2000 a deep reform of its 1913 nationality law, which liberalized nationalization to those that are not of German ancestry, in a context marked by strong anti-immigrant sentiment among the population (Morjé Howard 2008). The automatic granting of nationality to *Aussiedler* (ethnic Germans) that could barely (if at all) speak German or share cultural traits, and that would need costly integration courses, was becoming ever harder to justify in the face of German-born, yet non-nationals, for whom there was no legal possibility to become German. German-born Turks for instance would often speak fluent German, study and work in Germany without ever having the possibility to apply for citizenship. It is with the SPD-Greens Schroeder government in 1998 and with, in sight, the idea of guaranteeing the possibility of integration, that the reform of nationality law was heralded and carried out, under the criticism of the CDU/CSU opposition. Differently, integration measures were carried out, mostly by employers, Länder and NGOs, even though the central government placed financial means at their disposal (Sussmuth 2009).

Similarly to the other countries already mentioned, the issue of integration in Belgium society emerged in the 1980s when migrants were still mostly seen as temporary stayers (Mandin 2014). As in Germany, the first initiatives in this domain did not come from the authorities but rather from private actors, such as labour unions and migrant associations, until a set of law was passed in the 1980s, reforming nationality acquisition on the one hand and conferring the competence on integration to the Communities on the other. The creation of a Centre for Equal Opportunities and Opposition to Racism in the 1990s, in charge of combatting discrimination and facilitating social inclusion, further institutionalized integration. Integration in Belgium is a matter that has attracted soaring attention with the steady increase of electoral successes of the Vlaams-Belang in Flanders over the past 30 years (Petrovic 2012), an attention that crystalized around Muslims in the aftermath of the terrorist attacks on the Twin Towers in the US (Mandin 2014).

Similarly, migration reached the Austrian political agenda in the 1980s, mainly pushed and politicized by the ascent of Jörg Häider's FPÖ and, to a lesser (yet significant) extent, the Greens (Kraler 2011). The advent of the end of the 30-year long Grand Coalition in Austria with the entry of the FPÖ in government in February 2000 pushed immigration and integration issues further onto the agenda. Despite the resignation of Häider at the head of the FPÖ under the sanctions of the other 14 EU member states, some of the measures foreseen in the 2000s coalition programme were put forth in July 2002's reform.

In Denmark and the Netherlands (see the next section for more details), the issue of integration has occupied successive government agendas and public attention, from the 1980s onwards, and rapidly became a pivotal issue in politics.

As can be seen from the foregoing, the climate was gently pushing integration to the fore. The adoption of the Treaty of Amsterdam created a remote policy competence, the development of which has revolved around security and border controls in the aftermath of the terrorist attacks on the Twin Towers in 2001. But integration at the national level had already taken consistent steps and was on the agenda of half of the member states of the then EU-15. At EU level though, the priority was still internal security. A quick look at the composition of the Justice and Home Affairs Council meetings held from 1999 to 2002 shows an overwhelming representation of national Ministries of the Interior and Justice. Two exceptions are Sweden, which sent a Minister with a wide and vague portfolio (the so-called "Minister for International Development Cooperation, with responsibility for Migration and Immigration"), and, most importantly, Denmark, which from 2001 and the formation of the new government, sent a Minister for Refugees, Immigration and Integration. When Denmark took up the Presidency of the Council of the European Union, it took a leap forward to place the issue on the European agenda, a move that would gain momentum through the succession of three Presidencies, almost one after another over a short time-span, and that were eager to anchor integration onto the EU agenda.

SOFT-EUROPEANIZATION AND UPLOAD OF PREFERENCES: A CAUSAL MECHANISM

The fact that integration was dealt with at national level in most EU countries at the time was evidently not enough for it to become an EU policy. Being linked to legal immigration, and border control; in a word, to sovereignty, the issue was still sensitive and not prone to harmonisation. The creation of an EU policy on immigration, one of the most unlikely policies to be Europeanised (Faist and Ette 2007), represented the first step towards the possibility of an EU role in the integration of third country nationals. This convergence between institutional and situational elements created a fertile ground for further development. But there was still a long way to go from there to the solid anchorage of integration onto the EU agenda.

This section argues that the mechanism that took the policy to the EU sphere can be defined as a process of preferences upload in the bottom-up phase of soft-Europeanization. "Europeanization is like one of those bumblebees that seem to defy the laws of aerodynamics, yet they fly", as Exadaktylos and Radaelli wrote (2012: 17). The acceptation of Europeanization has been widely debated in the existing literature since the late 1990s and its definition remains fairly open today.[18] Most of the time,[19] it refers to a top-down logic, assuming the top is the EU and the bottom is the member states, and describes the effects of EU membership onto member states (Featherstone 2003). Another approach considers Europeanization in a more bottom-up fashion, examining the role of member states in setting the agenda and making policies at EU level (Richardson 2012). In a seminal article, Börzel (2002) links the two approaches. She posits that, in order to reduce the costs of implementation of EU outputs, member states are incentivised to upload their domestic policies to the EU level. In doing so, they reduce the adaptation effort to be produced at a later stage. Member states thus compete (however with different resources and therefore different strategies) to

[18] This is acknowledged by numerous students of Europeanization; see inter alia Radaelli (2003b), Bache (2005), Caporaso (2007), and Richardson (2012).

[19] I here make abstraction of the studies dealing with the divide neo-functionalism—inter-governmentalism that occupied a good deal of the discourse prior to the studies framed in terms of Europeanization. Previous studies were concerned with the emergence of a European polity and, indeed, proceeded in a bottom-up fashion.

have their policies adopted at EU level. In a similar, yet different, manner, Radaelli (2003b: 30) defines Europeanization as being:

> processes of (a) construction, (b) diffusion, and (c) institutionalization of formal and informal rules, procedures, policy paradigms, styles, 'ways of doing things', and shared beliefs and norms which are first defined and consolidated in the making of EU public policy and politics and then incorporated in the logic of domestic discourse, identities, political structures, and public policies.

Europeanization is here understood as a circular process of co-construction of norms that goes up to the EU sphere before coming back down in the domestic environment. This in turn should feed into the process of co-construction of norms and so on.

In Radaelli's as in Börzel's conception, there is room for member states trying to upload their policy preferences, although this is more evident in Börzel. But whilst Börzel's analysis revolves mainly around legal acts such as Directives and Regulations (mostly regulatory policies), Radaelli mentions public policy as a whole, and therefore includes less legally binding policy instruments. This is a notable difference in the case I am dealing with since the EU competence in matters of integration of third country nationals was inexistent at the time. As a consequence, the most likely manner in which EU norms could be adopted was by resorting to soft law, which considerably decreases the costs of further implementation, especially when there is no evaluation, benchmarking, or reporting activities.

Although these two definitions are clearly relevant for the case at hand, this chapter is more concerned with one phase of the process of Europeanization: how a national policy becomes, to some extent, an EU policy; how the EU obtains a say in a policy field from which it is *de jure* excluded.

Drawing on Scharpf's actor-centred institutionalism (1997) and notably on the importance he gives to institutions (see Chapter 2), I argue in the remainder of this section that the mechanism in question puts on stage the interaction between: (i) a necessary condition; i.e. the soft provisions deriving from the institutional context increase the acceptability of EU instruments at EU level; (ii) a sufficient condition; i.e. the preferences of the member states holding the Presidency of the Council eager to push the issue onto the EU agenda and their success in doing it; and (iii) an intervening (or facilitating) factor; i.e. the readiness of the Commission to occupy a policy space without ever impinging on member states' exclusive competence.

Soft Law: A Necessary Condition

Soft law is a set of non-binding provisions supposed to guide behaviours. To take a more formal and classic definition, soft law is a set of "rules of conduct which in principle have no legal force but which nevertheless may have practical effects" (Snyder 1993: 198). At EU level, soft law is a way to organise cooperation in realms where the treaty base for action is thin or inexistent or where interests are diverging and no agreement other than that can be reached (Radaelli 2003a, 2008). The Open Method of Coordination (OMC) has been a popular tool to ensure member states pursue similar goals without resorting to harmonisation.[20] Applied to immigration though, it blatantly failed.[21] The OMC is not just soft law; it implies reporting activities, benchmarking achievements against European counterparts, evaluating the measures taken and so on. It is a light structure, though not as light as branded. In order for member states to be willing to work together on the topic, the policy approach needed to be softer. In order to ease cooperation, any compulsion had to be removed. Only thus could cooperation at the EU level become acceptable.[22]

Member States' Preferences and the Role of the Presidency: The Sufficient Condition

The passage from national agenda to the EU agenda is a matter of political activism from specific actors who wish to sell their policy to other actors (Elgström 2000; Princen 2007). Of course, such activism does not necessarily pay off, since policies or national agendas are in competition

---

[20] See Chapter 2 for a more thorough description of the OMC. See also Borràs and Jacobsson (2004) and Kröger (2009).

[21] Chapter 2 provides more detail on this. See also Caviedes (2004) and Vellutti (2007).

[22] This is notably corroborated by one interviewee who holds that, what eased cooperation at EU level, was the fact that there was no compulsion whatsoever, the fact that member states could literally sign up for something without ever having to implement it.

with others and not all of them successfully end up on top of the EU political agenda. In the case of migrant integration, member states are key actors when it comes to placing their concerns onto the EU agenda. Since the Commission had no competence on the matter, it did not have the monopoly on the initiative, and since the Commission did not have a conditional agenda-setter role because of the application of the unanimity rule,[23] member states were the most likely agenda-setter candidates. In the context of an inexistent EU policy and in the absence of a clear legal basis, there was little chance to see integration rising further up the EU agenda. That said, Presidencies of the Council played a significant role in this regard.

The Presidency of the Council was initially established for functional motives and with a view to ensure political continuity (Wallace 1985). Functional motives because someone had to attend to the Council's business organization and Council meetings needed to be chaired. As for continuity, rotating Presidencies allowed for negotiations to keep going over time. For a long time, the Presidency has been regarded as an "office without power" (Tallberg 2003: 1), a mere mediator or administrative manager. Tallberg however questioned this restricted role, notably by operating a distinction between agenda-shaping, agenda-setting, agenda-structuring and agenda exclusion. The Presidency may not conform to the traditional acceptation of agenda-setting—he suggested—but it can surely influence it via a rich repertoire of means at its disposal. Tallberg thus introduced the notion of agenda-shaping, covering the capacity to set the agenda (agenda-setting), to structure it (agenda-structuring) and to exclude some issues from being treated (agenda exclusion). All three are mutually exclusive modes the Presidency can resort to in order to shape the agenda. The main contribution of Tallberg though is not so much the conceptualisation of different means of power but rather (at least for our purpose here) the break with the conventional wisdom that would look at the Presidency as a merely functional body. Christiansen (2006: 151) corroborates, arguing: "the Presidency is anything but an innocent functional creation", it grants individual governments holding it the possibility to prioritise certain issues and manage the EU agenda accordingly. This does not guarantee success for the member state in question insofar as the agenda is also sensitive to

---

[23] This point is presented in greater detail in Chapter 2 but see also Tsebelis (2013).

exogenous events (specific crisis, as, for instance, September 11, 2001) or long-term goals (accession of the Central and Eastern European Countries) or to the influence of other member states; but this opens an opportunity to the Presidency to push forward its preferences.

In the case at issue, Presidencies were successful in transferring their preferences to the EU level. Why is this so? As already stated, the topic is sensitive. So why is it that member states agree that one of them places the issue on the agenda? This, I argue, is due to the necessary condition. The fact that any initiative in that domain necessarily consists in soft law, member states have the possibility to adopt a text without ever having to give effect to it. Considering that there exists a culture of consensus within the Council, even when it comes to sensitive issues such as immigration-related ones (Aus 2008), it is oftentimes difficult to stand out and refuse a text. If the text at issue is soft law, then no member state has any interest in breaking the informal consensus rule for a text that it will not be obliged to eventually implement.[24] Resultantly, the chances of success of the member state proposing the issue being coordinated at EU level are considerably increased. In addition, the member states holding the Presidency organise their semester with a number of encounters to discuss their priorities in order to reach common positions before any proposal is put to the vote. In this manner, the Presidency has the opportunity to build consensus on specific issues, a consensus easier to reach where potential outputs are soft instruments.

The Circumscribed Activity of the Commission: An Intervening Factor

Once the member states place the issue on the agenda, the Commission has to give effect to the decisions made in Council's instances. As well established by the existing literature, the Commission has the ability to play the policy entrepreneur (Hooghe 1996; Cram 1997). It is decisive that the Commission remains within the boundaries of its role, exploiting the margins to a reasonable extent without reaching too far, in which case the issue could be removed from the agenda (the failed OMC in

---

[24] Another element which probably entered into play along with the fact that law was to be soft, is the fact that the Council's meetings were made up of representatives of ministries of the interior mostly (except for Denmark and Sweden; see above) with interests allegedly lying with security and border controls more than with integration.

2001 or some of the Directives rejected as seen in Chapter 2 are good examples). This condition is indubitably linked to the soft-law condition referred to above. Importantly though, the Commission has managed to remain within the boundaries of acceptability established by the member states but also managed to gain momentum to develop a sounder integration policy, notably via the creation of a fund for integration. If the OMC was refused in 2001, the policy as it stood in 2007 featured all the aspects of one.

THE ACTORS AT PLAY: THREE PRESIDENCIES AND THE COMMISSION

Three Presidencies with Joint Preferences

The Danish Presidency: Pulling the Trigger
After a first appearance at the European Council in Tampere, 1999, integration was scarcely touched upon. It appeared again in the conclusions of the European Council in 2002, in Seville, which ended the Spanish presidency and opened onto the Danish one. The conclusions adopted set, in general terms, the objective of striking "a fair balance" between border management and integration and asylum.[25] When they took up the Presidency in July 2002, the Danes had as a top priority the successful enlargement to the East that was to occur in 2004. This was a long-term goal already established that the Presidency inherited. But the Presidency also had an agenda of its own regarding the AFSJ—a top priority of the Amsterdam treaty—and, notably, one on integration.

Integration issues had been of pivotal importance for Danish public opinion and (consequently) for Danish politics for a long while. On the agenda since the 1980s, they became more and more salient in the 1990s to the point of being the central issues of the 1998, 2001, and 2005 election campaigns (Mouritsen and Hovmark Jensen 2014). This importance was sanctioned with the adoption of the Integration Act in 1999 and the creation in 2001 of a Ministry for Refugees, Immigrants and Integration, the oft-abbreviated "Ministry of Integration". The latter Ministry was set up under Rasmussen's minority government, backed by the overtly xenophobic Danish People's Party (Thränhardt 2014).

[25] European Council (2002: 7).

When the Danish Presidency came in in July 2002, integration was tossed onto the European agenda by the duo Haarder-Espersen. As soon as the Presidency began, a conference was held on successful labour integration (the very same month the Presidency started). The Danish Presidency strongly advocated more cooperation on integration matters. In September 2002, the Danish Presidency held an informal Justice and Home Affairs Council on immigration and integration.[26] In October of the same year, the Danes organised a Justice and Home Affairs Council[27] in which cooperation regarding integration at the level of the Justice and Home Affairs Council was discussed. Overall, the Council Conclusions on integration were not particularly ambitious in their content. They recalled member states' commitment to integration, as already stated in previous Council meetings, and called for more cooperation on the matter. Yet, these Conclusions were particularly important in several respects: (i) the Danish semester had been marked by a series of events relating to integration and, accordingly, the Conclusions dedicated some more importance to the topic with the adoption of a set of 13 generally worded conclusions, thus placing the issue on the European agenda; (ii) instead of being merged under a more general migration chapter, integration was dealt with in a section dedicated to it, thereby intimating the idea that integration is, or should be, a policy in its own right at EU level; and (iii) finally, the conclusions highlighted the importance of exchanging information concerning valuable experiences and national policies on integration (what would later become the National Contact Points on Integration[28]; see Box 3.1), and the backing of such initiatives with some EU-funding.[29] Such conclusions, rather vague in their formulation, were "adopted without major difficulties and even warmly welcomed by some member states" (Urth 2005: 170).

Integration was a strength for Denmark comparatively to other European countries since they had, at the time, the most developed

---

[26] Danish EU Presidency (2002).

[27] JHA Council (2002), paragraphs 10 and 11.

[28] An idea that would be exploited by the Commission to systematise the initiative. See next section on the Commission.

[29] An idea put forth by Commissioner Vitorino a month before. See next section on Commission.

policy on the matter (along with the Dutch). Since Presidencies represent the opportunity for member states to leave a mark on EU integration, the Danes allegedly intended to "market" their own policy.[30] In addition to that, a structural impediment is likely to have had a bottleneck effect on Danish priorities. Since Denmark had entirely opted out of Title IV TEC covering immigration, and since the achievement of the AFSJ was highly salient at the time, notably due to the forthcoming enlargement,[31] there was little that Denmark could actually do other than organising intergovernmental cooperation.[32] Integration was ideal in this respect since there was no sound competence for it, no other way to proceed than that of mere "light" coordination.[33] Integration was also, at the time, envisaged by the Danish Presidency as a way to counterbalance terrorism by acquainting immigrants coming from different backgrounds with democratic and more generally Western values. As a matter of fact, the Danish integration policy was mainly targeted at Muslims, who were perceived as observing different value systems, especially after September 11, 2001 (Mouritsen and Hovmark Jensen 2014). The convergence of these two factors; i.e. the impossibility for the Danes to work out Title-IV-related measures and their state-of-the-art integration policy, spurred the Danes to fill in the then widespread security paradigm with more integration to European values. That said, despite their eagerness to promote their integration policy, the Danes did not propose any *substantive* policy developments, they did not attempt to give a direction to the policy. Rather, their focus was set on initiating *procedural* developments by creating a venue for exchanging experiences in the domain (and within which they could eventually promote their policy). Even so, the Conclusions' phrasing did not foretell the shape such an exchange would take, thus leaving some room for the Commission to exploit (see the section on the Commission below).

[30] This is how an interviewee phrased it.

[31] JHA Council (1999).

[32] They actually had the possibility to orchestrate advancement on the AFSJ but that did not represent much interest for them insofar as they were legally limited in their participation. Soft coordination mechanisms were therefore of greater interest for the Danes since they could push forward their own policy.

[33] So argues an interviewee.

> **Box 3.1—The National Contact Points on Integration**
> The National Contact Points on Integration were initially envisaged under the Danish presidency of the Council of the EU in 2002. The network was operationalised by the European Commission that constituted it as an expert group made up of high-ranking officials, mostly from Interior ministries, with a view to exchange experiences and positions on the development of integration at EU level. The NCPIs are not part of the Comitology but rather consist of an informal network meeting under the auspices of the Commission to facilitate exchange of information and experiences, as well as to inform policy-making at EU level.

The Greek Presidency: A Bandwagon Effect

The Greek presidency immediately succeeded the Danish one in January 2003. Greece, at the time, was not much concerned with the integration of foreigners. A long-standing emigration country, it observed its first sizeable arrivals when the USSR collapsed, in spite of its lagging economic development (Kasimis 2012). The construction of a borderless area inevitably placed Greece as one of the southern gates of the EU. Affected by influxes of irregular migration, Greece's policies from the 1990s onwards have been characterised by a reactive approach of emergency handling: regularising irregular stays, combatting illegal employment and so forth. Integration was not on the agenda, even though a couple of measures "on paper" were adopted (ELIAMEP 2014) so that when Greece took on the Presidency, the impetus given by the Danes was likely to fade. So feared Commission's staff. As one of the interviewees recalls:

> We were sort of a bit disappointed when Greece took on the Presidency... we thought: 'we're gonna lose the sort of commitment to work on [integration]

But it did not happen. Instead, the Greek Presidency prolonged the run-up initiated by the Danes. They notably set up a collaborative project to plan their Presidency ahead, spurred on by an international think tank. In the Summer of 2002, the Greek government, along with the Migration Policy Institute (MPI), created the Athens Migration Policy

Initiative (AMPI) with a view to define the priorities of the Greek Presidency with respect to the development of the AFSJ, which was a top priority at the time. The initiative was that of the MPI, a Washington-based think tank presided by Dr. Demetrios Papademetriou, an American scholar of Greek origins with close connections to the Greek government. Papademetriou persuaded the Greek government to prepare the discussions at the Council with input from the research community (Pratt 2015). Within the AMPI, a number of informal workshops gathering senior civil servants took place to discuss issues and their solutions as well as the acceptation of integration that should guide integration policies. In the same fashion, an international two-day conference took place in Athens in May 2003, gathering world-leader scholars on migration and senior policy-makers "to discuss the key policy challenges facing the EU and its Member States relating to migration" (MPI 2003).

As a result, the Council conclusions adopted in Thessaloniki on June 20, 2003, at the end of the Greek Presidency, conceded an important place to integration. Whereas enlargement and the constitutional treaty ranked as top priorities, nearly a fourth of the conclusions explicitly dealt with integration.[34] The document endorsed some of the Commission's proposals formulated some 17 days before in a Communication.[35] The latter Communication notably worded integration as a 'two-way process', a formulation that would punctuate the policy at EU level up to the present day.[36] The conclusions also laid down the (unclear) idea of common basic principles as a result of the cycle of seminars, reflections and exchanges; it insisted on the usefulness of exchanging information, notably through the endorsement of the National Contact Points on Integration. It also acknowledged the importance of a wide range of actors being involved, but reaffirmed the state's prevalence in steering policy-making.[37] For all these reasons, the European Council of Thessaloniki was an important moment for the construction of the European integration policy but, first and foremost, it bore witness to the fact that integration had finally reached the EU agenda.

---

[34] European Council 11638/03 (2003).

[35] COM (2003) 336 final.

[36] See, for example, the CBPs (Box 3.2) or else the Council Decision on the European Integration Fund (see Chapter 4).

[37] European Council 11638/03 (2003).

The Dutch Presidency: Integration Anchored

The attention on integration somewhat died down after the Greek Presidency when Italy took over the Presidency in July 2003, leaving the call for common principles hanging. Despite a programme that was initially common to Greece and Italy, proposed ahead at the end of 2002, Italy had different preferences. Its plans indeed granted importance to the development of the AFSJ, but integration was not on the agenda. Italy's governing coalition led by Berlusconi and comprising *Lega Nord* and *Alleanza Nazionale* as main partners had other priorities: combatting illegal immigration and preserving public order (Di Quirico 2003). Bearing witness to it is the Bossi-Fini law passed a year before, introducing criminal sanctions for migrants in an irregular situation.

Italy is characterised by extensive sea borders in the Mediterranean and, consequently, by great exposure to immigration. Ireland, in a different fashion, does not present the same features but took on the Italian programme when it succeeded to Italy at the Presidency in the first half of 2004. Firstly, the Irish Presidency focused on the conclusion of the enlargement to Central and Eastern Europe with much fanfare and in fact, this is how it made its mark. Secondly, the conclusion of the process leading to the Constitutional Treaty was a major focus. As another issue of importance since the Treaty of Amsterdam, the progress of the AFSJ was on the table even though framed in an all-security fashion with a focus on police cooperation, the fight against drugs and organised crime and illegal immigration.[38]

Then came the Dutch Presidency in the second half of 2004. A number of initiatives as regards integration at EU level had already been taken but they were limited thus far to the exchange of information and best practices. As the European Council concluded in Thessaloniki,[39] if there were to be cooperation in the field of integration amongst member states, there needed to be a somewhat common approach to the issue, a frame of reference to understand the direction future policy developments could take. The Netherlands embraced this task and set out to define these Common Basic Principles on integration. The task was not easy as these principles needed to meet certain challenges. Firstly, they had to cover different realities and needed to be applicable across

---

[38] Irish EU Presidency (2004).
[39] European Council 11638/03 (2003).

member states. Secondly, as the very first substantive instrument proposed, this set of principles had to be acceptable to all parties. Therefore, the Dutch would have to build consensus on their content. Finally, and perhaps most importantly, it was not clear to member states what the eventual purpose of such principles would be (Urth 2005). Reassuring national administrations about their non-binding character and involving them in their definition were prime objectives.

The Netherlands already had a sound expertise on integration policies. It had been a prized destination country since WWII. Refusing to see itself as a country of immigration, the first integration policies came when politicians understood immigration was no temporary phenomenon. This led to the design of the first integration policies in the 1980s (Bruquetas-Callejo et al. 2011). Relatively depoliticised an issue at first, policies unfolded until immigration and integration became prominent in public opinion as a result of social tensions at the turn of the twenty-first century.[40] The dominant perception was that integration policies had failed and that social cohesion was in peril. The rise of populist parties, and figures such as Pim Fortuyn and Geert Wilders exploiting already existing tensions, further increased the saliency of integration and primed tougher migration policies. Dreadful events such as the attacks on the Twin Towers and the assassination of film-maker Theo van Gogh in 2004 reinforced that logic. From a formerly multicultural approach to integration, policies turned to more civic-integration-like measures (Bruquetas-Callejo et al. 2011).

Given its long-standing experience in handling integration policies, the Netherlands was far ahead of other member states in the matter (along with Denmark). It had developed a sound system of integration courses that it was willing to disseminate to other member states; which it did, notably through the NCPIs. Soon after its promotion campaign, Austria, Belgium, Denmark, Estonia, Finland, France, Germany, Sweden and the UK adopted civic integration requirements and tests (Jacobs and Rea 2008). Integration was held very dear by Dutch authorities, they were willing to cooperate at EU level but only so long as it did not interfere with their own policy.[41] In this respect, they fiercely opposed

[40] See Bruquetas-Callejo et al. (2011), Blom (2014), and Fischler (2014) for more on this.

[41] See Bourdrez (2010).

the OMC put forth in 2001 and considerably changed the purposes of the Family Reunification Directive by imposing integration require-ments on candidates (Bruquetas-Callejo et al. 2011). The existence of a soft framework however opened the possibility for the Dutch to put forth their integration policy without risking any change to it. It also allowed them to attempt to improve their image, severely damaged by the rise of populism and xenophobic discourse by politicians such as Geert Wilders.[42] If the idea of writing down common basic principles to guide member states came up at Thessaloniki, it is the Dutch that looked after their drafting. In fact, the call for principles had been made in an unclear fashion and, as Helene Urth recalls: "The sentence was inserted by a member state during the initial negotiations and survived without particular attention paid to it through to the European Council" (Urth 2005: 171).

The Dutch actually came forth with a set of principles ahead of their Presidency to take place in the second half of 2004.[43] They used the recently created NCPI network to discuss them and sound out their acceptability by member states before they were sent for official scrutiny before the SCIFA (Strategic Committee on Immigration, Frontiers and Asylum) and COREPER. Before the NCPI's 6th meeting, of April 28, 2004, the Dutch circulated a "brainstorming paper" presenting some ideas with respect to the development of the CBPs. They asked their counterparts to think about the said paper and feed into it with ideas and comments.[44] The Dutch NCPI then presented a "presidency paper" enriched with NCPIs' insights, at an informal meeting of the SCIFA in July, to prepare their policy programme as to the AFSJ content. The paper introducing the CBPs was welcomed by the member states and the Commission, gathered in the SCIFA formation.[45] A new (confiden-tial) document (enriched with SCIFA's comments) was then sent back to the NCPIs with comments. The Dutch included the comments and presented it for a first discussion at the September 15–16, 2004 SCIFA

---

[42] Ibid.

[43] See document Migrapol-Integration 27. Note that Migrapol documents are not available to the public but may be requested from the European Commission via its access-to-document web interface.

[44] Ibid.

[45] Migrapol-Integration 33.

meeting. The matter then left the NCPIs' hands to be officially discussed within the SCIFA, in coordination with the Dutch NCPI, which would manage the liaison. The Presidency paper presenting the CBPs[46] was sent to the SCIFA on September 9, 2004 and the CBPs were eventually adopted during a Justice and Home Affairs Council[47] held on November 19, 2004. Through all these steps, the Dutch regularly consulted their counterparts and integrated their comments, thus increasing the acceptability of the document.

From official scrutiny to adoption, the CBPs have little changed. Only one objection perhaps is worth noting. Spain had presented an amendment that sought to include an explicit reference to the maintenance of cultures and languages of origin.[48] Such amendment was however not well received by the other member states (Carrera and Wiesbrock 2009). Overall, the Common Basic Principles are rather vague formulations oscillating between different general positions such as multiculturalism and civic integration. CBP1 however frames the set of principles as leaning more towards multiculturalism.[49]

The Dutch Presidency also coincided with the end of the Tampere Programme, the 5-year roadmap for the implementation of the AFSJ, so that the Dutch not only had steered the adoption of a framework for EU policy-making, but were also in a position of laying down the future of an integration policy at EU level, which they did with the drafting and further adoption of the Hague Programme,[50] covering the years 2005–2010. The Hague programme reaffirmed the importance of integration, and policies and initiatives to make it happen. Once again, integration was given a chapter of its own, reinforcing the idea that it was a policy field in its own right, and this for the five years to follow.

If the development of the integration policy is marked by moments such as the summit in Tampere or that in Thessaloniki, different sources underline that such policy developments are due to the activism of three

---

[46] Council of the European Union 12258/04 (2004).

[47] JHA Council (2004).

[48] See notably Council of the European Union 12258/04 (2004).

[49] For an extensive analysis of the CBPs, see Mulcahy (2011: 32).

[50] European Council (2005).

member states (Urth 2005). As one interviewee, working on the integration policy within the Commission's DG Home Affairs, reckons:

> I don't think the Commission could have done that on its own. Even if they were strong and all, I don't think they could have come forward with the Common Basic Principles and so on [the rest of the integration policy].

But the Commission did not stand on the side of the road. On the contrary, the relative activism of the three countries echoed the search for competence of a newly created Directorate General in the Commission.

Box 3.2—The Common Basic Principles

- CBP 1: "Integration is a dynamic, two-way process of mutual accommodation by all immigrants and residents of Member States."
- CBP 2: "Integration implies respect for the basic values of the European Union."
- CBP 3: "Employment is a key part of the integration process and is central to the participation of immigrants, to the contributions immigrants make to the host society, and to making such contributions visible."
- CBP 4: "Basic knowledge of the host society's language, history, and institutions is indispensable to integration; enabling immigrants to acquire this basic knowledge is essential to successful integration."
- CBP 5: "Efforts in education are critical to preparing immigrants, and particularly their descendants, to be more successful and more active participants in society."
- CBP 6: "Access for immigrants to institutions, as well as to public and private goods and services, on a basis equal to national citizens and in a non-discriminatory way is a critical foundation for better integration."
- CBP 7: "Frequent interaction between immigrants and Member State citizens is a fundamental mechanism for integration. Shared forums, intercultural dialogue, education about immigrants and immigrant cultures, and stimulating living conditions in urban environments enhance the interactions between immigrants and Member State citizens."

- CBP 8: "The practice of diverse cultures and religions is guaranteed under the Charter of Fundamental Rights and must be safeguarded, unless practices conflict with other inviolable European rights or with national law."
- CBP 9: "The participation of immigrants in the democratic process and in the formulation of integration policies and measures, especially at the local level, supports their integration."
- CBP 10: "Mainstreaming integration policies and measures in all relevant policy portfolios and levels of government and public services is an important consideration in public policy formation and implementation."
- CBP 11: "Developing clear goals, indicators and evaluation mechanisms are necessary to adjust policy, evaluate progress on integration and to make the exchange of information more effective."

New Competences for a New Commission DG

The entry into force of the Treaty of Amsterdam brought some change to the Commission's structure. The Commission, which previously had a small Justice and Home Affairs unit, was henceforth provided with a Directorate General for Justice and Home Affairs (DG JHA), a suitably staffed division that would be able to work out a European policy, make proposals and so forth. As explained in Chapter 2, the Commission had proposed a two-step policy development that ended up failing. That said, a policy space was opening under the lead of three member states: Denmark, Greece and the Netherlands. If the Commission was refused the opportunity to steer the process through the OMC in 2001, it was not to stand as a mere observer.

If it is nowadays clear that the Commission is able to act as a "purposeful opportunist", unravelling its composition shows that it is true for the Commission in its relation with other EU bodies and member states, but also within the Commission, in the interaction between its different units (Cram 1997: 146; but see also Hooghe 1996). In this regard, it is interesting to see how the Commission, and the Immigration and Asylum Unit within DG for Justice and Home Affairs, carved out a competence for itself.

Lessons from a Failed OMC: The Commission's Contained Activism

Under the lead of Commissioner Vitorino, an OMC on immigration comprising a whole section on integration was proposed in July 2001 but was never put forth by the Council. Despite being regarded as a soft instrument, the organisation of cooperation under the Commission's supervision was not to the taste of member states (Caviedes 2004). Considering the much debated, and still debated at the time, couple of directives touching upon legal migration,[51] working out a policy of integration appeared more difficult than previously thought. In addition, the legal basis for integration as such was extremely thin: no explicit mention of it appeared in primary law until the adoption of the Lisbon Treaty. Thus far, integration was handled within a unit under DG Employment and Social Affairs and was presented as a corollary to the free circulation of labour (Guiraudon 2003). With the entry into force of the Treaty of Amsterdam, immigration found a legal basis but integration as such did not.[52] That said, since there was henceforward a DG in charge of immigration, it made little sense to leave integration under DG Employment. As a matter of fact, the division on immigration and asylum in DG Home was staffed with officers taken from DG Employment.

If the Commission was to play a role, it had to proceed cautiously. The Danish Presidency had proven there was an actual will to cooperate on integration, but it had also shown that the manner in which it was done was important. There was no room for harmonization (as the Constitutional Treaty would bear witness to[53]) no will for benchmarking and other finger-pointing sessions (as the failed OMC showed), but the availability to exchange information and best practices in the most flexible way.[54] And the Commission would follow the path set by the member states.

---

[51] Chapter 2 provides more detail on this.

[52] The treaty provision the closest to integration was article 63 (3) (a) TEC providing that measures be adopted as to "conditions of entry and residence, and standards on procedures for the issue by Member States of long term visas and residence permits, including those for the purpose of family reunion". Integration was first mentioned in primary law in the Constitutional Treaty. It notably excluded legal harmonisation in this domain. The Constitutional Treaty, however, was never adopted, making the treaty of Lisbon the first official reference to integration in primary law.

[53] Integration was first mentioned in primary law in the Constitutional Treaty, which notably excluded legal harmonisation in this domain.

[54] This point notably came out from the interviews conducted and documents retrieved. See also Bourdrez (2010).

The Danish Presidency opened the floor to integration with a conference in July 2002 on successful labour integration (see above). In September of the same year, the European Economic and Social Committee organized a conference on the role of civil society in promoting integration, in which Commissioner Vitorino participated. In his speech, Vitorino outlined the Commission's view on the matter (Vitorino 2002a), a view that would become systematized in a future Communication from the Commission.[55] Most importantly, Vitorino announced:

> I have decided to establish a programme of preparatory actions to promote integration of immigrants over the period 2003-2005 (...) to support networks and the transferal of information and good practices between stakeholders in order to facilitate open dialogue and identify priorities for a European integration policy. (Vitorino 2002a: 5)

Preparatory actions would finance transnational projects across the EU over the period 2003–2005 for a total of €4 million per year. These actions would be entitled the INTI Programme, a programme through which the Commission would directly finance projects gathering civil society organizations and subnational authorities. Despite a very modest amount, the fund was deemed very successful and laid the path towards a more sizeable financial instrument, the European Integration Fund (KANTOR Management Consultants 2009).

A month later, the Danish Presidency continued with a JHA Council in October 2002. The Council announced greater cooperation through the "establishment of national contact points in the member states" for the exchange of information between member states.[56] But as Helene Urth recalled, "the intentions of the Danish Presidency went no further than a list of names which could be used to facilitate contact and which was initially established by the Council secretariat by the end of the Danish Presidency" but the Commission was "determined to use this opportunity to improve cooperation" and "took the initiative to create a forum" for the exchange of information and good practices, a forum the Commission "could rely upon when developing new initiatives in

[55] COM (2003) 336 final.
[56] JHA Council (2002).

the field" (Urth 2005: 170).[57] As such, the National Contact Points on Integration were created; they would meet as an informal committee convened and steered by the Commission.[58] These encounters were to become the place where all new initiatives would be sounded out and discussed even before starting an official procedure.[59] This is where the Common Basic Principles were first presented by the Dutch Presidency; this is also where the Handbooks on Integration were discussed, not to mention the first ex-ante impact assessment and the draft Decision relating to the European Integration Fund yet to come. The first NCPI meeting took place in March 2003 and it is interesting to see that the Commission, which had been refused an OMC in 2001, proposed a study (commissioned by the Commission) on benchmarking integration policies be presented to the NCPIs.[60] Such a study was in fact presented in the second NCPI meeting[61] in July 2003.

During the very same JHA Council, Commissioner Vitorino announced the preparation of a Communication on Immigration, Integration and Employment[62] to underline the need for more migrant integration. It was the joint effort of DG Employment *and* DG Home Affairs and pointed out the necessity to integrate migrants into the labour market *and* into society if the member states wanted to reach the Lisbon goals of an employment rate of 70%. Considering Europe's aging population and the migrants already present in the EU, integration was presented as a means to realize the potential of migration.[63] This Communication was released in June 2003. It presented a particular view of integration. The idea was to overcome economic integration to move towards a "holistic" conception, taking into account cultural and religious diversity, citizenship, participation and political rights.[64] The Communication thereby defined a set of priorities to be tackled

---

[57] See also COM (2003) 336 final: 29.

[58] See documents Migrapol-Integration 2–61 notably.

[59] See amongst other Migrapol-Integration 27; 40; 42; 43; 48.

[60] Migrapol-Integration 4.

[61] Migrapol-Integration 11. See also Urth (2005).

[62] COM (2003) 336 final.

[63] Vitorino (2002a).

[64] COM (2003) 336 final: 18.

and placed itself on the path of further development. Notably, the Commission insisted on the need to collect more information to monitor integration across the EU in a comparable fashion; e.g. establishing benchmarks at EU level.[65] The Commission also proposed to monitor the development of the common immigration policy through the elaboration of annual reports.[66] A first such report[67] was delivered in 2004, based on a questionnaire passed to NCPIs to update shared information on existing policies at national level.

The developments of this policy field increasingly looked like an OMC. The Common Basic Principles acted like an umbrella for the whole policy by defining the concept of integration and therefore, in a way, the goals to be achieved. The National Contact Points on Integration created occasions for encounters, the exchange of views and national developments. The Commission's annual reports and the development of indicators of integration would play the role of benchmarks. The adoption of a European Integration Fund would eventually create an obligation to report on activities carried out. Indeed, this is not an OMC as such, but rather a sort of patchwork of different instruments that stitched together may seem like one. It is interesting to note that building up an OMC for the integration of third country nationals has been the underlying intention of Commissioner Vitorino all along. At a conference given in October 2004 at the seat of the European Policy Centre, he reaffirmed his intention to launch an OMC. But there has never been any decision in this direction. The recipe for success of this quasi-OMC actually appears to be the absolute flexibility of the instruments, the possibility for member states to control the process all along, and having a Commission that is not steering but following the pace set by member states.[68] As one interviewee from the European Commission recalls,

---

[65] Ibid., p. 35.

[66] Such initiative was immediately endorsed by the European Council of Thessaloniki (European Council 2003).

[67] COM (2004) 508 final.

[68] This point is corroborated by the interviews conducted for this research.

> you get the instructions from the Ministerial meetings (…). They leave the Commission quite room for manoeuvre" but "you're working with the member states (…) they will go as far as they want to go. You can encourage them and suggest things to them but if they don't want to do it, then they just don't do it.

The OMC implied a strong role for the Commission and especially reporting activities by the member states, which member states were not keen to do (Caviedes 2004). This, however, somewhat changed with the inception of the European Integration Fund, which shattered the strictly intergovernmental approach followed thus far (see below).

Building a Castle from Scratch: DG EMP and DG JHA

> They [DG JHA] were building a castle, which is what you do when you want to increase your power (…). Our Director wanted to have a big DG, as big and powerful as DG Employment (…), we wanted to have the same as DG Employment. It was a Church fight.

This is how one of the interviewees, working for the Commission's DG for Justice and Home Affairs, summarises the driver of the DG's activity in the course of an interview. What she said is another way to say that the Commission is by no means a monolith unit but rather a "multi-organisation" (Cram 1997: 153): different DGs have different drivers and different resources. The emergence of new competences, and a new DG, engenders a redefinition of who does what and how, it reshuffles political opportunities. The new DG, therefore, must make some room for itself. Formerly, the integration of foreigners informally fell under the competence of DG V or else DG Employment, Industrial Relations and Social Affairs. In charge of social affairs, its role encompassed social inclusion of vulnerable groups, migrants belonging to that category.

DG Employment is one of the original Directorates of the Commission and, despite the rather weak EU social policy at the outset and its tumultuous relationships with various sectoral interests (Cram 1997), it enjoyed considerable influence, notably through the management of the European Social Fund. From 1958 until the adoption of the treaty of Amsterdam, it had a unit, Unit D.4, the activity of which revolved around free movement of workers, migrant integration and anti-racism. The creation of a DG legally in charge of "visas, asylum, immigration and other policies related to free movement of persons"

(Title IV TEC) necessarily called into question the attribution of the competence of migrant integration to DG Employment. That said, the attribution of the competence to DG Employment had some legitimacy. Already in charge of integration at the time, it had the institutional and personnel resources; having for its remit the fight against social exclusion, a then prevalent paradigm,[69] its action was justified for the inclusion of migrants. But the Treaty of Amsterdam created an "Area of Freedom, Security and Justice", three words that together called for a common policy that should not be completely security oriented, as called for by the Seville summit[70]; a common policy that, in the words of the Commissioner, must be "well balanced".[71] As he put it:

> This balance will be required throughout the different phases of the policy and should take into account the following elements: ensuring the respect for the 1951 Geneva Convention and particularly the principle of 'non refoulement', the legitimate aspiration of third-country nationals to better living conditions and the taking into account of the reception capacity of the Member States and of the Union as a whole.

But instead of being expropriated from DG Employment, the issue was split into two separate, autonomous, objectives. One would regard integration in the labour market and would be taken care of by DG Employment; the other would regard social and cultural aspects, and would be handed to DG JHA. Consequently, a part of the staff formerly working within DG Employment was transferred to DG JHA. Such a divide was the result of intense debate and negotiations.[72] What is of particular interest is the capacity Vitorino showed in instrumentalising a larger policy agenda to increase DG JHA's scope of action,[73] a strategy already used by DG Employment (Cram 1997; Guiraudon 2003).

---

[69] See above for more on the social inclusion paradigm. See also Murard (2002), Guiraudon (2003).

[70] European Council (2002).

[71] Vitorino (2002b: 8). Note that the rhetoric of a well-balanced policy that truly covered freedom and justice, and not only security, has been punctuating the documents emanating from EU institutions (see notably COM [2005] 123 final, establishing a framework programme on solidarity and the management of migration flows).

[72] So recalled some of the interviewees.

[73] Vitorino (2002a). See also COM (2003) 336 final.

Whereas DG Employment had the significant European Social Fund, DG JHA had no clear budget available, no appropriation.[74] In spite of that, Vitorino announced in September 2002 the allocation of some funding for the integration of third country nationals under the scope of DG JHA.[75] He linked the issue of social integration to that of unemployment and exclusion, two themes relating to DG Employment but at the core of the Lisbon goals: an employment rate of 70% for growth, thus anticipating a Communication on immigration, integration and employment[76] that would only be released in June 2003, a Communication common to the two DGs. Notably, the Communication placed integration as the factor for the realization of the potential of immigration, a phrasing that would punctuate future documents. Briefly, the Communication underscores the fact that the population in Europe is ageing and the EU will face, in the coming years, shortages of workforce and skills. But the discourse is nonetheless cautious. Immigration cannot realistically be the only answer; so no, the doors of the EU are not swinging open. Rather, the Communication points to the under-exploitation of resources and thus for the need to tap into the existing workforce through the better integration of migrants.[77] Based on the Labour Force Survey, the Commission underlines the differential in employment rates between EU nationals and non-EU nationals across the EU.[78] Whereas 64.4% of EU nationals are employed, only 52.7% of non-EU nationals are in work. Migrants are also over-represented in risky sectors, undeclared work, and, in many cases, they occupy positions that do not match their skills and qualifications.[79] Integration is therefore not only a matter of labour market integration strictly speaking, but also a matter of social, cultural and political integration, as these elements are perceived to be obstacles on the road to labour market integration too.[80]

Resultantly, the Commission adopted the INTI Programme for preparatory actions for the integration of third country nationals in 2003.

[74] See the yearly budgets available to the Commission, available at http://eur-lex.europa.eu/budget/www/index-en.htm.

[75] Vitorino (2002a).

[76] COM (2003) 336 final.

[77] See notably Section 2 of COM (2003) 336 final.

[78] COM (2003) 336 final: 53.

[79] Ibid., p. 19.

[80] In this respect, see also COM (2004) 508 final.

A small fund of €18 million in total that, however, set the basis for a larger one still to come. The INTI Programme was a fund directly handled by the European Commission for transnational projects involving 4–5 countries over the period 2003–2006. According to the evaluation conducted, it aroused great interest on the part of integration stakeholders (Kantor Management Consultants 2009). More than 570 proposals were submitted from 20 countries; the remaining 7 countries participated as partners to given projects. The perceived and evaluated success of the INTI Programme made the case for demanding increased Community funding (Urth 2005). For the multiannual financial framework 2007–2013, the Commission proposed more importance be granted to integration[81] through the establishment of a framework programme on solidarity and the management of migration flows,[82] a financial instrument to support the construction of the (so-called well balanced) AFSJ. This programme comprised four funds: the European Border Fund, the Return Fund, the European Refugee Fund and the European Integration Fund. Altogether, the four funds initially amounted to €5.866 million[83] for the financial perspective 2007–2013; €1771 million would be dedicated to integration so that 20% at least of the 2.2 million/year new legal residents could benefit from integration measures.[84] Reflecting the fact that the AFSJ was "one of the main priorities of the European Union for the years to come, to be supported through substantially increased financial means",[85] the first proposal of the Commission for the 2007–2013 period tripled the formerly very low level of expenditure allocated to freedom, security and justice by 2013 (Laffan and Lindner 2005). Such appropriations were however halved by the end of the decision-making process, mostly because member states preferred to maintain a redistributive budget model to the reformed model inspired by the Sapir Report and more growth-oriented.[86]

---

[81] COM (2004) 101 final/2.

[82] COM (2005) 123 final.

[83] Ibid.

[84] COM (2004) 101 final/2. Note that the figure for the coverage announced (here 20%) was risen to 30% in future documents; see notably SEC (2005) 435: 44.

[85] COM (2005) 123 final: 14.

[86] For more on this topic, see Schild (2008), Rant and Mrak (2010), and Dür and Mateo (2010).

Inevitably, the budget for the integration of third country nationals suffered a severe cut with dire consequences on its scope of application: from €1771 million, it shrunk to €825 million.

Notwithstanding, from no competence at all, DG JHA (which changed name in the meantime) acquired substantial means over a short time-span and decidedly carved out a competence for the integration of third country nationals. Certainly of limited breadth; but still a competence.

CONCLUSION

The failed attempt at engaging member states in an OMC in 2001 did not bode well for an EU integration policy. Immigration was mostly conceived and framed as a security issue that called for security answers. It is therefore under the guise of the fight against social exclusion that the first measures in this respect took place. Migrants constituting a category at risk of exclusion, their integration would fall under the competence (to a very limited extent) of DG Employment. At national level, integration had been an issue of concern for at least half of the EU-15 since the 1980s. By 2003, almost all EU-15 member states had in place some sort of integration policy. I argue in this chapter that the passage to the EU occurred thanks to a combination of three elements. Firstly, integration measures had to be of a soft nature. The long and heated debate around the Family Reunification and Long-Term Residence Directives, and the failure of the OMC in 2001, proved that the way to approach integration measures mattered. If any integration policy was to unfold at EU level, it had to be soft. Secondly, the will of three Presidencies of the Council—the Danish, the Greek and the Dutch—over a reduced time-span was sufficient to trigger, follow up and anchor integration onto the EU agenda. Thirdly, the Commission played a very important role of facilitator. Executing the wishes of the Council, it proved capable of developing a policy within its margins of acceptability, exploiting them to flesh out a policy. In parallel, the Commission also proved capable of carving out a role in integration for itself, notably through the creation of funding opportunities. Mobilising a wider agenda aimed at increasing the employment rate across the EU, the Commission gained momentum in the field and created the European Integration Fund, a systematic instrument, the design of which would reflect the weak competence on the matter at EU level and the ensuing decision-making process (Chapter 4).

REFERENCES

SCHOLARSHIP AND EXPERT REFERENCES

Aus, J. P. (2008). The Mechanisms of Consensus: Coming to Agreement on Community Asylum Policy. In D. Naurin & H. Wallace (Eds.), *Unveiling the Council of the European Union: Games Governments Play in Brussels* (pp. 99–120). Basingstoke: Palgrave Macmillan.

Bache, I. (2005). *Europeanization and Britain: Towards Multi-level Governance?* Paper prepared for the EUSA 9th Biennial Conference in Austin, Texas, March 31–April 2.

Bigo, D. (1996). *Polices En Réseaux: L'éxpérience Européenne.* Paris: Presses de la Fondation nationale des sciences politiques.

Bigo, D. (2002). Security and Immigration: Toward a Critique of the Governmentality of Unease. *Alternatives: Global, Local, Political, 27* Special Issue, 63–92.

Blom, S. (2014). *Local Migration and Integration Policies in Amsterdam.* (Fondazione ISMU KING Project, In-Depth Study, No. 16).

Borràs, S., & Jacobsson, K. (2004). The Open Method of Co-ordination and New Governance Patterns in the EU. *Journal of European Public Policy, 11*(2), 185–208.

Börzel, T. A. (2002). Pace-Setting, Foot-Dragging, and Fence-Sitting: Member State Responses to Europeanization. *JCMS. Journal of Common Market Studies, 40*(2), 193–214.

Bourdrez, L. (2010). *The EU Policy on the Integration of Third-Country Nationals. "A Two-Way Process?".* Master's thesis, University of Amsterdam.

Bruquetas-Callejo, M., Garcés-Mascareñas, B., Penninx, R., & Scholten, P. (2011). The Case of the Netherlands. In G. Zincone, R. Penninx, & M. Borkert (Eds.), *Migration Policymaking in Europe: The Dynamics of Actors and Contexts in Past and Present* (pp. 129–165). Amsterdam: Amsterdam University Press.

Cantle, T. (2001). *Community Cohesion: A Report of the Independent Review Team.* London: Home Office.

Caporaso, J. (2007). The Three Worlds of Integration Theory. In P. R. Graziano (Ed.), *Europeanization: New Research Agendas* (pp. 23–34). Basingstoke: Palgrave Macmillan.

Carrera, S. (2008). *Benchmarking Integration in the EU: Analyzing the Debate on Integration Indicators and Moving It Forward.* Gütersloh: Bertelsmann Foundation.

Carrera, S., & Wiesbrock, A. (2009). Civic Integration of Third-Country Nationals Nationalism Versus Europeanization in the Common EU Immigration Policy. *Centre for European Policy Studies.*

Castles, S., de Haas, H., & Miller, M. J. (2013). *The Age of Migration: International Population Movements in the Modern World* (5th ed.). Basingstoke: Palgrave Macmillan.

Caviedes, A. (2004). The Open Method of Co-ordination in Immigration Policy: A Tool for Prying Open Fortress Europe? *Journal of European Public Policy, 11*(2), 289–310.

Checkel, J. T. (2005). *It's the Process Stupid! Process Tracing in the Study of European and International Politics* (ARENA Centre for European Studies Working Papers, University of Oslo, No. 26).

Christiansen, T. (2006). The Council of Ministers: Facilitating Interaction and Developing Actorness in the EU. In J. Richardson (Ed.), *European Union: Power and Policy-Making* (3rd ed.). New York: Routledge.

Collier, D. (2011). Understanding Process Tracing. *PS. Political Science & Politics, 44*(04), 823–830.

Cram, L. (1997). *Policy-Making in the European Union: Conceptual Lenses and the Integration Process.* New York: Taylor & Francis.

Di Quirico, R. (2003). Italy, Europe and the European Presidency of 2003. *Notre Europe, Research and European Issues, 27.*

Duez, D. (2008). *L' Union Europeenne et L'immigration Clandestine: De La Securite Interieure a La Construction de La Communaute Politique.* Bruxelles: Editions de l'Universite de Bruxelles.

Dür, A., & Mateo, G. (2010). Bargaining Power and Negotiation Tactics: The Negotiations on the EU's Financial Perspective, 2007–2013. *JCMS: Journal of Common Market Studies, 48*(3), 557–578.

Elgström, O. (2000). Norm Negotiations. The Construction of New Norms Regarding Gender and Development in EU Foreign Aid Policy. *Journal of European Public Policy, 7*(3), 457–476.

ELIAMEP. (2014). Migration in Greece Recent Developments in 2014. *Hellenic Foundation for European and Foreign Policy.*

Exadaktylos, T., & Radaelli, C. M. (2012). Looking for Causality in the Literature on Europeanization. In T. Exadaktylos & C. M. Radaelli (Eds.), *Research Design in European Studies: Establishing Causality in Europeanization.* Basingstoke: Palgrave Macmillan.

Faist, T., & Ette, A. (2007). The Europeanization of National Policies and Politics of Immigration: Research, Questions and Concepts. In T. Faist & A. Ette (Eds.), *The Europeanization of National Policies and Politics of Immigration: Between Autonomy and the European Union* (pp. 3–31). New York: Palgrave Macmillan.

Favell, A. (2001). *Philosophies of Integration: Immigration and the Idea of Citizenship in France and Britain* (2nd ed.). New York: Palgrave Macmillan in association with Centre for Research in Ethnic Relations, University of Warwick.

Featherstone, K. (2003). Introduction: In the Name of "Europe". In K. Featherstone & C. M. Radaelli (Eds.), *The Politics of Europeanization* (pp. 3–26). New York: Oxford University Press.

Fischler, F. (2014). *Integration Policy Netherlands Country Report* (Interact Research Report 2014/15).

Guiraudon, V. (2003). The Constitution of a European Immigration Policy Domain: A Political Sociology Approach. *Journal of European Public Policy, 10*(2), 263–282.

Guild, E. (2001). *Immigration Law in the European Community.* The Hague: Kluwer Law International.

Heidbreder, E. (2014). *When Multiple Levels Meet Migration: The Specific Challenges of a EU Immigration Regime* (Fondazione ISMU, KING Project, Desk Research Paper, No. 3).

Hollifield, J. F. F. (1992). *Immigrants, Markets, and States: The Political Economy of Postwar Europe.* Cambridge: Harvard University Press.

Hooghe, L. (1996). Building a Europe with the Regions: The Changing Role of the European Commission. In L. Hooghe (Ed.), *Cohesion Policy and European Integration: Building Multi-level Governance.* Oxford: Oxford University Press.

Huysmans, J. (2000). The European Union and the Securitization of Migration. *JCMS: Journal of Common Market Studies, 38*(5), 751–777.

Jacobs, D., & Rea, A. (2008). *The End of National Models? Integration Courses and Citizenship Trajectories in Europe.* Paper presented at the European Union Studies Association. 17–19 May.

Kantor Management Consultants. (2009). *The Evaluation of the INTI Program Framework Contract for Evaluation and Evaluation Related Services.* Kantor Management Consultants.

Kasimis, C. (2012). Greece: Illegal Immigration in the Midst of Crisis. *Migration Policy Institute.* Available at http://www.migrationpolicy.org/article/greece-illegal-immigration-midst-crisis. Last Consulted November 16, 2016.

Kraler, A. (2011). The Case of Austria. In G. Zincone, R. Penninx, & M. Borkert (Eds.), *Migration Policymaking in Europe. The Dynamics of Actors and Contexts in Past and Present* (pp. 21–60). Amsterdam: IMISCOE Research Series.

Kröger, S. (2009). The Open Method of Coordination: Underconceptualisation, Overdetermination, De-politicisation and beyond. *European Integration online Papers, 13*(1).

Kundnani, A. (2012). Multiculturalism and Its Discontents: Left, Right and Liberal. *European Journal of Cultural Studies, 15*(2), 155–166.

Laffan, B., & Lindner, J. (2005). The Budget. In H. Wallace, W. Wallace, & M. A. Pollack (Eds.), *Policy-Making in the European Union* (5th ed., pp. 191–212). Oxford: Oxford University Press.

Mahoney, J. (2010). After KKV: The New Methodology of Qualitative Research. *World Politics, 62*(1), 120–147.

Mandin, J. (2014). *An Overview of Integration Policies in Belgium* (Interact Research Report 2014/20).

Mathieson, J., Popay, J., Enoch, E., Escorel, S., Hernandez, M., Johnston, H. and Rispel, L. (2008). *Social Exclusion. Meaning, Measurement and Experience and Links to Health Inequalities. A Review of Literature* (WHO Social Exclusion Knowledge Network, Vol. Background Paper 1).

Morjé Howard, M. (2008). The Causes and Consequences of Germany's New Citizenship Law. *German Politics, 17*(1), 41–62.

Mouritsen, P., & Hovmark Jensen, C. (2014). *Integration Policies in Denmark* (INTERACT Research Report 2014/06).

MPI. (2003). Press Release: Top Migration Experts to Meet in Athens Under the Leadership of the Migration Policy Institute and the Auspices of the Greek Presidency of the EU to Discuss Migration Issues of Concern to Europe. *Migration Policy Institute.* Available at http://www.migrationpolicy.org/news/top-migration-experts-meet-in-athens. Last Consulted October 21, 2016.

Mulcahy, S. (2011). *Europe's Migrant Policies: Illusions of Integration.* Basingstoke: Palgrave Macmillan.

Murard, N. (2002). Guilty Victims: Social Exclusion in Contemporary France. In P. Chamberlayne, M. Rustin, & T. Wengraf (Eds.), *Biography and Social Exclusion in Europe: Experiences and Life Journeys.* Bristol: Policy Press.

Noiriel, G. (2006) *Le Creuset Francais: Histoire de L'immigration, XIXe–XXe Siecles.* Paris: Seuil.

Penninx, M., Garcés-Mascareñas, B., Protasiewicz, P. M., Schwarz, H., & Caponio, T. (2014). *European Cities and Their Migrant Integration Policies A State of the Art Study for the Knowledge for Integration Governance (KING) Project.* (Fondazione ISMU, KING Project, Overview Paper No. 5).

Petrovic, M. (2012). Belgium: A Country of Pemanent Immigration. *Migration Policy Institute.* Available at http://www.migrationpolicy.org/article/belgium-country-permanent-immigration. Last Consulted October 21, 2016.

Pratt, S. (2015). EU Policymaking and Research: Case Studies of the Communication on a Community Immigration Policy and the Common Basic Principles for Integration. In P. Scholten, H. Entzinger, R. Penninx, & S. Verbeek (Eds.), *Integrating Immigrants in Europe: Research-Policy Dialogues* (pp. 117–131). Amsterdam: IMISCOE Research Series.

Princen, S. (2007). Agenda-Setting in the European Union: A Theoretical Exploration and Agenda for Research. *Journal of European Public Policy, 14*(1), 21–38.

Radaelli, C. (2003a). *The Open Method of Coordination: A New Governance Architecture for the European Union?* (Vol. 1). Stockholm: Swedish Institute for European Policy Studies.

Radaelli, C. (2003b). The Europeanization of Public Policy. In K. Featherstone & C. M. Radaelli (Eds.), *The Politics of Europeanization* (pp. 27–56). New York: Oxford University Press.

Radaelli, C. M. (2008). Europeanization, Policy Learning, and New Modes of Governance. *Journal of Comparative Policy Analysis: Research and Practice, 10*(3), 239–254.

Rant, V., & Mrak, M. (2010). The 2007–2013 Financial Perspective: Domination of National Interests. *JCMS: Journal of Common Market Studies, 48*(2), 347–372.

Richardson, J. (2012). Supranational State Building in the European Union. In J. Richardson (Ed.), *Constructing a Policy-Making State? Policy Dynamics in the EU*. Oxford: Oxford University Press.

Rubio-Marín, R. (2004). *Immigration as a Democratic Challenge: Citizenship and Inclusion in Germany and the United States*. Cambridge: Cambridge University Press.

Schain, M. (2010). Managing Difference: Immigrant Integration Policy in France, Britain, and the United States. *Social Research: An International Quarterly, 77*(1), 205–236.

Scharpf, F. W. (1997). *Games Real Actors Play: Actor-Centered Institutionalism in Policy Research*. Boulder: Westview Press.

Schild, J. (2008). How to Shift the EU's Spending Priorities? The Multi-annual Financial Framework 2007–2013 in Perspective. *Journal of European Public Policy, 15*(4), 531–549.

Schnapper, D. (1994). The Debate on Immigration and the Crisis of National Identity. *West European Politics, 17*(2), 127–139.

Snyder, F. (1993). Soft Law and Institutional Practice in the European Community. In S. Martin (Ed.), *The Construction of Europe: Essays in Honour of Emile Noel* (pp. 197–225). Boston: Kluwer Academic Publishers.

Sussmuth, R. (2009). The Future of Migration and Integration Policy in Germany. *Migration Policy Institute*. Available at http://www.migration-policy.org/research/future-migration-and-integration-policy-germany. Last Consulted January 15, 2017.

Tallberg, J. (2003). The Agenda-Shaping Powers of the EU Council Presidency. *Journal of European Public Policy, 10*(1), 1–19.

The Economist. (2001, 27 September). Charlemagne; Antonio Vitorino. *The Economist*.

Thiesse, A.-M. (2001). *La Création Des Identités Nationales: Europe XVIIIe–XXe Siècle*. Paris: Éditions du Seuil.

Thränhardt, D. (2014). *The State of European Integration Governance: A Comparative Evaluation* (Fondazione ISMU, KING Project, Desk Research Paper, No. 7).

Tsebelis, G. (2013). Bridging Qualified Majority and Unanimity Decisionmaking in the EU. *Journal of European Public Policy, 20*(8), 1083–1103.

Urth, H. (2005). Building a Momentum for the Integration of Third-Country Nationals in the European Union. *European Journal of Migration and Law, 7*(2), 163–180.

Vanhercke, B. (2012). Social Policy at EU Level: From the Anti-poverty Programmes to Europe 2020. *European Social Observatory,* Vol. VC/2012/0658.

Van Wolleghem, P. G. (2016). *Migrations and Policy Cycle in the UK: Overview of Recent Trends* (Fondazione ISMU, Working Paper Series).

Velluti, S. (2007). What European Union Strategy for Integrating Migrants? The Role of OMC Soft Mechanisms in the Development of an EU Immigration Policy. *European Journal of Migration and Law, 9*(1), 53–82.

Vennesson, P. (2008). Case Studies and Process Tracing Theories and Practices. In D. Della Porta & M. Keating (Eds.), *Approaches and Methodologies in the Social Sciences: A Pluralist Perspective* (4th ed., pp. 223–239). Cambridge, NY: Cambridge University Press.

Vitorino, A. (2002a). *Closing Speech at the Conference on the Role of Civil Society in Promoting Integration, SPEECH/02/371.* Paper presented, Brussels.

Vitorino, A. (2002b). Interview with Mr. António Vitorino, European Commissioner for Justice and Home Affairs. *Immigration, Asylum and Social Integration, European Communities.*

Wallace, H. (1985). The Presidency of the Council of Ministers of the European Community: Tasks and Evolution. In C. O. Nuallain (Ed.), *The Presidency of the European Council of Ministers.* London: Routledge.

Wischenbart, R. (1994). National Identity and Immigration in Austria— Historical Framework and Political Dispute. *West European Politics, 17*(2), 72–90.

Zincone, G., Penninx, R., & Borkert, M. (2011). *Migration Policymaking in Europe: The Dynamics of Actors and Contexts in Past and Present.* Amsterdam: IMISCOE Research Series.

EU Acts and Other Official Documents

COM. (2003). 336 Final—European Commission (2003). *Communication from the Commission on Immigration, Integration and Employment.*

COM. (2004). 101 Final/2—European Commission (2004). *Communication from the Commission to the Council and the European Parliament. Building our Common Future Policy Challenges and Budgetary Means of the Enlarged Union 2007–2013.*

COM. (2004). 508 Final—European Commission (2004). *Communication from the Commission to the Council, the European Parliament, the European*

Economic and Social Committee and the Committee of the Regions. First Annual Report on Migration and Integration.

COM. (2005). 123 Final—European Commission (2005). *Communication from the Commission to the Council and the European Parliament Establishing a Framework Programme on Solidarity and the Management of Migration Flows for the Period 2007–2013.*

Council of the European Union 12258/04. (2004). *Common Basic Principles for Immigrant Integration Policy in the European Union.*

Danish EU Presidency. (2002). *Press Release: Informal Meeting of the Ministers in the Area of Justice and Home Affairs.*

European Commission. (1998). *Action Plan of the Council and the Commission on How Best to Implement the Provisions of the Treaty of Amsterdam on an Area of Freedom, Security and Justice.*

European Council. (1999). *Tampere European Council 15 and 16 October 1999, Presidency Conclusions.*

European Council. (2001). *European Council Meeting in Laeken 14 and 15 December 2001, Presidency Conclusions.*

European Council. (2002). *Seville European Council 21 and 22 June 2002, Presidency Conclusions.*

European Council 11638/03. (2003). *Thessaloniki European Council 19 and 20 June 2003, Presidency Conclusions.*

European Council 15915/05. (2005). *Financial Perspective 2007–2013.*

Irish EU Presidency. (2004). *Programme of the Irish Presidency.*

JHA Council. (1999). *Action Plan of the Council and the Commission on How Best to Implement the Provisions of the Treaty of Amsterdam on an Area of Freedom, Security and Justice, 1999/C 19/01.*

JHA Council. (2002). *2455th Council Meeting, Luxembourg, 14/15 October 2002.*

JHA Council. (2004). *2618th Council Meeting, 19 November 2004, Brussels.*

SEC. (2005). 435 Final—European Commission (2005). *Commission Staff Working Document Annex to the General Programme Solidarity and Management of Migration Flows Extended Impact Assessment.*

CHAPTER 4

The European Integration Fund: Principles, Decision-Making and Output

With the adoption of the Treaty of Amsterdam and the integration of immigration-related policies under the first pillar, a window of opportunity for an EU integration policy was swinging open. Even though the main lens through which immigration was perceived was security, a competing paradigm embedded the fight against social exclusion in EU policies. At national level, most countries had already taken initiatives towards consistent integration policies. In spite of that, no competence was transferred to the EU in this respect. Only article 63 (a) (3) touched upon legal immigration, a remote reference (if ever one) to integration.[1] But from 1999 to 2005, significant steps were taken towards the construction of an EU integration policy. At the instigation of the Danish, Greek and Dutch Presidencies of the Council of the EU, a series of soft instruments were adopted, decided upon by the Council, and brought to bear by the Commission. The Commission, which had just acquired a new competence, and a new DG, was determined to implement the Tampere Milestones, a set of orientations adopted in 1999. With a proposal for an Open Method of Coordination (OMC) in 2001, it covered it all. Such a proposal was however never discussed. The Commission drew the conclusion that it had to advance cautiously; and so it did, by

---

[1] Handoll (2012: 45) qualifies the use of the said legal basis for integration as a "creative one".

© The Author(s) 2019
P. G. Van Wolleghem, *The EU's Policy on the Integration of Migrants*, Palgrave Studies in European Union Politics,
https://doi.org/10.1007/978-3-319-97682-2_4

remaining within the limits established by the member states. If the latter were willing to cooperate in the EU sphere, the form of such cooperation mattered a great deal: softer than soft (read: less binding than the OMC) was the rule. This did not prevent the new DG from building up power, notably by placing integration within a wider and prevalent agenda: the Lisbon Goals of an employment rate of 70%. In that way, DG Justice and Home Affairs (JHA) clung to DG Employment's priority in order to gain momentum. In 2002, a preliminary fund (the INTI programme) was announced by Commissioner Vitorino, set by DG JHA and directly managed by it. This paved the way for the establishment of a bigger and more comprehensive fund, the European Integration Fund (see Chapter 3).

The European Fund for the Integration of third country nationals (EIF) was decided upon on 25 June 2007 with the adoption of Council Decision 2007/435/EC at the unanimity of the member states, on the basis of article 63 (a) (3) TEC. It is a fund amounting to €825 million to be spent over the period 2007–2013 for projects aimed at easing the integration of non-EU nationals across the EU in accordance with nationally-defined programmes. Since the EU had no formal competence in the domain, the Council Decision did not provide for a clear European approach to integration, but proposed to support national policies leaning onto European-defined principles. From another perspective, the permanence of unanimity voting in this field is synonymous with little delegation from the member states to the EU, which likely translates into great discretion left to member states by EU outputs and a limited role for the Commission.[2]

This chapter traces the process[3] that led to the adoption of the fund whilst taking account of the institutional setting and constellation of actors, it highlights member states' preferences, bones of contention and

---

[2] On delegation aspects, see Chapter 2; but see also Franchino (2004, 2007). Chapters 5 and 6 are concrete cases of implementation of EU outputs in case of limited delegation.

[3] Just like Chapter 3, this chapter employs process tracing to establish the mechanism at play. Whereas the mechanism in Chapter 2 was defined as an upload of preferences, the mechanism at play in this chapter appears to be more strictly concerned with bargaining. For more on process tracing, see (Checkel 2005; Vennesson 2008; Mahoney 2010; Collier 2011). For more on the data used here, see the appendices to this book.

bargaining outcomes.[4] The first part emphasises the key characteristics of the fund and the principles at its foundation. I notably show that, as adopted, the EIF displayed flexible features, enabling member states to use the fund with considerable discretion. The second part takes the reader through the policy-making process. I show how such a process led to the elimination of constraining clauses on the one hand; and on the other, I look into the most disputed features of the fund, namely, those relating to the distribution of the money available. Since the amount available for the EIF over the 7 years of implementation is fixed beforehand, the negotiation takes on the aspect of a zero-sum game.

The EIF: Features and Principles

Functioning of the Fund

Objectives, Specific Objectives and Priorities

The objectives the fund was to address were not at the centre of the negotiation process. From the outset, the Commission proposal contained rather widely framed objectives that would fit member states' very different needs. As per Council Decision,[5] the general objective of the fund is to "support the efforts made by the member states in enabling third country nationals (...) to fulfil the conditions of residence and to facilitate their integration into European societies". Such general objective is then split into specific objectives,[6] priorities and specific priorities.[7] They will be introduced in turn.

There are four specific objectives (see Box 4.1). They frame the overall intents and purposes of the fund, and guide member states' use of it. The vague formulation preceding them; i.e. "the fund shall contribute to the following specific objectives" does not make it clear whether all four objectives must be tackled or to what extent they should be addressed.[8]

---

[4]Chapter 2 provides useful definitions with regard to concepts such as institutional setting and constellations of actors. More generally, see Scharpf (1997).

[5]Council Decision 2007/435/EC, article 2.

[6]Ibid., article 3.

[7]Both defined in C. (2007) 3926 final.

[8]In what proportion of the fund and, more importantly, in what implementation years.

These objectives are further broken down into 19 eligible actions (again, vaguely worded[9]).

> **Box 4.1—The Objectives of the EIF**
> a. facilitation of the development and implementation of admission procedures relevant to and supportive of the integration process of third-country nationals;
> b. development and implementation of the integration process of newly-arrived third-country nationals in Member States;
> c. increasing of the capacity of Member States to develop, implement, monitor and evaluate policies and measures for the integration of third-country nationals;
> d. exchange of information, best practices and cooperation in and between Member States in developing, implementing, monitoring and evaluating policies and measures for the integration of third-country nationals.

Another set of indications is delineated in the Commission Decision[10] defining the strategic guidelines for the implementation of the fund. This Decision establishes four priorities (see Box 4.2 for a summary). Such priorities should be addressed following more stringent rules: "When preparing their draft multi-annual programme, Member States should target throughout the available Community resources under this Fund to at least three of the priorities listed below, among which priorities 1 and 2 are mandatory". Here again, such provision allows room for manoeuvre in different ways. The rule for addressing them does not specify whether member states should address these mandatory priorities every year or what share of the fund should be dedicated to them. In addition, priority 1 (which is mandatory; see Box 4.2) casts a wide net: providing for the implementation of the CBPs is tantamount to: (i) referring to the general objective of the fund and (ii) referring to 11 short-worded, widely defined principles. Finally, these priorities consistently overlap with the objectives referred to above.

---

[9] I do not list them here as it would be too lengthy, see article 4 of the Council Decision 2007/435/EC for more

[10] C. (2007) 3926 final.

Box 4.2—The Priorities of the EIF

Priority 1: Implementation of actions designed to put the 'Common Basic Principles for immigrant integration policy in the European Union' into practice.

Priority 2: Development of indicators and evaluation methodologies to assess progress, adjust policies and measures and to facilitate co-ordination of comparative learning.

Priority 3: Policy capacity building, co-ordination and intercultural competence building in the Member States across the different levels and departments of government.

Priority 4: Exchange of experience, good practice and information on integration between the Member States.

A third and last set of indications consists of specific priorities. These are optional and their implementation relies on a financial incentive (Chapter 5 looks into the effect of such financial incentives). More specifically, the EIF, as any other EU fund, provides for a co-financing principle. As a rule, 50% of a project is financed by the EU, but EU contribution may reach 75% where the state addresses specific priorities. As a derogation, member states falling under the cohesion fund receive 75% co-financing, irrespective of them addressing specific priorities. There are in total five specific priorities (see Box 4.3 for a summary). Here again, they are defined in a rather loose manner and may be addressed by the member states for very different purposes for at least two reasons. First of all, the fact that there exist five specific priorities multiplies the probability a member state, regardless of its specifics, has a ground reality suitable for addressing them. That is, the five specific priorities as they stand offer a pretty diverse panorama which procures a vast array of choices. For instance, specific priority 2, regarding specific target groups, is wide enough to match different situations.[11] The wording of the other specific priorities, too, leaves room for interpretation and different usage. This is notably the case for specific priority 3, relating to "innovative introduction programmes and activities". Under this wording, Carrera and Faure

---

[11]As C. (2007) 3926 final phrases it: "Actions, including introduction programmes and activities, whose main objective is to address the specific needs of particular groups, such as women, youth and children, the elderly, illiterate persons and persons with disabilities".

Atger (2011) show how member states retain great room for manoeuvre. Secondly, there is a consistent overlap between priority 1 and the specific priorities. Priority 1 aims to put the CBPs into practice and reads:

> The Commission Communication on 'A Common Agenda for Integration: Framework for the Integration of third-country nationals in the European Union' [COM (2005) 389 final] puts forward a series of concrete measures designed to put the Common Basic Principles into practice, and is a reference document in this respect. The 'Handbook on integration for policy-makers and practitioners' (...) is a useful complement. The implementation of measures and good practice described in these two documents should be greatly encouraged.[12]

The first document cited [i.e. COM (2005) 389 final] provides specific policy recommendations that consistently overlap with the fund's specific priorities in many instances.

Box 4.3—The Specific Priorities of the EIF
Specific priority 1: Participation as a means of promoting the integration of third-country nationals in society.
Specific priority 2: Specific target groups.
Specific priority 3: Innovative introduction programmes and activities.
Specific priority 4: Intercultural dialogue.
Specific priority 5: Involvement of the host society in the integration process.

Programming, Spending and Control Mechanisms
The fund is implemented through the elaboration of a Multi-Annual Programme covering the period 2007–2013 by the member state and its approval by the Commission. The Commission shall ensure the member state's multiannual programme tackles the objectives pursued by the fund. The multiannual programme is then broken down into annual programmes, in their turn validated by the EU Commission, according to the same criteria.

---

[12]C. (2007) 3926 final.

Since the responsibility for integration policies lies with member states, they retain great room for manoeuvre regarding programme drafting and implementation, despite the approval of programmes by the Commission (Carrera and Faure Atger 2011). Here, a distinction between substantive and procedural control mechanism is in order. On the procedural side, the Commission has the power to ensure that the use of the fund respects the principle laid down in the financial regulations; namely lawful and sound financial management. This is a considerable power given the fact that the fund is spent via shared management, so that the member state spends and the Commission controls (as opposed to direct management; i.e. the Commission spends directly). Accordingly, the Commission has the capacity to withhold payment of balance in the event of mismanagement. Such control mechanism is, however, limited to ill-practices. On the substantive side, the Commission has no power to force member states to address any specific issue. It may attempt to orientate member states' Multi-Annual Programmes on the basis of the objectives and priorities of the fund detailed in the section above but, as I have shown, these are loosely phrased and do not give the Commission much leverage.

The Principles Underlying the Fund

National Planning and European Framework: The CBPs as a Backdrop
Once the idea of a European Integration Fund was put on the table, critics did not take long to appear, mostly because the EU had no formal competence and member states were not all willing to let it chip in. Commissioner Antonio Vitorino announced his intention of creating a European Integration Fund as the new financial perspectives for 2007–2013 were being drafted, on the occasion of the Ministerial Integration Conference in Groningen, the Netherlands, November 9–11, 2004. Such a fund, he asserted, would ensure member states' views and priorities would be heard in the process.[13] The conference conclusions mention the "examination of all financial means available for the integration-related activities within the European institutions" but ministers seemed to have very different views of what should be done in this regard and, despite intensive discussion, no agreement could be

---

[13] Migrapol-Integration 43rev.

reached.[14] Vitorino's announcement was nonetheless reaffirmed by his successor Frattini at the JHA Council[15] held on November 19, 2004.

Establishing an integration fund at EU level was a delicate matter. There was no competence at the time at EU level. The French and Germans had made clear their scepticism in this respect.[16] The freshly signed Constitutional treaty in its article III-267(4) included a reference to integration; providing for the possibility of the EU to support national policies but excluding legal harmonisation. But the treaty was never ratified and the treaty of Nice was still the one in force. The only legal basis available was that of legal migration (Article 63 (a) (3) TEC), the use of which was put into question, notably by the German representative at the NCPI meeting on January 28, 2005.[17] The matter therefore pertained exclusively to member states, as was constantly recalled throughout EU documents.[18] Consequently, implementation would be the responsibility of the member states.[19] As a matter of fact, the Decision establishing the fund reaffirms the prevalence of the state on several occasions. Article 2 for instance makes it clear that the objective of the fund is to "support" member states' efforts, thereby restraining the possibility of the Commission to affect the content of national policies.

Nevertheless, somewhat of a common approach to integration was adopted on the very same occasion as when Vitorino announced his will to create a fund.[20] This common approach consisted in the Common Basic Principles (CBPs) on integration, a set of principles aimed at providing a "coherent European Union framework" within which member states should elaborate their integration policies.[21] The European Integration

---

[14] Council of the European Union 15434/04 (2004).

[15] Migrapol-Integration 43rev.

[16] Migrapol-Integration 40; 52; corroborated by the interviewees.

[17] Migrapol-Integration 52.

[18] This was notably recalled at the Thessaloniki Summit in October 2003 [European Council 11638/03 (2003)]; in the Commission's preliminary impact assessment for the fund (Migrapol-Integration 48); in the Commission proposal for a fund [COM (2005) 123 final], to cite a few examples.

[19] Council Decision 2007/435/EC.

[20] Council of the European Union 15434/04 (2004).

[21] European Council 11638/03 (2003); see also COM (2005) 389 final.

Fund was thought of as a way to embody the EU framework on integration, to promote the implementation of the Common Basic Principles (Pratt 2015). As the first discussion paper about the fund stated[22]:

> The Integration Fund will support the development of national integration strategies which take into account the common basic principles for immigrant integration policy in the European Union.

References to the implementation of the CBPs through the EIF are plentiful and citing them all would be lengthy, cumbersome and repetitive. Hereafter are some examples. The Decision establishing the fund for instance recalls in recital (28) that the objective of the latter is "to promote the integration of third country nationals in the host societies of member states within the framework of the Common Basic Principles". Article 16 (2) states that the guidelines giving effect to the priorities of the Community for each of the fund's objective should promote the CBPs. Article 17 indicates that multi-annual and annual programmes must consider the CBPs. The elaboration by the Commission of the strategic guidelines for the implementation of the fund should also give effect to the common basic principles. Such guidelines notably refer to a Commission Communication aimed at strengthening the implementation of the CBPs.[23]

From the outset, the EIF was thus placed in a limbo between the exclusive national competence and the European framework. Even though the CBPs were designed so that they would focus on key areas and shared problems rather than on national practices in order to increase their acceptability (Pratt 2015), and even though they were adopted on the unanimity of the member states, their practical implementation as per Multi-Annual Programmes was found to be underwhelming (Carrera and Faure Atger 2011).

Implementing Solidarity: A Fund for Integration
The EIF is part of the General Programme on Solidarity and Management of Migration Flows[24] as introduced with the new financial

---

[22] Migrapol-Integration 42: 2.
[23] See C. (2007) 3926 final and COM (2005) 389 final.
[24] COM (2005) 123 final.

perspective for the period 2007–2013 (see above). The objective of this programme is to organise solidarity between member states in the face of unevenly distributed migration flows. In terms of integration, the principle of solidarity lied in the fact that EIF annual amounts would be distributed between member states according to the number of legal residence permits granted rather than on the basis of member states' capacity to take care of integration. Solidarity thus far was implemented through the cohesion policy, with objective distribution criteria (at least after the 1988 reform). The cohesion policy aimed to reduce disparities between member states in terms of average population wealth compared to the EU average. The solidarity principle as conceived with the integration fund made abstraction of the differentiated capacity of member states to organise integration policies and considered the actual number of migrants that should benefit from integration policies. As the Discussion Paper presenting the fund[25] put it, it is:

> a new form of solidarity in order to support the efforts of Member States in enabling third country nationals of different cultural, religious, linguistic and ethnic backgrounds to settle and take actively part in all aspects of European societies.

Accordingly, the target established was cross-national (as opposed to state-based). Estimates across the EU by averaging within-country results showed that about 15% of migrants effectively participated in integration programmes. With the introduction of the fund, the Commission announced that the objective was to cover 30% of the target population, which doubled the coverage in relative terms but which consisted in a significant increase in the absolute number of beneficiaries given the constant increase of influxes over the 2000s. So double coverage but with more and more beneficiaries implied significant resources be deployed. The Commission proposal therefore calculated that the adequate amount to meet the objective was €1771 billion[26] over the period 2007–2013. However, the European Council agreement of December 15–16, 2005 over the financial perspective for the period 2007–2013 significantly cut the allocation of immigration and

---

[25] Migrapol-Integration 42: 2.

[26] COM (2005) 123 final: 11; see SEC (2005) 435: 44 for a detail of the calculation.

solidarity-related funding.[27] The overall budget for the heading on Citizenship, Freedom, Security and Justice was more than halved (heading 3)[28] which entailed a reduction of the European Integration Fund too (cut by 53%) shrinking the overall amount from €1771 billion to €825 million.

The issue of integrating migrants was, at the time, not untouched by EU policies. As a matter of fact, migrants being a group vulnerable to social inclusion, they naturally fell under the scope of the European Social Fund (ESF; see Guiraudon 2003). The ESF however reflected an old reasoning; namely, that integration should be achieved on the economic front, and that social integration would naturally follow. Accordingly, the ESF treated integration of vulnerable groups as depending on their participation in the labour market, but did not target migrants. When the Commission started to consider the idea of an integration fund,[29] merging new money in old structures was considered as a policy option. That is, instead of launching a new policy instrument that would require implementation, the already greased ESF machine could have been augmented of the same amount. To that option, the creation of a new fund that would explicitly and exclusively target third country nationals was preferred. In that manner, the use of EU money would be conditioned to address integration of non-EU nationals, without any possibility to derogate. The inception of a new instrument however inevitably opens a round of negotiations. The unanimity voting rule on top of that meant that uncertainty loomed over the final outcome (see Chapter 2). As Helene Urth (2005: 176) put it: "[t]he Fund must be agreed in the Council by unanimity which may prove to be difficult. Some countries are highly in favour, some believe that the subsidiarity principle is prevailing and that Community funding, therefore, should not be provided".

[27] See Chapter 3; but see also Schild (2008).

[28] Commission proposal for the financial perspectives [COM (2004) 487 final] and accompanying document [SEC (2005) 494 final] proposed that a total of €24.705 billion euro be dedicated to heading 3. But the document adopted by the European Council [European Council 15915/05 (2005)] provided for a more limited amount; €10.270 billion euros would be allocated to the same heading.

[29] See Commission's ex-ante impact assessment SEC (2005) 435. See also Migrapol-Integration 48 and 54.

THE POLICY-MAKING PROCESS: WHO GETS WHAT AND HOW?

From the moment the discussion left the National Contact Points on Integration to final adoption of the EIF, just over two years had passed, in the course of which the fund was discussed. Surprisingly, little discussion concerned directly substantive policy points, sending the analysis back to a henceforth famous adage in political science, uttered by Lasswell in 1936: "Who gets what, when and how" (see Lasswell 1936). As a matter of fact, four main issues arose. Two were linked to the way the fund would be spent. They were solved without much discussion. Two others constituted the bones of contention and mostly touched upon the who-gets-what question. Accordingly, this section will first look into the principle of additionality and principle of partnership. Then I will go through the main disputes: the distribution key and the target group. Before going any further, it ought to be said that the four points developed hereafter are part of a package deal that concerns the provisions common (to some extent) to the four funds part of the General Programme Solidarity and Management of Migration Flows (European Border Fund, European Refugee Fund, Return Fund and European Integration Fund). Resultantly, cross-fund bargains were possible, and were actually observed, notably in the case of Greece which entered a reservation on the EIF. Note in addition that the EIF was the only of the four funds to be adopted by unanimity, as pertaining to legal immigration matters (see Chapter 2).

Additionality and Partnership; or How the Spending of the Fund Became Flexible

Both the principle of additionality and the principle of partnership were introduced by the Commission with the reform of the EU cohesion policy in 1988 (Bachtler and Mendez 2007), in an attempt to bypass national governments and organise decentralisation (Hix 2005). The principle of additionality aimed at ensuring that EU funding would not substitute national expenditure, whilst the partnership principle provided for the participation of national, supranational, but especially subnational actors, in the design and implementation of programmes adopted in the framework of the cohesion policy. The 1988 reform constituted a ground-breaking shift as it would drastically change the relationship between different levels of policy-making, embedding a shift from rather hierarchical relationships to a more network dynamic. According to Marks, this was "the leading edge of a system of multilevel governance" (Marks 1993: 401; see also Bache 2010, for an analysis of the principle of partnership). Moulded into the structural funds' model,[30] the European Integration Fund originally contained the two principles, but the principle of additionality was removed altogether and the partnership principle was considerably weakened.

The Additionality Principle
The process that led to the removal of the principle of additionality was rather straight forward. In a SCIFA meeting in September 2005, Germany, France, the Netherlands, Austria and Hungary raised questions about the functioning of the principle.[31] They were subsequently joined by Slovenia in February 2006. The Slovene delegation came forth with a note to the Commission and other member states, in which it declared that the principle of additionality implies that member states are capable of guaranteeing national budgetary resources for the engagement of the EU fund and that this puts into question the reasonableness of a fund implementing so-called solidarity. It proposed amending the text so that contributions from the fund may, to some extent, replace national expenditure. For the Slovene delegation, a true principle of solidarity would account for the differentiated capacity to secure national budgetary resources, especially where no policy had ever existed.[32] Implementing a whole new policy without being able to use EU funding would imply further efforts of policy building. Resultantly, the principle of additionality was removed altogether, despite concerns from Sweden and the Commission.[33] In September 2006, Sweden entered a scrutiny reservation on the removal of such a principle[34] but lifted its reserve by the end of the month.[35]

---

[30] During the negotiation phase, the Commission declared having 'copied' the provisions regarding spending rules from the structural funds [Council of the European Union 5578/06 (2006)].

[31] Council of the European Union 12802/05 (2005).

[32] Council of the European Union 6735/06 (2006).

[33] Council of the European Union 9385/06 (2006).

[34] Council of the European Union 12524/06 (2006).

[35] Council of the European Union 13407/06 (2006).

> **Box 4.4—The Principle of Additionality as in Commission Proposal**
> *Article 11*
> **Additionality**
>
> 1. Contributions from the Fund shall not replace public or equivalent expenditure by a Member State.
> 2. The Commission shall, in cooperation with each Member State, verify additionality mid-term by 31 December 2012 and ex-post by 31 December 2015.

The principle as per the Commission proposal stated that national public expenditure should not be replaced by EU funding. Beyond that, it provided that the Commission verify the implementation of the principle twice over the period, thus keeping member states in check, to a certain extent.[36] The removal of such a principle has far-reaching consequences. Together with the principle of co-financing, it gives the opportunity for governments to merge EU funding within their national expenditure. This likely creates unbalances in principle, since member states that already have a sound integration policy in place are in a better position to use the fund than member states that must create an integration policy *ex-nihilo*. This likely engenders conflicting purposes: the usability of the fund and its intent to implement solidarity. If a member state is hampered in its use of the fund, third country nationals do not benefit from integration policies and the objectives pursued by the fund are undermined. Solidarity according to the distribution of migrants across Europe is not implemented. But, as Slovenia advanced, keeping the additionality principle is also risky and could have even direr consequences.

Considering the foregoing, the safest option in the face of the member states that had no integration policy beforehand was to remove such a principle. Such removal however reduces the Commission's capacity to influence (from the substantive standpoint) member states spending the money available, since they are legally given the opportunity to replace some of their own funding for integration with the funding granted by the EIF.

---

[36] COM (2005) 123 final.

The Partnership Principle

The partnership principle is the cornerstone of the structural funds, the principle that set off multilevel governance (Marks 1993; Bache 2010). As Bache (2010: 59) posits,

> In the normative debates, the rise of governance is often understood as the rise of heterarchy and the diffusion of power, but it can also reinforce hierarchies and mask underlying power relations. Partnership, as a prominent instrument of governance, should be investigated with both of these possibilities in mind.

Even if provided for in the structural funds rules, the effectiveness of the partnership principle is dependent on a pre-existing balance of territorial relations within a member state so that member states willing to keep their hold of a given policy could effectively do so (Bache 2010). The principle of partnership organises, in theory at least, the relationship between different policy-making levels. For the structural funds, the principle of partnership encompasses supranational, national and subnational levels in the design and implementation of programmes. Initially, the EIF followed the exact same rule.[37]

As per Commission proposal,[38] partnership in the ambit of the EIF mirrors that of the structural funds. It was to include a wide range of actors all along the process, from preparation to implementation, monitoring and evaluation. Gradually, the principle was emptied of its requirements and filled with options. Whilst paragraph 1 mentioned the bodies that "shall" be part of the partnership, the final version listed those that "may" be included. In the same vein, the second sentence of paragraph 2 was removed altogether. In other words, what was supposed to be a partnership principle ended up being an invitation to associate bodies other than governments to the management of the EIF. Wide margins of discretion were thus granted to member states' central administrations. Firstly, the "broad and effective" partnership would now count the bodies the state wishes to associate to the process; secondly, the latter process was considerably shrunk since "preparation, implementation, monitoring and evaluation" were cancelled without being replaced. Shortly, the principle became an empty shell.

[37] Council of the European Union 5578/06 (2006).
[38] COM (2005) 123 final.

Box 4.5—The Partnership Principle Before and After	
Partnership as per Commission proposal	*Partnership as per Council Decision*
1-Each Member State shall organise, in accordance with current national rules and practices, a partnership with the authorities and bodies which it designates, namely	Each Member State shall organise, in accordance with current national rules and practices, a partnership with the authorities and bodies which are involved in the implementation of the multiannual programme or which, according to the Member State concerned, are able to make a useful contribution to its development
(a) the implementing authorities designated by the Member State for the purposes of the management of the interventions of the European Social Fund and other competent regional, local, urban and other public authorities	Such authorities and bodies may include the competent regional, local, urban and other public authorities, international organisations and bodies representing civil society such as nongovernmental organisations, including migrant organisations, or social partners
(b) any other appropriate body representing civil society, non-governmental organisations, including the social partners	
Each Member State shall ensure broad and effective involvement of all the appropriate bodies, in accordance with national rules and practices	This partnership shall include at least the implementing authorities designated by Member States for the purpose of the management of the interventions of the European Social Fund and the responsible authority of the European Refugee Fund
2-The partnership shall be conducted in full compliance with the respective institutional, legal and financial jurisdiction of each partner category	2-Such partnership shall be conducted in full compliance with the respective institutional, legal and financial jurisdiction of each partner category
The partnership shall cover preparation, implementation, monitoring and evaluation of the multiannual programmes	

As a unique check, the Commission asked member states to explain how they intended to implement the principle in their Multi-Annual Programme; i.e. once and for all, so to speak. As Carrera and Faure Atger (2011) note, most member states considered the principle as a consultation moment with other authorities in charge of allocating other funds (which is made mandatory in the Decision) and ministries; a one-off consultation on the occasion of the drafting of the Multi-Annual Programme. In most cases, no further consultation was conducted for the drafting of the annual programmes or for the actual implementation or monitoring. Beyond frequency, consultation is not co-decision; so that the role attributed to such partners was by no means binding for the member state.

The principle of partnership as provided for in the EIF decision is thus by no means comparable to that of the structural funds, because in the case of the EIF, it grants considerable leeway to the member state.

Distribution Key and Target Group; The Bones of Contention

The definition of the target group and the distribution key are closely related topics. If the distribution key defines how to cut the pie, the definition of the target group provides the knife. Emphasising flows of migrants for the distribution of amounts poses the question of how one defines flows. As said above, flows regard the number of third country nationals that recently obtained a residence permit. Yet, at EU level, there exist different sorts of permits, further broken down at national level. Should the distribution key consider as residents migrants with a seasonal work permit? Is it the same as foreigners reuniting with their family? In normative terms, this opens an endless debate in a desirability cloak. In policy terms though, it is a determinant of member states' respective allocations. Italy and Spain, for instance, resort to a seasonal workforce for their agriculture, allegedly more than their counterparts in relative terms. They are thus likely to support their inclusion in the target group with a view to inflate the number of migrants qualifying for the "flow" category. Other countries like, say, the Baltic countries, have more interest in relaxing the boundaries of the target group so that their share of stateless persons (read: Russians who stayed after the collapse of the USSR) can be counted in the distribution key under the "stock" category.[39]

That said, a third provision weakens the link between the distribution key and target group: a specific provision explicitly excluding some categories of migrants for the calculation of the amounts.[40] Despite the importance of the latter provision, it did not crystallise oppositions as much as the target group and the distribution key.[41] The two provisions

---

[39] This was actually a point of discussion during the negotiation of the fund.

[40] See article 14 of Commission proposal in COM (2005) 123 final.

[41] Council of the European Union 12999/06 (2006).

at issue remain therefore closely intertwined as a different target group can justify a change in the distribution key (see below). Analysing them separately may thus prove a delicate, yet necessary task. It is important to separate them from an analytical standpoint for at least three reasons: (i) the two lines of conflict on the two issues do not perfectly overlap one another; (ii) the two issues progressed at a different pace; and (iii) theoretically, the distribution key and the target group regard two different moments, respectively how to allocate the amount in the first place and how to use it afterwards.[42] For these reasons, the two items will be treated in turn.

A caveat is in order here. This section attributes preferences and their respective salience to member states on these two aspects. Not all member states are placed on the spectrum because their positions could not be determined through thorough survey of official documents and interviews with key actors. Note though that the importance of the EIF for the member states was somewhat eclipsed by the negotiation of the European Border Fund, discussed at the same time within the same committees.

Target Group: A Widely Worded Provision Removed

Initially, the target group was loosely worded. Any non-EU national who would not fall under the EU asylum legal framework was to be eligible for actions financed under the EIF. The provision even provided for the possibility of pre-migration support to integration.[43] Accordingly, member states had the possibility to spend the fund at their discretion. At the time, the budget forecast announced a fund of €1771 million, a significant amount that allowed, in a way, for a widely defined target group. But with the budget revisions introduced in the prospect of the 2007–2013 financial perspective, the budget available for the EIF was reduced to €825 million.[44] This prompted the Presidency to propose a revision of the overall purpose of the fund, notably through reducing the scope of the target group. Instead of considering third country nationals in the

---

[42] The wider the target group, the more member states with a small number of migrants are able to actually use the fund when it comes to implementation. A narrower definition, concerning newly arrived third country nationals for instance, renders the actual use of the fund more difficult for those countries with lower influxes.

[43] So-called pre-departure measures; see COM (2005) 123 final: 120.

[44] See Chapter 3 for more on this point.

Fig. 4.1 Member states' preferences on the definition of the target group

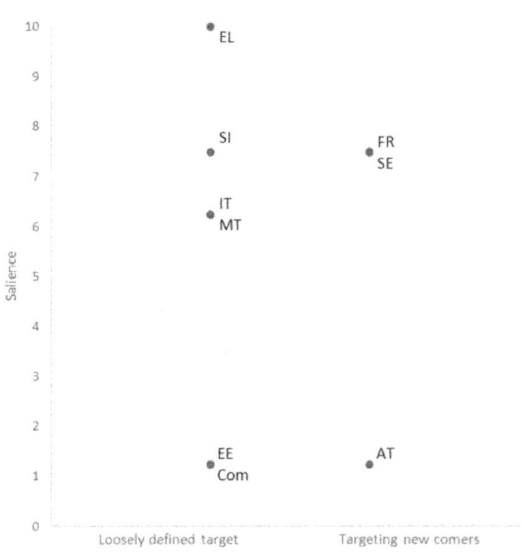

territory and would-be migrants, the Presidency proposed that the fund address newly-arrived third country nationals.[45] This was considered in a further SCIFA meeting and two views came up as possible options.[46] On the one hand, a loose definition of the target group could facilitate member states' use of the available funding; an option in accordance with the Commission's original proposal. On the other hand, the option favoured by the Presidency, the acceptation of "newly-arrived" migrants could be linked to the long-term residence status; would be eligible migrants with a residence permit of one year or more and that would not qualify for the long-term residence permit. Diverging opinions amongst member states emerged. The most visible disagreement opposed supporters of an inclusive and flexible definition of the target group to those that favoured targeting newly arrived third country nationals. Such opposition can be graphically summarised on a Cartesian plane with member states' positions on the abscissa and the saliency of such positions on the ordinates (Fig. 4.1). Since the issue presents itself in a binary fashion, member states are placed either at one point or the other. Saliency is

[45] Council of the European Union 7214/06 (2006).
[46] Council of the European Union 8091/06 (2006).

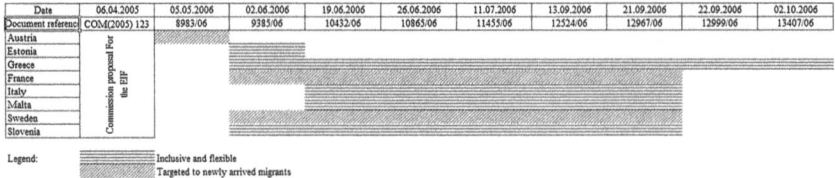

Fig. 4.2   Timeline: member states' positions on the target group

represented on a scale ranging from 1 to 10 and was calculated by counting the number of times their position was recalled in the process[47] (see Fig. 4.1; see also Fig. 4.2 for a timeline representation).

Considering that consensus will eventually require unanimity, it is likely that the more distant the positions are from one another, the harder it will be to convince any member state to yield.[48] The probability of reaching a consensus does not only depend on the distance between positions but also on how dear, so to speak, a member state holds its position. In the case at issue, salience is the greatest for Greece, followed by Slovenia, France and Sweden, all three at the same level. The Commission and Austria are the agenda setters. The Commission has proposed the original version of the text, putting forward a flexible definition of the target group in the first place.[49] Such position is important as it set the baseline, a baseline not questioned until the fund was reduced. Austria, then holding the Presidency of the Council, proposed an alternative in the ambit of the budgetary restriction and made clear it would rather opt for a more targeted instrument.[50] The one as the other did not express further opinion, therefore placing themselves on the plane with a low saliency for their position.[51] Altogether, the position of

[47] Member states had in total 8 opportunities to voice their concern regarding the definition of the target group. Greece entered a reservation on the matter and held its position from the beginning to the very end when it lifted its reservation. It is thus placed at the top of the figure. Estonia cast its comment once and therefore ranks lower on the saliency scale. Note that I placed saliency on a 0–10 scale.

[48] See Chapter 2 for more on this point. More generally, see Tsebelis (2001).

[49] COM (2005) 123 final.

[50] Council of the European Union 7214/06 (2006); 8091/06 (2006).

[51] It is likely that the saliency of their respective positions is underestimated. Since they formulated the alternatives, they came to the fore with their preferences (although they need to be acceptable for the member states) rather than sided for the one or the other so

the Commission does not matter much,[52] if not for setting the baseline, whereas that of Austria could as it delineated the possible alternatives. That said, the alternatives cannot take too much distance from what the other member states are ready to accept.

The issue of the target group stood from May to October 2006. It appeared with the change in the financial perspective. Austria, holding the Presidency at the time, announced that as a consequence of the diminution of the budget to the AFSJ, the EIF amount would diminish, too, and that its scope should be reduced accordingly.[53] Austria thus put forth a compromise text displaying the two options already mentioned, clearly siding in favour of a fund addressing newly arrived third country nationals.[54] Differently, the Commission's favoured option was that of a wide target group granting more flexibility to member states.[55] Since the two camps could not be reconciled, the issue was tasked to a sub-committee of the SCIFA, the Working Party on Migration and Expulsion, for a technical scrutiny of the proposal.[56] A month later; e.g. at the beginning of May, no agreement was found. As official documents phrase it: "[f]ollowing extensive examination of the said provisions, it became evident that the envisaged exclusive limitation of the scope related to the newly arrived third country nationals was felt to be inflexible".[57] Resultantly, the article defining the target group was simply removed, in spite of the concerns of France and Sweden, and to the contentment of Estonia, Greece and Slovenia, which insisted discretion was necessary to meet specific needs due to the different stages of development of their integration policies.

Despite the removal of the article itself, the opposition went on. France and Sweden notably upheld their position by expressing their concern as to the removal of the article.[58] Indeed, maintaining the

that there is the possibility that their expressed position is more salient. There is however no way to test this hypothesis; I thus consider the conservative option the safest and attribute them saliency following the same rule as for the others.

[52] Since the text may be amended the same way it may be accepted, see Chapter 2 for more on this. See also Tsebelis (2013).

[53] Council of the European Union 7214/06 (2006).

[54] Council of the European Union 8091/06 (2006); 8373/1/06 (2006).

[55] Council of the European Union 8373/1/06 (2006).

[56] Ibid.

[57] Council of the European Union 9028/06 (2006): 1.

[58] Council of the European Union 9385/06 (2006).

references to the newly-arrived foreigners weighs in with the debate on the distribution key. If the fund targets newcomers, then a higher percentage of the variable amount distributed according to the number of newcomers makes a lot of sense (see below). Greece and the other defendants of a loosely defined target group maintained their position, too. Notably because, if the article explicitly dealing with the target group was cancelled, references to newly arrived third country nationals were still made with respect to the general objective of the fund. Article 2 for instance provided that "[t]he fund shall primarily focus on actions relating to the integration of newly arrived third country nationals",[59] a rather vague formulation for which Greece entered a reservation. Whereas most of the countries' opinions faded at one moment or another, Greece maintained its reservation until the end. The likely reason is the same as that explaining why some member states wanted a more targeted instrument: it justifies the distribution key granting more importance to flows (in the event that the fund addresses integration of new-comers) or stocks.

In summary, the negotiation process on that aspect led to the withdrawal of the article on the target group for more flexibility in the spending of the fund. References to newly arrived third country nationals remained but were loosely phrased so that member states would enjoy discretion in the spending of the fund. The outcome mirrors a "least common denominator" approach (Tsebelis 2013: 14) or the incomplete contract mentioned in the delegation literature.[60] To the question why some member states would advocate less flexibility in the fund's spending, the most plausible answer lies in the role of the target group's definition in the determination of the distribution key. A reference to newcomers justifies a certain split of the fund whilst a more flexible notion reshuffles the cards. It is interesting in this regard to see the respective positions (and salience of the latter) of Greece, Slovenia, France and Sweden on the two issues by comparing Figs. 4.1 and 4.3: France and Sweden strongly advocate prevalence of flows over stocks of migrants and a fund targeted at newcomers; whilst Greece and Slovenia strongly advocate the exact opposite. In a nutshell, the distribution key is indeed the most relevant issue, at the core of the "who gets what and how" question.

---

[59] Council of the European Union 10432/06 (2006).

[60] For an overview, see *inter alia* Kassim and Menon (2003) but see also Chapter 2 of this book.

The Distribution Key

Continuing the discourse started at the end of the last section, there is indeed a link between the target group and the distribution key. A certain target justifies a certain distribution. No target reshuffles the cards and enlarges the margins of negotiation on the distribution key.

The Commission's proposal put forth a threefold distribution key governing member states' allocations. At the time, the EIF was worth €1771 million. The fund would be distributed via: (i) a fixed amount different for old and new member states; (ii) a percentage of the fund as a function of the total number of third country nationals legally residing in the member state over the previous three years; i.e. the stock of migrants; and (iii) a percentage of the fund as a function of the number of third country nationals who have obtained a residence permit over the previous three years; i.e. flows of migrants.

The fixed part was initially established at €300,000 for EU15 member states whilst the 10 states that joined in 2004 and 2007 would receive €500,000. The rest of the fund would be split according to the following shares: 40% for the stock of migrants; 60% for the flows. Such precedence of flows over stocks considerably affects the allocation of funding. Likewise, the cumulated fixed allocations determine what remains to be distributed according to variable amounts. The fund as designed by the Commission favours distribution to so-called new member states (or EU+12) that receive a higher yearly fixed amount. But such distribution was not to everyone's taste. Depending on whether one has more (or expects more) incoming fluxes or has more settled migrants, one receives more or less. In addition, the higher the fixed amount, the lower the remainder to be split. A member state that expects a higher share of the fund according to variable amount (irrespective of whether flows or stocks prevail; typically EU15 states) has all interests to lower the fixed amount. Conversely, a country with little flows (of legal migrants; this is important since some countries, like Italy, Greece or Spain may receive a lot of immigrants but not all of them will eventually obtain a residence permit) or stock gains from higher fixed amounts. Considering that the total sum that can be spent over the seven years of the programme can under no circumstances be exceeded, the negotiation of the Commission's proposal endorses all the features of a zero-sum game in which what is given to one is taken from the other. Here, two lines of conflict can be distinguished, although closely related: one regards the fixed amount whilst the other concerns more directly the distribution key for variable amounts.

Fig. 4.3 Member states' preferences as to variable amounts

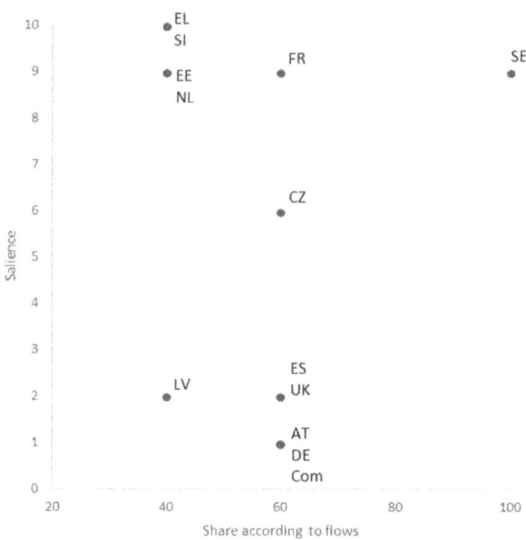

Regarding the variable amounts first, Fig. 4.3 represents member states' position as to the share that should be granted according to flows of migrants (on the abscissa; see also Fig. 4.4 for a timeline representation). The ordinate axis concerns the salience of such a position.[61] France and Sweden display a salient preference for a higher share of the fund distributed according to flows of migrants. They face Greece, Slovenia, Estonia and the Netherlands, preferring precedence be given to stocks with the issue being salient as well. Another group comprising Latvia, Spain, the United Kingdom Austria and Germany[62] shows mild salience for positions following the same divide. Considering the divide regardless of saliency, it appears there are more countries expressing

---

[61] Salience in this respect is measured through the number of times a member state expresses its opinion on the matter along the decision-making process. From the moment the issue first arose, to the end of the decision-making process, member states had the possibility of expressing their opinion ten times. Greece here again expressed its position the most often. As for the positions, I considered the first one ever expressed. Note though that positions changed very little in the process. Sweden passed from a 100 to 80% whereas France passed from 60 to 80%.

[62] Austria and Germany's position were not expressed during the official process but before that, when the matter was approached in the NCPIs committee. The Commission's

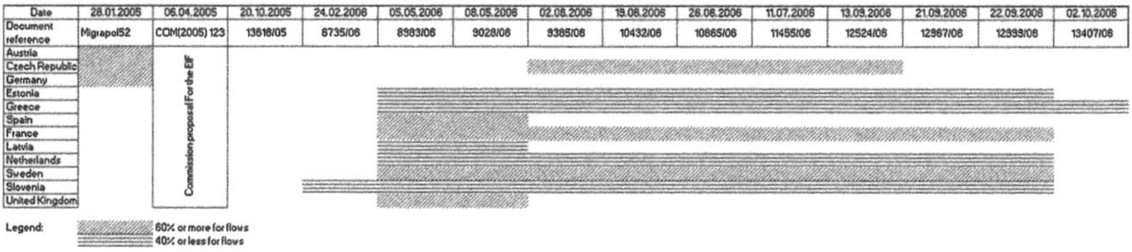

Date	28.01.2005	06.04.2005	20.10.2005	24.02.2006	05.05.2006	08.05.2006	02.06.2006	19.06.2006	26.06.2006	11.07.2006	13.09.2006	21.09.2006	22.09.2006	02.10.2006
Document reference	Migrapol 52	COM(2005) 123	13618/05	8735/06	8983/06	9028/06	9385/06	10432/06	10865/06	11455/06	12524/06	12967/06	12893/06	13407/06
Austria														
Czech Republic														
Germany														
Estonia														
Greece														
Spain														
France														
Latvia														
Netherlands														
Sweden														
Slovenia														
United Kingdom														

Legend: 60% or more for flows
40% or less for flows

Fig. 4.4 Timeline: member states' positions on the distribution key

their preference for flows than for stocks (Sweden, France, the Czech Republic, Spain, the United Kingdom, Austria and Germany). These countries also have, arguably, more bargaining power (Brams and Affuso 1985; Hosli 1995; Cross 2012): economically stronger, it is less costly for them to walk away from the negotiation table than it is for others (even though it is unlikely in practice). Most of them also already had a sound integration policy in place with considerable national public funding, thus reducing the importance of the EIF and increasing their negotiating position. But since the decision rule is unanimity, there is still the possibility, in theory, that a country with less bargaining power block the adoption of a bill (Buchanan and Tullock 1958; Tsebelis 2001).

As for the fixed amounts (see Table 4.1), the hypothesis formulated above is verified: the countries less likely to gain from the variable amounts (those with no or little immigration history) advocate higher fixed amounts, irrespective of their preference for the variable amount distribution. Conversely, advocates of lower fixed amounts are countries with a long migration history.

At the end of the process, Greece, a fierce defendant of its position, yielded. All member states were granted the same fixed amount of €500,000 per year (instead of a differentiated or lower amount) and the variable amount would be split with 60% for flows, 40% for stocks. How did we get there?

The first spark came in February 2006. In a note addressed to the SCIFA in anticipation of a forthcoming meeting,[63] the Slovene

proposal, at the unofficial stage provided precedence be given to stocks (Migrapol-Integration 42). The Commission reversed the distribution key before officially issuing its proposal on the demand of the Austrian, German and Czech delegations. I consider this as the clear expression of a preference.

[63] Council of the European Union 6735/06 (2006).

Table 4.1   Member states' position on the fixed amount

	Higher share for flows	Lower share for flows	Unexpressed
Higher fixed amount	CZ, Com	SI, LV	HU, MT, CY
Lower fixed amount	FR, DE	NL	
Unexpressed	SE, AT, ES, UK	EL, EE	

Delegation proposed the distribution key be reversed to place more emphasis on stocks (60%) rather that fluxes (40%). By mid-March, Estonia, Greece, Latvia, but also the Netherlands, rallied such positions, whereas France, the UK and Spain were in favour of retaining the proposed distribution key.[64] In this respect, Sweden took the stance of asking that 100% of the fund be used for fluxes, due to the fact that the fund is targeted at newly arrived third country nationals.

Ahead of this meeting, the Presidency, realising the necessity of reducing the overall budget for the four funds, opened a discussion on the possibility of decreasing fixed amounts.[65] Whilst France advocated such reduction, Greece seemed[66] to be in favour of a same fixed amount of €500,000 for all countries. A group of states made up of the Czech Republic, Cyprus, Latvia, Hungary, Malta and Slovenia, declared their preference for the text proposed by the Commission (so a higher amount for EU+12 countries). They were later joined by Cyprus and Greece[67] in June 2006. A meeting of the SCIFA to discuss the Presidency's compromise text took place on May 11, 2006. On this occasion, a number of issues were further discussed. Instead of decreasing fixed amounts, as France suggested, the text equalled all of them to €500,000, thereby supporting the stance of the Czech Republic, Cyprus, Latvia, Hungary, Malta and Slovenia. As for the distribution key, the compromise text maintained the proposition laid down by the Commission; i.e. emphasis on fluxes over stocks. The new combination of the two provisions triggered fresh warnings across the board; from the Czech Republic, Greece, Estonia, Italy, France, the Netherlands, Sweden and Slovenia.[68]

[64] Council of the European Union 8983/06 (2006).
[65] Council of the European Union 7214/06 (2006).
[66] Council of the European Union 8983/06 (2006).
[67] Council of the European Union 10432/06 (2006).
[68] Council of the European Union 9385/06 (2006).

By September 2006, the distribution key was still on the table. France and Sweden clung to the emphasis on influxes and asked 80% be dedicated to them. Estonia, Greece, the Netherlands and Slovenia stuck to their position, too, and asked that 60% be dedicated to stocks. With time passing and the issue still standing, the matter left SCIFA to reach COREPER.[69] But whilst most opponents reached a common position in COREPER, Greece maintained its preference for an emphasis on stocks[70] through its scrutiny reservation on article 2, defining the general objective of the fund, a reservation holding since June 2006.[71] Greece lifted its reservation a few days after,[72] without any change being made, paving the way for formal adoption in Council. The overall process actually led to little formal change from the Commission proposal. Notwithstanding, these changes are worth pointing out. If the original distribution key was kept, the annual fixed amount increased by €200,000 for 14 EU member states,[73] decreasing the remaining amount to be distributed by the same figure. Originally, the overall fixed amount for the 7 years of the fund was to be €71.4 million; that is 8.65% of the total amount. After the change, fixed amounts equalled €91 million; 11% of the total amount. This notably reduced the remaining amount to be further distributed.

Greece has been a fundamental player all along. By entering a reservation it would not lift until the very end of the process, to the point of threatening the adoption of the vote, it proved the most determined to obtain satisfaction. In fact, it is only after Greece lifted its reservation that the text could move to the vote. Greece, however, lifted its reservation without obtaining what it wanted. Why is this so? It is always arguable that opposing a text is good as long as the finger-pointing is not too precise. Standing against the bill works if the member state is not the only one to want to amend the text. Alternatively, being the one that says no is a considerable pressure in spheres where consensus-seeking logics reign.[74] Accordingly, Greece could have yielded when support for its position faded. More likely though, Greece would have obtained

---

[69] Council of the European Union 12999/06 (2006).

[70] Council of the European Union 13407/06 (2006).

[71] Council of the European Union 10865/06 (2006).

[72] Council of the European Union 13407/06 (2006).

[73] Let us recall that Denmark opted out of policies linked to the AFSJ; hence a reference to 14 of the EU15 countries.

[74] See Chapter 2 for more on this. See also Aus (2008).

concessions on another (related) policy, in a typical log-rolling fashion. As the Decision was included in a package deal, Greece could have bargained on other fronts and obtained a more favourable distribution key in one of the other three funds under discussion.[75]

Conclusion

Without a strong foothold on integration matters and with a rule providing for unanimity decision-making, the adoption of a fund at EU level that would consistently enforce a European view of integration was unlikely (see Scharpf's actor-centred institutionalism as described in Chapter 2). This chapter shows that the decision-making process led to a fund with widely defined objectives, flexible implementation rules, and for which most of the attention has focused on the who-gets-what question. In summary, the negotiation revolved around easing the requirements for spending and getting more to spend, two sides of the same coin.

From the outset, the proposal from the Commission set a series of objectives that would be endorsed by the member states without much discussion. Casting a wide net, these objectives allowed member states to use the fund according to their priorities. This is also due to the fact that, lacking a competence on the matter, all the EU could do was support national policies. The negotiation of the Commission's proposal reinforced member states' grip on the fund as some of the principles established with the reform of the cohesion policy in 1988; i.e. principles of additionality and partnership, were either removed or weakened. Accordingly, member states were legally given the opportunity to replace their own funding for integration with the funding granted by the EIF, and they were under no obligation to consult subnational bodies or third sector organisations for the programming, implementing or evaluating phases of the fund. In addition, implementation was made more discrete with the suppression of a clear, binding reference to the target group. In this manner, member states could use the fund with more flexibility whilst the control mechanism in the Commission's hands progressively faded. As a result, the way member states would plan to use the fund would likely depend on their respective preferences (Chapter 5).

---

[75] So holds one of the interviewees who happened to participate in the negotiations of the fund.

REFERENCES

SCHOLARSHIP AND EXPERT REFERENCES

Aus, J. P. (2008). The Mechanisms of Consensus: Coming to Agreement on Community Asylum Policy. In D. Naurin & H. Wallace (Eds.), *Unveiling the Council of the European Union: Games Governments Play in Brussels* (pp. 99–120). Basingstoke: Palgrave Macmillan.

Bache, I. (2010). Partnership as an EU Policy Instrument: A Political History. *West European Politics, 33*(1), 58–74.

Bachtler, J., & Mendez, C. (2007). Who Governs EU Cohesion Policy? Deconstructing the Reforms of the Structural Funds. *JCMS: Journal of Common Market Studies, 45*(3), 535–564.

Brams, S. J. & Affuso, P. J. (1985). New Paradoxes of Voting Power on the EC Council of Ministers. *Electoral Studies, 4*(2), 135–139.

Buchanan, J. M. & Tullock, G. (1958). *The Calculus of Consent: The Foundations of Constitutional Democracy.* Indianapolis: Liberty Fund. Available at: http://www.econlib.org/library/Buchanan/buchCv3c7.html. Last Consulted November 12, 2016.

Carrera, S., & Faure Atger, A. (2011). *Integration as a Two-Way Process in the EU? Assessing the Relationship Between the European Integration Fund and the Common Basic Principles.* Brussels: Centre for European Policy Studies.

Checkel, J. T. (2005). *It's the Process Stupid! Process Tracing in the Study of European and International Politics* (ARENA Centre for European Studies Working Papers No. 26). University of Oslo.

Collier, D. (2011). Understanding Process Tracing. *PS. Political Science & Politics, 44*(4), 823–830.

Cross, J. P. (2012). Everyone's a Winner (Almost): Bargaining Success in the Council of Ministers of the European Union. *European Union Politics, 14*(1), 70–94.

European Council 15915/05. (2005). Financial Perspective 2007–2013.

Franchino, F. (2004). Delegating Powers in the European Community. *British Journal of Political Science, 34*(2), 269–293.

Franchino, F. (2007). *The Powers of the Union: Delegation in the EU.* Cambridge: Cambridge University Press.

Guiraudon, V. (2003). The Constitution of a European Immigration Policy Domain: A Political Sociology Approach. *Journal of European Public Policy, 10*(2), 263–282.

Handoll, J. (2012). Integration Policy in the European Union: The Question of Competence. In Y. Pascouau & T. Strik (Eds.), *Which Integration Policies for Migrants? Interaction Between the EU and Its Member States* (pp. 15–50). Nijmegen: Wolf Legal Publishers.

Hix, S. (2005). *The Political System of the European Union* (2nd ed.). Basingstoke: Palgrave Macmillan.

Hosli, M. O. (1995). The Balance Between Small and Large: Effects of a Double-Majority System on Voting Power in the European Union. *International Studies Quarterly, 39*(3), 351.

Kassim, H., & Menon, A. (2003). The Principal-Agent Approach and the Study of the European Union: Promise Unfulfilled? *Journal of European Public Policy, 10*(1), 121–139.

Lasswell, H. D. (1936). *Politics; Who Gets What, When, How.* New York: Whittlesey House, McGraw-Hill Book Co.

Mahoney, J. (2010). After KKV: The New Methodology of Qualitative Research. *World Politics, 62*(1), 120–147.

Marks, G. (1993). Structural Policy and Multilevel Governance in the EC. In A. W. Cafruny & G. G. Rosenthal (Eds.), *The State of the European Community.* Boulder: Lynne Rienner.

Pratt, S. (2015). EU Policymaking and Research: Case Studies of the Communication on a Community Immigration Policy and the Common Basic Principles for Integration. In P. Scholten, H. Entzinger, R. Penninx, & S. Verbeek (Eds.), *Integrating Immigrants in Europe: Research-Policy Dialogues* (pp. 117–131). Amsterdam: IMISCOE Research Series.

Scharpf, F. W. (1997). *Games Real Actors Play: Actor-Centered Institutionalism in Policy Research.* Boulder: Westview Press.

Schild, J. (2008). How to Shift the EU's Spending Priorities? The Multi-annual Financial Framework 2007–13 in Perspective. *Journal of European Public Policy, 15*(4), 531–549.

Tsebelis, G. (2001). *Veto Players: How Political Institutions Work.* Princeton: Princeton University Press.

Tsebelis, G. (2013). Bridging Qualified Majority and Unanimity Decisionmaking in the EU. *Journal of European Public Policy, 20*(8), 1083–1103.

Urth, H. (2005). Building a Momentum for the Integration of Third-Country Nationals in the European Union. *European Journal of Migration and Law, 7*(2), 163–180.

Vennesson, P. (2008). Case Studies and Process Tracing Theories and Practices. In D. Della Porta & M. Keating (Eds.), *Approaches and Methodologies in the Social Sciences: A Pluralist Perspective* (4th ed., pp. 223–239). Cambridge, NY: Cambridge University Press.

EU Acts and Other Official Documents

C (2007) 3926 Final—European Commission. (2007). *Commission Decision of 21/VIII/2007 Implementing Council Decision 2007/435/EC as Regards the Adoption of Strategic Guidelines for 2007 to 2013.*

COM (2004) 487 Final—European Commission. (2004). *Communication from the Commission to the Council and the European Parliament. Financial Perspectives 2007–2013.*

COM (2005) 123 Final—European Commission. (2005). *Communication from the Commission to the Council and the European Parliament Establishing a Framework Programme on Solidarity and the Management of Migration Flows for the Period 2007–2013.*

COM (2005) 389 Final—European Commission. (2005). *Communication from the Commission to the Council, the European Parliament, the European Economic and Social Committee and the Committee of the Regions. A Common Agenda for Integration—Framework for the Integration of Third-Country Nationals.*

Council Decision 2007/435/EC. (2007). *Establishing the European Fund for the Integration of Third-Country Nationals for the Period 2007 to 2013 as Part of the General Programme Solidarity and Management of Migration Flows.*

Council of the European Union 5578/06. (2006). *Note.*

Council of the European Union 6735/06. (2006). *Note.*

Council of the European Union 7214/06. (2006). *Note.*

Council of the European Union 8091/06 (2006). *Note.*

Council of the European Union 8373/1/06. (2006). *Note.*

Council of the European Union 8983/06 (2006). *Note.*

Council of the European Union 9028/06 (2006). *Note.*

Council of the European Union 9385/06. (2006). *Note.*

Council of the European Union 10432/06. (2006). *Revised Note.*

Council of the European Union 10865/06. (2006). *Outcome of Proceedings.*

Council of the European Union 12524/06. (2006). *Note.*

Council of the European Union 12802/05. (2005). *Outcome of Proceedings.*

Council of the European Union 12999/06. (2006). *Introductory Note.*

Council of the European Union 13407/06. (2006). *Note.*

Council of the European Union 15434/04. (2004). *Information on the Ministerial Conferences of Groningen (9–11 November 2004) and of Rotterdam (6–7 July 2004).*

European Council 11638/03. (2003). *Thessaloniki European Council 19 and 20 June 2003, Presidency Conclusions.*

SEC (2005) 435 Final—European Commission. (2005). *Commission Staff Working Document Annex to the General Programme Solidarity and Management of Migration Flows Extended Impact Assessment.*

SEC (2005) 494 Final—European Commission. (2005). *Commission Working Document Technical Adjustments to the Commission Proposal for the Multiannual Financial Framework 2007–2013.*

CHAPTER 5

Why Implement Without a Tangible Threat? the Effect of a Soft Instrument on National Migrant Integration Policies

The European Integration Fund was adopted in 2007, after a policy on integration came into existence at EU level (Chapter 3). The way this policy emerged and the rules in use (formally and informally) led to the adoption of a fund that would grant wide margins for manoeuvre to member states (Chapter 4). Considering the specific institutional environment thereby set (Chapter 2), the question of the implementation of a fund relying on soft law arises. Over the past 20 years, the study of policy-making has argued in favour of softer regulation. The New Management school has advocated smarter regulation, suggesting the desirability of a shift from command-and-control instruments to incentive-based ones (Grabosky 1995), whilst Multilevel Governance scholars have advocated less hierarchical and more co-operative processes (Hooghe and Marks 2001). At EU level, the Lisbon Strategy gave birth to the Open Method of Coordination (OMC; see Chapter 2), intended to bypass the crippled community method in delicate policy realms. Yet, to date, studies of the implementation of EU outputs are still very much focusing on EU directives, leaving, by the same token, the study of primary and secondary law (mainly Regulations and Decisions)

This Chapter reproduces the contents published in Van Wolleghem (2017) © 2017 University Association for Contemporary European Studies and John Wiley & Sons Ltd.

© The Author(s) 2019
P. G. Van Wolleghem, *The EU's Policy on the Integration
of Migrants*, Palgrave Studies in European Union Politics,
https://doi.org/10.1007/978-3-319-97682-2_5

implementation to lawyers. Now that enthusiasm for the OMC has passed, leaving behind a series of case studies, thorough descriptions and hypotheses about its cognitive impact, little attention has been paid to other policy instruments and their implementation across EU member states.

This chapter shifts the focus to the top-down Europeanization phase and delves into the mechanisms that govern the implementation of the European Integration Fund's (EIF) soft law provisions across EU member states. I argue that the design specific to a policy instrument determines the actors disputing its implementation. Drawing from different strands in the existing literature, I develop a series of hypotheses to answer the question: what explains variation in implementation in the absence of a threat from above? Considering the EIF as soft law,[1] I show that much is placed under the discretion of governments. I posit that: in the event of low oversight by the EU Commission, as is the case for the implementation of EU law, and in the absence of horizontal oversight, as is supposed to be the case for the OMC, member states may be prevented from free-riding thanks to the effect of oversight from below (Cremona 2012; Dai 2005; Featherstone 2005). That is, member states will tend to pursue their own agenda unless public opinion or civil society organizations play the watchdogs. These hypotheses owe their place in my model to the constant endeavour of the European Commission to render its funding activities visible to the wide public and its will to empower non-profit organizations through financing rules. I thus show that the policy instrument used determines the influential actors in the game and their respective resources, which in turn may determine the outcome of the implementation process.[2] Empirical evidence is drawn from the application of time-series cross-section methods to an original dataset.[3]

This chapter starts by bridging the literature on compliance, OMC and policy instruments in order to delineate a policy-specific approach. The features of the EIF are then recapitulated in order to show the extent to which it is a soft law instrument. The third part presents four

---

[1] Despite the fact that the EIF was adopted through Council Decision, the provisions it includes are of a soft law nature. See below for more on this. See also Trimikliniotis (2012).

[2] See Chapter 2 for more on this point.

[3] Time-series cross-section models are nowadays well known in the academic community so that there is no need to go in-depth on the method here (see notably Beck 2006). Models' specifics and the data used are detailed in the appendices.

hypotheses regarding its implementation, which I then test in the empirical section (followed by post-estimation analyses).

A Policy Specific Approach to Implementation: Compliance, Flexibility and Instruments

This chapter bridges the literature on compliance, OMC and policy instruments. Studies on compliance have produced cross-country and cross-sectoral explanations as to *why* member states comply with EU directives (Treib 2014). This literature has offered two main series of explanations. On one end of the spectrum, state-based approaches usually contend that implementation depends on capacity. Structural (poverty, government efficiency, culture) or organizational (federalism, corporatism) features determine a state's capacity to abide by its European duties.[4] This stance is, however, vulnerable to severe criticisms in that it suggests that, over a broad range of policy fields, some countries will systematically tend either to comply or not comply. Yet, sector-specific interests matter and this cannot be accounted for by state-based explanations. Empirically, there appears to be more variation across the different policies within countries than amongst countries.[5]

At the other end of the spectrum, preference-based explanations have initially consisted of two branches. One has posited the impact of the goodness of fit between EU outputs and national institutional frameworks (Börzel and Risse 2003) whilst the other has centred its analysis on the game between veto points (Haverland 2000; Giuliani 2003). Both approaches have, however, proven to be only 'sometimes-true theories' (Falkner et al. 2005, 2007). Further developments of preference-based explanations have nonetheless blossomed, geared up with sector-based preferences arguments (see inter alia Steunenberg 2007; Steunenberg and Rhinard 2010). These studies aim at testing the role that preferences in specific policy sectors play in the implementation of EU outputs.

---

[4] Such an approach can be found in inter alia Mbaye (2001), Pridham (1994), Lampinen and Uusikylä (1998), König and Luetgert (2008), Falkner et al. (2005, 2007), Falkner and Treib (2008).

[5] So found Thomson et al. (2007), König and Luetgert (2008), König and Mäder (2014), Börzel (2000).

With the advent of the Open Method of Coordination (OMC), a new strand in the literature on EU outputs has aimed at explaining *how* soft instruments (the OMC) affect member states' preferences (Kröger 2009). Concentrating mostly on processes, scholars put emphasis on learning (Knill and Lenschow 2005; Radaelli 2008), peer-pressure through benchmarking (Borràs and Jacobsson 2004) or naming and shaming (Büchs 2007).

Interestingly, in answering different questions, compliance studies and OMC studies have brought to light similar causal mechanisms. Capacity, veto-players or goodness of fit have been put to the fore (Saurugger and Terpan 2013). The reason lies in the fact that the two phenomena under study share a similar feature: compliance. Even though soft law is not binding law, it can exert an important influence on member states' behaviour (Tholoniat 2010). Therefore, there is (non-)compliance (or 'resistance' to) with hard law as with soft law; what changes are the sources and degree of coercion exercised.[6] In the case of directives, high coercion is applied and embodied by the Commission which may launch a legal action for failure to comply with EU obligations. In the case of soft law, mild coercion is instead exercised and it comes from different sources that may be European counterparts or national actors. This is where the third literature, on instruments, comes into play. It revolves around Lowi's early statement that policies determines politics (Lowi 1964; see Chapter 2) and posits that the instrument matters. It determines the actors, the sectoral interests that are going to affect its implementation[7]; hence the need for a policy-specific model of explanation.

As mentioned, with soft-steering instruments, Commission oversight is no longer a threat, which makes member states' commitment to objectives difficult to ensure (Dehousse 2005; Tholoniat 2010). If constraint from above is limited, it may come from the sides or even from below. Horizontal constraint refers mainly to the OMC and the principle of benchmarking or peer-pressure it contains. Finally, constraint may come from below, from the power the constituency holds to constrain the actions of politicians through the threat of electoral sanctions, and from the consent or opposition organized interests may voice (Featherstone 2005; Dai 2005; Cremona 2012). The latter source of constraint is the

---

[6] On this aspect, see notably Salamon (2000), Gunningham and Sinclair (1998).

[7] Different strands in policy tool literature agree on this point; see notably Gunningham and Sinclair (1998), Kassim and Le Galès (2010).

most relevant for this chapter and the relevant actors ought to be identified accordingly.

In designing a policy specific model of explanation, this chapter is at the cross-roads of these three sets of literature: it considers the *actors* likely to affect implementation in order to explain *why* member states implement or 'resist' *soft law* instruments. In order to allow cross-country comparison, I inspire my acceptation of implementation from the literature on compliance. That is, several works employ timeliness as a proxy for compliance with EU Directives, thereby limiting implementation to transposition (e.g. formal notice of national implementation measures) and ignoring application and enforcement.[8] Despite its limits, this strategy allows cross-national comparison of member states' behaviour. In a similar fashion, I consider member states' response rate to soft law; that is, how much they declare in their annual programmes that they implement, or how much they show (passive) resistance by declaring they do not implement.[9]

When Policy Determines Politics: The Implementation of the EIF

Immigration is a new item of EU law. Barely mentioned in the Maastricht treaty, it was enshrined for the first time in EU primary law by the Treaty of Amsterdam. Even then, the integration of foreigners was scarcely touched upon. It was first dealt with in a Commission proposal for an OMC on immigration[10] that was, however, not put forward by the Council (Caviedes 2004). This did not prevent the Commission from advancing its agenda through a patchwork of different soft law instruments, sometimes called 'quasi-OMC' (Carrera 2008: 6). Two of these instruments form the core of the EU integration policy: (i) the Common Basic Principles (CBPs), a set of 11 short principles intended to guide the policies of member states; (ii) the European Integration Fund (EIF), a financial instrument aimed at implementing the CBPs.

---

[8] For more on this, see Börzel (2001) and Treib (2014).

[9] Note that, whilst this chapter looks into an implementation phase close to that of transposition for Directives, Chapter 6 delves into the next phase, close to that of application of Directives.

[10] COM (2001) 387 final; see Chapter 1 for more on this.

Why the EIF is a Good Example of Soft Law Implementation

The EIF presents particular features that make it a soft law instrument *par excellence*. Pertaining to a realm in which the EU had no formal competence[11] until the entry into force of the Treaty of Lisbon makes soft law the unique mode of action accessible to EU institutions; but unlike most of the soft instruments used thus far, the EIF is not an OMC: there is no institutionalized peer-pressure through benchmarking or the like. Touching upon immigration, it is a rather sensitive and salient policy field in which member states are likely to follow their own agenda.

The EIF is a rather small envelope of €825 million financing integration projects over the period 2007–2013. Around 93% of it is spent on national programmes on the basis of a yearly-calculated allocation. Amounts are indicative and conditional upon a member state's willingness to engage them. Like most EU funds, the EIF operates on the principle of co-financing and programming: the member state financially commits to objectives announced in a multiannual programme, which is in turn further broken down into annual programmes; this commitment is supplemented by the EU fund. But, unlike most EU funds that provide a sound partnership principle (see Bache 2010), the EIF places governments at the centre of its implementation (see Chapter 4). There is a programming phase in coordination with the Commission, but the definition of the substantive content of the programmes remains largely dominated by the state (Carrera and Faure Atger 2011). There is a partnership principle here too, but it is very weak since governments may or may not open the programming phase to other actors.[12] Unlike other funds, no principle of additionality is provided for. The entire process therefore remains in the hands of governments, which have the option to neglect the fund's purposes and pursue their own. From an empirical perspective, the EIF eschews the problems that hamper comparative analysis of other soft law policies[13]: by providing funding opportunities, it is submitted to financial regulations and consequently member states are obliged to plan and report on their activities, which provides essential data for comparative analysis.

---

[11] The EIF was adopted on the basis of article 63 (3) (a) relating to legal immigration and ruled by unanimity voting.

[12] Council Decision 2007/435/EC, art. 10.

[13] Tholoniat (2010: 97) notes that in the first OMCs, members states 'tended to avoid peer review exercises or simply refused to report on progress' on sensitive issues.

How the EIF Works

The EIF Decision and related documents[14] establish the goals that shall be tackled by the fund. The use of the fund is submitted to more or less stringent rules (see Chapter 4). Some are rather vague (the "specific objectives" outlined in Chapter 4) whilst some others may be complied with ex-ante, in agreement with the Commission (the case of "priorities" summarised in Chapter 4); these two sets of rules make their empirical analysis difficult. I therefore consider the set of indications that is at the same time soft law and empirically traceable: a series of five specific priorities financially incentivized (hereinafter 'EU indications'). I test hypotheses as to how member states respond to these.[15] Note though that according to the fund's rules, individual projects are co-financed up to 50% by the EU. This contribution is increased to 75% where the state follows the indications. However, member states falling under the cohesion fund receive 75% from the fund, irrespective of whether they address them. Therefore, not every country has a financial incentive to follow EU indications. Notwithstanding, member states showed very different responses over the years. Figure 5.1 reports the mean and standard deviation of their implementation over the seven years of the EIF. Most member states observe sizeable dispersion around the mean, creating a hectic picture that cannot be accounted for by financial incentives. Another graphic representation (Fig. 5.2) shows the yearly distribution for each member state. It notably shows that dispersion around the mean is not due to a gradual increase or decrease in implementation, but forms an apparently random pattern.

The huge variation between and within member states in their response to EU indications poses a question that I formally phrase as follows: what explains variation in implementation in the absence of a credible threat from above? Structural and functional explanations can be discarded for several reasons. First of all, it is evident that such variation within countries cannot be explained by invariant structural features alone (Fig. 5.2 is quite telling in this respect). Secondly, EU indications

---

[14] See C. (2007) 3926 final.

[15] These indications, so-called 'specific priorities', are defined in C. (2007) 3926 final (see Chapter 3 for more on these). They regard inter alia: participation of migrants in integration policies; targeting vulnerable groups; innovative introduction programmes.

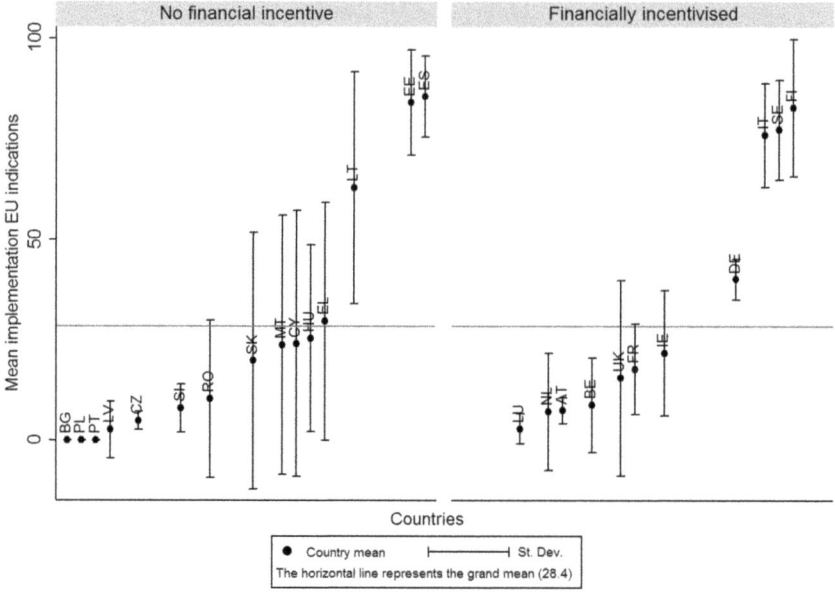

Fig. 5.1 Implementation of EU indications in percentage of total funding, by financial incentive, mean percentage and standard deviation

are worded in an ample and construable manner,[16] they are numerous and, hence, can satisfy a large array of situations on the ground, and they are not policies per se but orientations to be given to projects financed under the EIF.

HYPOTHESES TO THE TEST

As said earlier, soft law is not no law and there is indeed compliance with (or resistance to) soft law. What the driver of compliance is remains to be seen insofar as little legal coercion can be exercised by the Commission (as it is in the case of Directives) or other member states (as in the OMC). As far as the EIF is concerned, Commission oversight is limited to sound financial management and there is no horizontal monitoring device

[16] See Chapter 4; but see also examples in Carrera and Faure Atger (2011: 30).

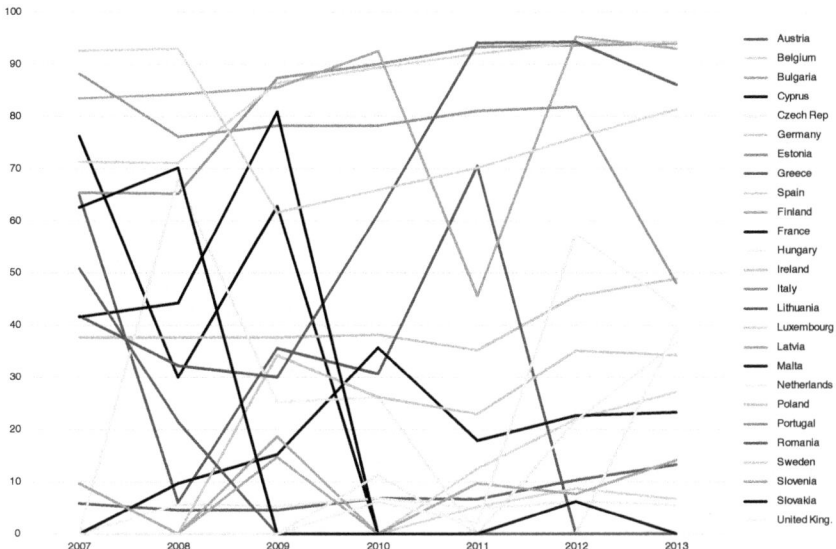

Fig. 5.2 Implementation of EU indications in percentage of total funding over the period 2007–2013

whatsoever. There remains a compliance mechanism from below, since politicians are answerable to a constituency that may or may not remove them from office from one mandate to another. I posit that the weak role of the two former control mechanisms accentuates the importance of the latter and that, under certain circumstances, civil society may exert strong oversight able to ensure compliance is sought by the implementers.

Why Public Opinion Should Matter

Many scholars have argued that policy-makers have limited attention available[17] and that society faces many issues simultaneously. Only a small number of issues are taken up by policy-actors and give rise to policy development. If policy-makers are interested in staying in office they must pay attention to the issues the public cares about (Green-Pedersen

---

[17] See notably Howlett and Giest (2012).

and Mortensen 2013). Yet, public opinion has rarely been studied in implementation scholarship and when it has, it focused on attitude towards EU integration (Treib 2014). In this fashion, rather little evidence has been found in support of it; only Mbaye (2001) found it had an impact. Furthermore, little account has been given to public opinion on specific issues. Spendzharova and Versluis (2013) succeeded in demonstrating the impact of public opinion attachment to environmental issues and compliance with environmental-related directives. Scrutinizing public opinion when it comes to implementing immigration-related policies is of compelling relevance. Immigration is decidedly a hot topic. As of 2004, numerous respondents to Eurobarometer 60 ranked immigration as one of the most important issues. In August 2015, Eurobarometer revealed that immigration was the foremost concern of the European public, more important than economic issues and unemployment (Les Echos 2015). Van Spanje and de Vreese (2011) and Luedtke (2005) have found that anti-immigration attitude has actual effects on MEPs' votes and support for the EU. Alonso and Fonseca (2011) found that immigration had also gained in saliency in party competition across Europe since WWII.

Essentially, public opinion is likely to matter. But what would be the foreseeable effect? It presents few difficulties to hypothesize the effect of low saliency. Inverting Lowi's argument (1964) that policies with direct consequences for public budgets are often highly salient to the public, I posit that a policy that is not really salient should not have consequences on public budgets. Resultantly, when the public is not attentive to the issue, the state has an incentive to minimize national spending by addressing EU indications and obtaining 75% co-financing from the EU. To paraphrase Susskind (2006: 279): 'the best way for a negotiator to satisfy his interests is to find a low-cost way (to him) of meeting the most important interests of his negotiating partners'. In that sense, government can yield to the financial incentive and concentrate on the issues that interest citizens the most. For those states that have no financial incentive in following EU indications, they may do so as a result of the reporting activities entailed by the fund which expose the way they implement it to other member states and EU institutions. They may thus be sensitive to peer-pressure or name-and-shame logics (as in a benchmarking exercise; see above).

Alternatively, the effect of high salience is uncertain. It could lead to "more Europe" in the implementation, be it for blame-shifting purposes or because public opinion supports EU integration. But high salience could also be linked to a more national policy. After all, immigration policies at national level have been built on national identities (Luedtke 2005). To put it differently, high salience is likely to matter to public policies 'but the direction of the effect is crucially dependent on the policy opinions expressed in the mass public' (Green-Pedersen and Mortensen 2013: 170). That said, the public's policy preferences in this respect are likely vague (Wren and McElwain 2009) and potentially conflicting[18] so that parties can hardly try and close the distance separating them from the public at large.[19] I therefore hypothesize that high salience leads to a political response in accordance with a government's position on the matter. Given that EU indications aim at implementing the CBPs, which define integration as a 'two-way process of mutual accommodation'[20] between migrants and nationals and therefore as departing from assimilation, a government is likely to implement these indications if it favours multiculturalism over assimilation.[21]

Hence,

H1: Low salience in public opinion prompts governments to implement EU indications.

H2: High saliency in public opinion combined with government preference for multiculturalism increase the likelihood of implementing EU indications.

---

[18] Eurostat data (2014) show conflicting positions in the public's attitude towards migrants for instance. Note that the public's preferences as to integration and/or how much Europe there should be in integration policy is more difficult to fathom.

[19] As a matter of fact, parties' policy preferences on the matter change very little over short periods of time. Policy preferences on multiculturalism for the period 1999–2014 have rarely moved of more than one point on a zero-to-ten scale.

[20] See the CBPs, Box 3.2.

[21] The concepts of assimilation and multiculturalism have been discussed a great deal in the specialized literature (see this book's introduction). They are here considered as a policy preferences. Assimilation refers to a policy position viewing integration as a one-sided process of adaptation whereby immigrants are to be incorporated into the host society (Brubaker 2001) whereas multiculturalism refers to the acceptance (and sometimes) promotion of long-term cultural differences (Kymlicka 1995).

Why Civil Society Organisations Should Matter

In ever slimmer states, administrative decentralization has increased and is often a favoured option to cut bureaucracies' expenses (Majone 1999). Delegation of the delivery of public services to non-profit organizations has become increasingly common. This is also how the EIF is supposed to work: programming is up to government whilst the ground implementation of projects falls to third parties, be they subnational bodies or third sector entities.[22] Civil society organizations (CSOs) are thus a good candidate for acting as surrogate regulators (Dai 2005; Gunningham and Sinclair 1998) and may push governments towards more implementation (Saurugger 2012). Note that, in order to act as surrogate regulators, CSOs must display sufficient financial and staff capacities to be co-implementers.

There are, however, different ways to look at the CSO-government relationship. They may interact in a confrontational manner and CSOs may exert pressure on the state to achieve their goals. Dai (2005) argues that civil society is likely to be empowered by the existence of an international norm that would allow it to exert pressure on a government's agenda. If we consider their interaction in a collaborative fashion, government and CSOs have a common interest in increasing the available resources to be distributed, in 'increas[ing] the size of the pie' (Susskind 2006: 281).

Beyond the CSO-government relationship, CSOs involved in migration issues have a policy position substantively close to the Commission's, for a number of reasons: (i) because of the long standing relationship between a Commission in search of input and output legitimacy[23] and CSOs seeking material and symbolic resources[24]; (ii) because the relationship between the Commission and CSOs on migration-related issues is not one of contentious politics but rather one of building up alliances (Geddes 2000); (iii) because the Commission's position is rather progressive and in line with the position of CSOs, as evidenced

---

[22] Commission Decision C. (2008) 795.

[23] See inter alia Scharpf (2003).

[24] For migration, see inter alia Geddes (2000), but see also the INTI programme; that is, NGOs directly financed by Commission for the integration of third country nationals.

at the 11th meeting of the European Integration Forum (April 2014), which gathered CSOs in Brussels to discuss integration matters.[25]

But since public opinion might already have an impact on government programming, the impact of organized civil society may be diminished in the sense that governments may favour public opinion over CSOs. So the impact of CSOs may be higher when there is low salience in public opinion, and arguably low salience in government. In the event the issue is salient for government, the government is likely to keep a firm grip on the programming phase. Conversely, if the issue is neither salient for the public nor for the government, government may loosen its grip and grant more room to CSOs. As Albaek et al. (2007) and Green-Pederson and Mortensen (2013) argue: in times of low salience in public opinion, subsystems (ensembles of interests groups, bureaucrats and experts) are likely to dominate policy-making.

Hence,

H3: Higher CSO capacity prompts governments to implement EU indications.

H4: The lower the salience of the issue for public opinion and for government, the higher the impact of CSO capacity on government's choice to follow EU indications.

The section that follows presents the results of the time-series cross-section regressions run.[26] Model (1) consists in a general specification aimed at testing hypotheses 1 and 3. Model (2) introduces a two-way interaction term in order to test hypothesis 2. Model (3) comprises a three-way interaction term to test hypothesis 4. All three models include controls. Firstly, given that the EIF is an incentive-based instrument, the incentive itself must be controlled for. Second, the weight that CSO capacity is likely to have on a government's choice is likely to depend on how much a government involves organized interests in policy-making (Saurugger 2007). I therefore introduce an index of corporatism to

---

[25] CSOs overwhelmingly considered the CBPs to be up-to-date and a fundamental framework for national policy-making. See Council conclusions of the Council and the Representatives of the Governments of the Member States on the integration of third-country nationals legally residing in the EU, June 2014. On the Commission's progressive position, see Geddes (2000).

[26] See appendices for the method.

control for it. Finally, I control for member states administrative capacity as proposed by the literature on compliance and OMC (see the appendices for more on method and operationalisation of variables).

EMPIRICAL ANALYSIS: THE RESPONSE OF MEMBER STATES TO THE INCENTIVE

The results yielded by my models, reported in Table 5.1 below, are mitigated.[27] Overall, governments are less likely to follow the EU's agenda when the issue is salient for public opinion (H1; model 1). The impact of public opinion is highly significant and its coefficient sizeable: an increase of one percentage point in public opinion's saliency is accompanied by a decrease of about one percentage point in implementation of EU indications. This relationship is highly linear which suggests a constant effect of public opinion rather than what I hypothesized. In a similar fashion, the model provides evidence of the impact of CSO capacity (H3; model 1), although not in the direction expected: the effect is negative, suggesting that Rasmussen et al. (2013: 250) may well be right in emphasizing the 'transmission belts' role assumed by civil society organizations. According to them, interest organizations 'link public "demands" and policy "supply"' (p. 250). Alternatively, reduced implementation could be due to the inclusion of more actors in the decision-making process, rendering consensus harder to attain, thereby hindering implementation (König and Luetgert 2008). Another plausible explanation could lie with the relatively low financial incentive the fund represents for CSOs, linked to their capacity to influence the programming phase. If national funding significantly outweighs EU funding, then CSOs may not be willing to burden themselves with further (optional) goals and, according to their capacity to influence government decision, they may push governments towards reduced implementation of EU indications. Further investigation should be conducted in this respect. The coefficient is somewhat significant and sizable since a one unit change is associated with a change of ten percentage points in the dependent variable.

---

[27] Coefficients are discussed irrespective of their statistical significance since: (a) the study does not rely on representative sampling but on a finite population; (b) the population is rather small; (c) statistical and substantive significance are two different things. See the appendices for more on this. See also Taagepera (2008) and Valentine et al. (2015) for a very interesting discussion on statistical significance.

Table 5.1 The determinants of EU indications implementation in 25 EU member states, 2008–2013

	Model (1)	Model (2)	Model (3)
Public opinion	−1.079***	−1.153	−1.175
	(0.374)	(0.940)	(2.261)
CSO capacity	−10.664**	−10.668**	2.355
	(5.303)	(5.319)	(16.321)
Financial incentive	−0.228	−0.226	−0.220
	(0.342)	(0.344)	(0.346)
Position on multiculturalism	−1.123	−1.182	−1.137
	(1.530)	(1.685)	(1.534)
Multiculturalism salience	6.151*	6.096*	7.457*
	(3.403)	(3.47)	(4.44)
Corporatism	7.667	7.549	8.269
	(1.0167)	(10.287)	(9.786)
Administrative capacity	9.966	10.082	8.797
	(10.396)	(10.516)	(10.184)
Public opinion * position on multi.		0.014	
		(0.165)	
Multi. Salience * CSO capacity			−1.334
			(2.305)
CSO capacity * Public opinion			0.174
			(1.68)
Multi. Salience * Public Opinion			0.106
			(0.364)
CSO capacity * Multi. Salience * Public opinion			−0.098
			(0.255)
Constant	14.659	15.112	2.987
	(16.604)	(17.465)	(22.469)
Random effects			
Country			
Std.D Year	4.370	4.386	4.572
	(0.915)	(0.936)	(0.95)
Std.D Constant	28.785	28.861	27.074
	(5.055)	(5.076)	(4.985)
Std.D Residual	12.204	12.250	12.258
	(0.881)	(0.889)	(0.896)
Model fit			
Prob. > Wald χ^2	0.0207	0.0367	0.0360
Multilevel vs. linear model; Prob. > χ^2	0.0000	0.0000	0.0000

Number of obs: 147; Number of groups: 25; Avg obs per group: 5.9
***$p < 0.01$; **$p < 0.05$; *$p < 0.1$; Std. error in parenthesis

Interestingly, the salience of multiculturalism for the government in office proves significant and positive, meaning that when the government cares about the issue it tends to use EU indications. The coefficient is also fairly sizeable: an increase of one point of salience for a government (a zero-ten scale variable) is accompanied by an increase of about six percentage points, therefore conflicting somewhat with salience for public opinion, but still less determining than the latter. This confirms the hypothesis that a government has limited attention available and cannot address all the issues a society is facing simultaneously. Yet another element worth reporting is the irrelevance of the financial incentive. Financial incentive is never significant and its coefficient is negative and almost null. This is an interesting policy conclusion inasmuch as, as it stands, financial incentive does not suffice to counterbalance preferences. This confirms Gunningham and Sinclair's view (1998) that financial incentive may be more efficient than command-and-control instruments—in that they rely on volition rather than on costly control mechanisms—but less reliable in driving behaviours.

No evidence is found in support of hypothesis 2 (model 2); in the event of high salience of the issue in public opinion, governments do not react according to their policy positions on the issue. Rather, governments are more likely not to follow EU indications. Consider that the coefficient of the two-way interaction term is not significant whatever the value of public opinion. More importantly, the marginal effect of a government's position increases very slightly as salience in public opinion increases whilst the confidence interval soars, ranging from about −30 to +30 (see Fig. 5.3).

Turning now to hypothesis 4 (model 3), it appears that ultimately a lot has to do with how much a government cares about the issue, and public opinion and CSO capacity only have a moderating effect (Fig. 5.4) that is not necessarily the one expected; i.e. CSO capacity has a non-positive effect on implementation (already shown with disconfirmation of hypothesis 3, model 1) whilst high salience in public opinion plays the expected role. The three-way interaction inserted in the model proves non-significant overall but scrutiny of the predictive margins at high and low levels of CSO capacity and public opinion[28] hints at a

---

[28] See the appendices for methodological details.

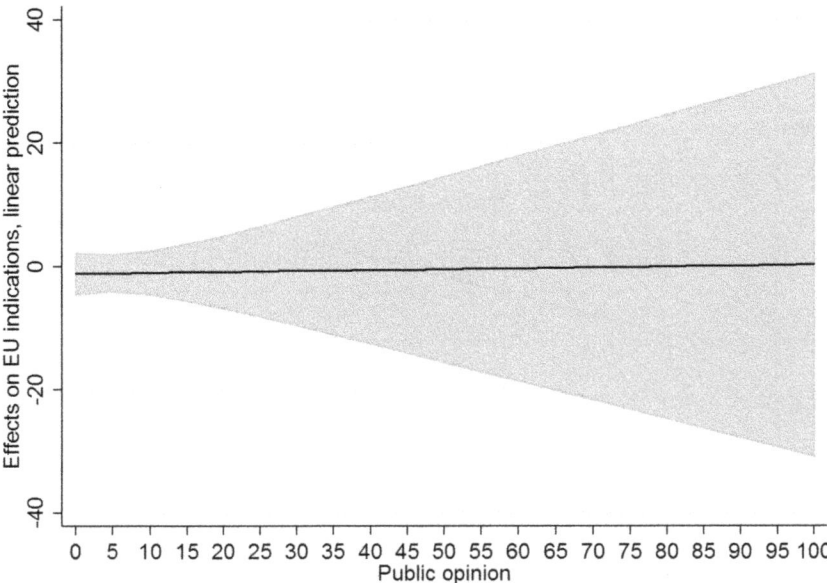

Fig. 5.3 Average marginal effect of governments' positions on implementation of EU indications, at different levels of public opinion (with 95% CI)

more nuanced picture. I do not graph confidence intervals, which would render Fig. 5.4 illegible, but I delineated the area where the predictive margins are significant at 95% or more (top right-hand corner). The first thing to notice is the non-significance of the marginal effect of salience for governments where CSO capacity and public opinion are high (dotted line). Their combined effect renders uncertain the impact of a government's salience, so to speak, whilst the coefficient is the flattest. Second, public opinion seems to make implementation more costly for governments since, when the former is high, salience for governments needs to be higher for governments to start implementing EU indications.[29] Third, the effect of high CSO capacity tends to shrink the effect

[29]The slope is the steepest for CSO low and PO high but implementation begins at a higher level of government salience (5 on the scale). Note however that this line meets the CSO-low-PO-low one towards government maximum salience.

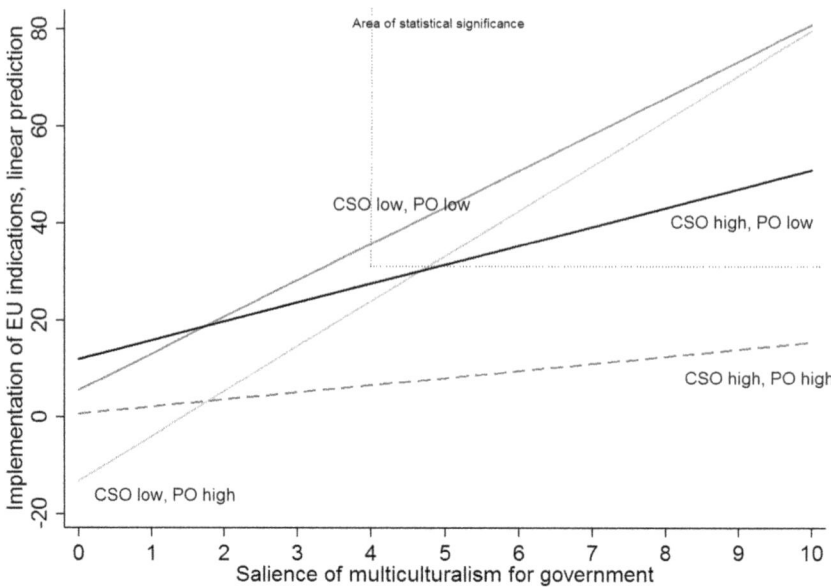

Fig. 5.4 Predictive margins of the effect of salience of multiculturalism for governments, at high and low levels of CSO capacity (CSO) and public opinion (PO)

of salience for governments when salience in public opinion is low. Finally, but most importantly, when both public opinion and CSO capacity stand at a low level, governments follow EU indications if multiculturalism is of some interest for them. Hypothesis 4 is thus disconfirmed in its direction (as was H3) but not in the sense that there is a relationship between a government's action and civil society as a whole (public opinion and CSO capacity).

ROBUSTNESS TESTS

This section is relatively technical but nonetheless useful to assess the soundness of the results obtained. The reader who is less interested in technicalities can skip to this chapter's conclusion.

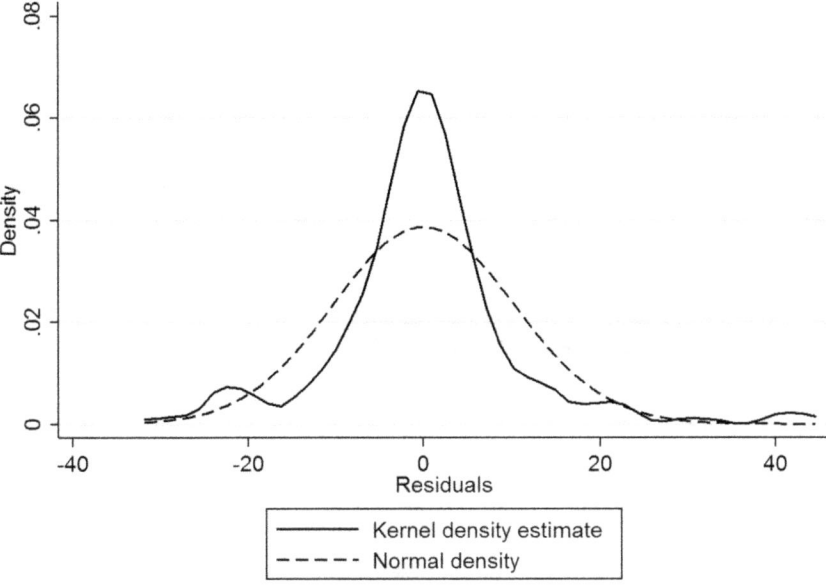

Fig. 5.5 Kernel density estimate of the distribution of residuals

Because it is impossible to run a zero-inflated beta regression the residuals are not normally distributed (Fig. 5.5). This is mainly due to the distribution of the dependent variable that counts a number of values equal to 0 and a number of values approximating 100 (Fig. 5.6). In spite of this, plotting residuals against fitted values shows a rather homoscedastic picture, with, however, potential influential observations (Fig. 5.7). The locally weighted smoothing curve (LOWESS prediction) does not seem to be dragged up or down by the latter. Dropping such observations does not change much the coefficients or their significance. They are therefore not influential enough to bias the estimates. I then look at potential influential level-two units (countries). For that, I compute Cook's D tests for the model, its fixed effect, and its random effect part (Table 5.2). I also compute DFBetas for each parameter

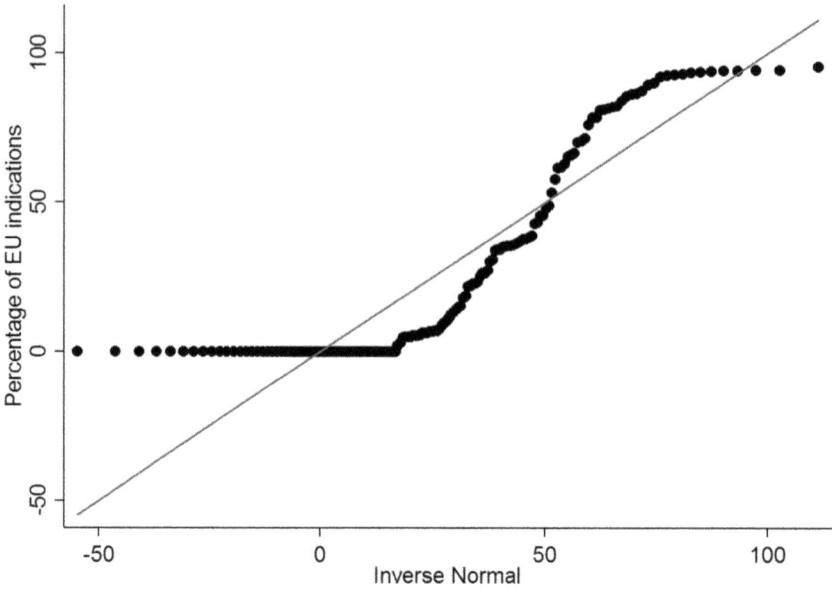

Fig. 5.6   Q-Q plot of the dependent variable, percentage of EU indications

(see Fig. 5.8). The two measurements point to allegedly influential countries. These are Italy, Greece, Lithuania, Slovakia, Cyprus, Slovenia Finland and the Netherlands.

I therefore run the same model, dropping the countries identified as plausibly influential (Table 5.3). Note that each time, 6 data points are dropped. From the results of the successive regressions, it appears that estimates are rather consistent across models, both in terms of magnitude and significance. Two main observations may be of relevance. First, dropping Italy somewhat changes the estimates' significance since administrative capacity now falls within the 90% confidence interval, which is never the case for all other models. Note also that the estimate for public opinion observes a sizeable change compared to the other partial models. Second, dropping Finland and the Netherlands decreases the significance of public opinion which passes from the 99% confidence interval to the 95% confidence interval. It also decreases the statistical

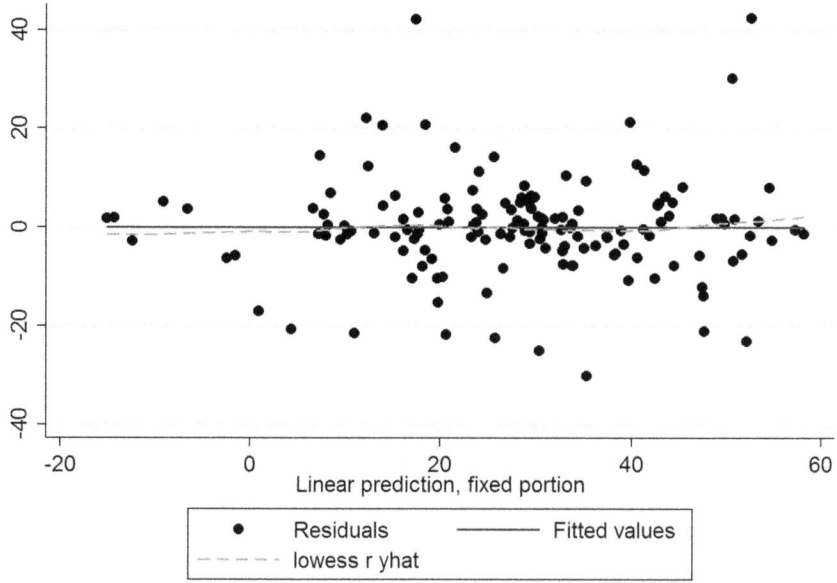

Fig. 5.7 Residuals vs. fitted values with linear prediction and LOWESS prediction

Table 5.2 Level-two units with Cook's D above the cut-off value

Level-2 unit	Cook's D	Cook's D, fixed	Cook's D, random
Greece	0.1500258	0.0663177	0.3732474
Italy	0.2340912	0.2627564	0.1576505
Lithuania	0.1174288	0.0210227	0.3745115
Slovakia	0.1469306	0.0405156	0.4307041
Cyprus	0.0785707	0.011576	0.2572232

Cut-off value = 0.1600

significance of the model as a whole but within the margins of the acceptable. A last element worth mentioning is the increase of almost six points of CSO capacity's coefficient when the Netherlands is dropped. Altogether, in the light of the foregoing, the model appears to be consistent across the partial regressions I ran.

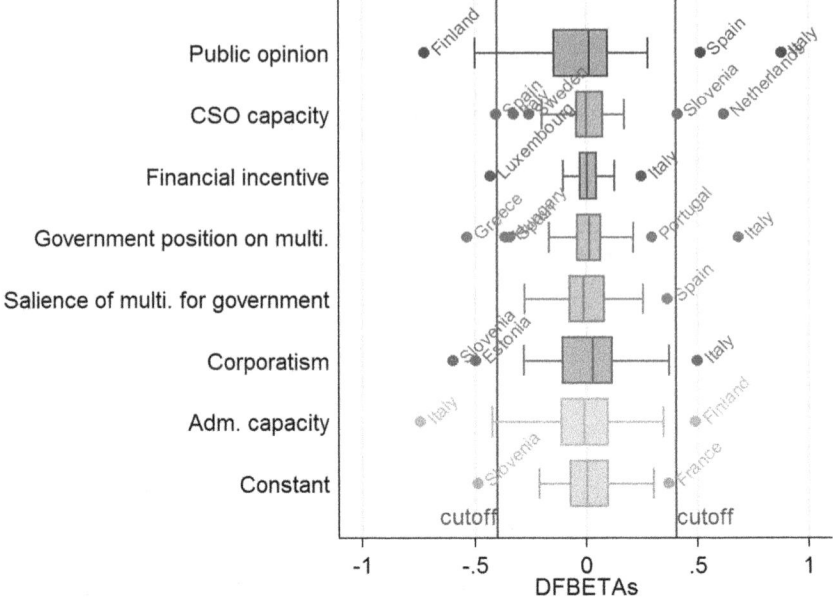

Fig. 5.8 Plot of DFBetas for level-two units for each parameter

Conclusion

The process that led to the adoption of the EIF rendered its implementation rather flexible. Consisting of soft law provisions, whether to address the indications made therein or not is up to national governments. But when it comes to studying the implementation of EU outputs, most research has focused either on the factors determining member states' compliance with Directives, or on the processes leading them to follow soft law provisions. This chapter is at the crossroads of these two strands and aims at identifying the factors determining the implementation of soft law provisions across member states. It seeks to answer the question: why do member states implement without a legal obligation to do so? In Chapter 2, I posited that institutions matter in the choice of actors. In this chapter, I have argued that, when it comes to implementation, the policy instrument matters. Like institutions (or rather: as an institution itself), the instrument determines the influential actors that in turn may affect implementation outcomes. Looking into the implementation of the European Integration Fund, I have posited that when

Table 5.3 Regression results when dropping potentially influential level-two units

	Full model	Drop IT	Drop EL	Drop LT	Drop SK	Drop CY	Drop SL	Drop FI	Drop NL
Public opinion	-1.079***	-1.41***	-1.026***	-1.158***	-1.18***	-0.981***	-1.105***	-0.807**	-0.992**
CSO capacity	-10.664**	-9.076**	-10.536*	-9.84*	-11.512**	-10.597*	-12.85**	-9.632*	-16.171*
Financial incentive	-0.228	-0.359	-0.205	-0.229	-0.229	-0.222	-0.272	-0.191	-0.2
Position on multicult.	-1.123	-2.161	-0.253	-1.224	-1.436	-1.066	-1.094	-1.188	-1.058
Multicult. salience	6.151*	6.074*	5.85*	6.412*	6.838**	6.416*	5.27	6.571*	6.198*
Corporatism	7.667	2.931	8.822	9.407	6.454	7.284	14.002	5.197	7.786
Administrative capacity	9.966	17.627*	6.343	8.849	14.337	9.553	10.086	4.739	11.017
Constant	14.659	11.346	14.633	13.221	9.548	12.666	23.397	13.095	16.962
Nb. of obs.	147	141	141	141	141	141	141	141	141
Nb. of Gps	25	24	24	24	24	24	24	24	24
Prob>χ^2	0.0207	0.0023	0.0206	0.0125	0.0051	0.0046	0.0123	0.0817	0.061

governments' preferences cannot be challenged by the Commission or bound by horizontal controls, they may be constrained by public opinion and Civil Society Organizations (CSOs). I have reached three main conclusions. Firstly, in the case of soft law, the main driver of implementation appears to be the salience of the issue for government: when the government cares about the issue, it is more likely to follow indications established at EU level. Secondly, public opinion and civil society organizations have a moderating effect able to counterweight government preferences. Thirdly, the financial incentive proves scantly capable of dragging the preferences of member states towards the EU's preferences. Overall, these three conclusions point to the fact that financial incentive is less effective as an enforcement means than the empowerment of actors who are in a good position to keep government in check.[30] At EU level, this implies that providing for a sound partnership principle may be more effective a policy option for the implementation of soft law than financial incentives.

Consequently, this chapter provides little evidence of a Europeanization process being under way. The response to EU soft provisions[31] is primarily guided, or mediated, by national actors and according to national logics. It is interesting, however, to observe the existence of a mechanism of compliance from below that may lead to more Europeanization if grassroots actors are mobilised and empowered.

If the main driver of implementation in the programming phase appears to be the salience of the issue for government, in the actual implementation; i.e. the commitment of the amounts distributed, the determinant of implementation seems to lie elsewhere (Chapter 6).

References

Scholarship and Expert References

Albaek, E., Green-Pedersen, C., & Nielsen, L. B. (2007). Making Tobacco Consumption a Political Issue in the United States and Denmark: The Dynamics of Issue Expansion in Comparative Perspective. *Journal of Comparative Policy Analysis: Research and Practice, 9*(1), 1–20.

Alonso, S., & Fonseca, S. C. d. (2011). Immigration, Left and Right. *Party Politics, 18*(6), 865–884.

---

[30] See the concept of fire alarm oversight as in McCubbins and Schwartz (1984); policy mix in Gunningham and Sinclair (1998).

[31] And here I endorse a definition of Europeanization close to that of Featherstone (2003), in a top down fashion; see Chapter 2.

Bache, I. (2010). Partnership as an EU Policy Instrument: A Political History. *West European Politics, 33*(1), 58–74.

Beck, N. (2006). *Time-Series–Cross-Section Methods*. No. draft as of June 5th 2006.

Borràs, S., & Jacobsson, K. (2004). The Open Method of Co-ordination and New Governance Patterns in the EU. *Journal of European Puölic Policy, 11*(2), 185–208.

Börzel, T. A. (2000). Why There Is No "Southern Problem". On Environmental Leaders and Laggards in the European Union. *Journal of European Public Policy, 7*(1), 141–162.

Börzel, T. A. (2001). Non-compliance in the European Union: Pathology or Statistical Artefact? *Journal of European Public Policy, 8*(5), 803–824.

Börzel, T. A., & Risse, T. (2003). Conceptualising the Domestic Impact of Europe. In K. Featherstone & C. Radaelli (Eds.), *The Politics of Europeanization* (pp. 57–82). Oxford: Oxford University Press.

Brubaker, R. (2001). The Return of Assimilation? Changing Perspectives on Immigration and Its Sequels in France, Germany, and the United States. *Ethnic and Racial Studies, 24*(4), 531–548.

Büchs, M. (2007). *New Governance in European Social Policy: The Open Method of Coordination*. Southampton: Palgrave Macmillan.

Carrera, S. (2008). *Benchmarking Integration in the EU. Analyzing the Debate on Integration Indicators and Moving It Forward*. Bertelsmann Foundation.

Carrera, S., & Faure Atger, A. (2011). *Integration as a Two-Way Process in the EU? Assessing the Relationship between the European Integration Fund and the Common Basic Principles*. Brussels: Centre for European Policy Studies.

Caviedes, A. (2004). The Open Method of Co-ordination in Immigration Policy: A Tool for Prying Open Fortress Europe? *Journal of European Public Policy, 11*(2), 289–310.

Cremona, M. (2012). Introduction. In M. Cremona (Ed.), *Compliance and the Enforcement of EU Law*. Oxford: Oxford University Press.

Dai, X. (2005). Why Comply? The Domestic Constituency Mechanism. *International Organization, 59*(02), 363–398.

Dehousse, R. (2005). La Méthode Ouverte de Coordination. Quand L'instrument Tient Lieu de Politique. In P. Lascoumes & P. Le Galès (Eds.), *Gouverner par les Instruments* (pp. 331–356). Paris: Presses de Sciences Po « Académique ».

Eurostat. (2014). Standard Eurobarometer 82 Autumn 2014.

Falkner, G., & Treib, O. (2008). Three Worlds of Compliance or Four? The EU-15 Compared to New Member States. *JCMS: Journal of Common Market Studies, 46*(2), 293–313.

Falkner, G., Treib, O., & Hartlapp, M. (2005). *Complying with Europe: EU Harmonisation and Soft Law in the Member States*. Cambridge: Cambridge University Press.

Falkner, G., Hartlapp, M., & Treib, O. (2007). Worlds of Compliance: Why Leading Approaches to European Union Implementation Are Only "Sometimes-True Theories". *European Journal of Political Research, 46*(3), 395–416.

Featherstone, K. (2003). Introduction: In the Name of "Europe". In K. Featherstone & C. M. Radaelli (Eds.), *The Politics of Europeanization* (pp. 3–26). New York: Oxford University Press.

Featherstone, K. (2005). "Soft" Co-ordination Meets "Hard" Politics: The European Union and Pension Reform in Greece. *Journal of European Public Policy, 12*(4), 733–750.

Geddes, A. (2000). Lobbying for Migrant Inclusion in the European Union: New Opportunities for Transnational Advocacy? *Journal of European Public Policy, 7*(4), 632–649.

Giuliani, M. (2003). Europeanization in Comparative Perspective: Institutional Fit and National Adaptation. In K. Featherstone & C. M. Radaelli (Eds.), *The Politics of Europeanization*. New York: Oxford University Press.

Grabosky, P. N. (1995). Counterproductive Regulation. *International Journal of the Sociology of Law, 23*(4), 347–369.

Green-Pedersen, C., & Mortensen, P. B. (2013). Policy Agenda-Setting Studies: Attention, Politics and the Public. In E. Araral, S. Fritzen, & M. Howlett (Eds.), *Routledge Handbook of Public Policy* (pp. 167–174). New York: Taylor & Francis.

Gunningham, N., & Sinclair, D. (1998). *Designing Smart Regulation*. Paris: OECD/International Energy Agency.

Haverland, M. (2000). National Adaptation to European Integration: The Importance of Institutional Veto Points. *Journal of Public Policy, 20*(1), 83–103.

Hooghe, L., & Marks, G. (2001). *Multi-level Governance and European Integration*. Lanham: Rowman & Littlefield.

Howlett, M., & Giest, S. (2012). *Routledge Handbook of Public Policy*. New York: Taylor & Francis.

Kassim, H., & Le Galès, P. (2010). Exploring Governance in a Multi-level Polity: A Policy Instruments Approach. *West European Politics, 33*(1), 1–21.

Knill, C., & Lenschow, A. (2005). Compliance, Competition and Communication: Different Approaches of European Governance and Their Impact on National Institutions. *JCMS: Journal of Common Market Studies, 43*(3), 583–606.

König, T., & Luetgert, B. (2008). Troubles with Transposition? Explaining Trends in Member-State Notification and the Delayed Transposition of EU Directives. *British Journal of Political Science, 39*(1), 163–194.

König, T., & Mäder, L. (2014). The Strategic Nature of Compliance: An Empirical Evaluation of Law Implementation in the Central Monitoring

System of the European Union. *American Journal of Political Science, 58*(1), 246–263.

Kröger, S. (2009). The Open Method of Coordination: Underconceptualisation, Overdetermination, De-Politicisation and Beyond. *European Integration Online Papers, 13*(1).

Kymlicka, W. (1995). *Multicultural Citizenship: A Liberal Theory of Minority Rights*. New York: Oxford University Press.

Lampinen, R., & Uusikylä, P. (1998). Implementation Deficit? Why Member States Do Not Comply with EU Directives? *Scandinavian Political Studies, 21*(3), 231–251.

Les Echos. (2015, August 1). L'immigration, Principale Preoccupation Des Europeens. *Les Echos*.

Lowi, T. J. (1964). American Business, Public Policy, Case-Studies, and Political Theory. *World Politics, 16*(04), 677–715.

Luedtke, A. (2005). European Integration, Public Opinion and Immigration Policy: Testing the Impact of National Identity. *European Union Politics, 6*(1), 83–112.

Majone, G. (1999). The Regulatory State and Its Legitimacy Problems. *West European Politics, 22*(1), 1–24.

Mbaye, H. A. D. (2001). Why National States Comply with Supranational Law: Explaining Implementation Infringements in the European Union, 1972–1993. *European Union Politics, 2*(3), 259–281.

McCubbins, M. D., & Schwartz, T. (1984). Congressional Oversight Overlooked: Police Patrols Versus Fire Alarms. *American Journal of Political Science, 28*(1), 165–179.

Pridham, G. (1994). National Environmental Policy-Making in the European Framework: Spain, Greece and Italy in Comparison. *Regional Politics and Policy, 4*(1), 80–101.

Radaelli, C. M. (2008). Europeanization, Policy Learning, and New Modes of Governance. *Journal of Comparative Policy Analysis: Research and Practice, 10*(3), 239–254.

Rasmussen, A., Carroll, B. J., & Lowery, D. (2013). Representatives of the Public? Public Opinion and Interest Group Activity. *European Journal of Political Research, 53*(2), 250–268.

Salamon, L. M. (2000). The New Governance and the Tools of Public Action: An Introduction. *Fordham Urban Law Journal, 28*(5), 1611–1674.

Saurugger, S. (2007). Democratic Misfit? Conceptions of Civil Society Participation in France and the European Union. *Political Studies, 55*(2), 384–404.

Saurugger, S. (2012). Beyond Non-compliance with Legal Norms. In T. Exadaktylos & C. M. Radaelli (Eds.), *Research Design in European Studies: Establishing Causality in Europeanization*. Basingstoke: Palgrave Macmillan.

Saurugger, S., & Terpan, F. (2013). Resisting EU Norms. A Framework for Analysis. *HAL Archives Ouvertes*.

Scharpf, F. W. (2003). *Problem-Solving Effectiveness and Democratic Accountability in the EU*. (MPifG Working Papers Vol. 3, No. 1).

Spendzharova, A., & Versluis, E. (2013). Issue Salience in the European Policy Process: What Impact on Transposition? *Journal of European Public Policy, 20*(10), 1499–1516.

Steunenberg, B. (2007). A Policy Solution to the European Union's Transposition Puzzle: Interaction of Interests in Different Domestic Arenas. *West European Politics, 30*(1), 23–49.

Steunenberg, B., & Rhinard, M. (2010). The Transposition of European Law in EU Member States: Between Process and Politics. *European Political Science Review, 2*(03), 495–520.

Susskind, L. (2006). Arguing, Bargaining, and Getting Agreement. In M. Moran, M. Rein, & R. E. Goodin (Eds.), *The Oxford Handbook of Public Policy* (pp. 269–295). New York: Oxford University Press.

Taagepera, R. (2008). *Making Social Sciences More Scientific: The Need for Predictive Models*. Oxford: Oxford University Press.

Tholoniat, L. (2010). The Career of the Open Method of Coordination: Lessons from a "Soft" EU Instrument. *West European Politics, 33*(1), 93–117.

Thomson, R., Torenvlied, R., & Arregui, J. (2007). The Paradox of Compliance: Infringements and Delays in Transposing European Union Directives. *British Journal of Political Science, 37*(4), 685–709.

Treib, O. (2014). Implementing and Complying with EU Governance Outputs. *Living Reviews in European Governance, 9*.

Trimikliniotis, N. (2012). The Instrumentalisation of EU Integration Policy: Reflecting on the Dignified Efficient and Undeclared Policy Aspects. In Y. Pascouau & T. Strik (Eds.), *Which Integration Policies for Migrants? Interaction Between the EU and Its Member States* (pp. 109–128). Nijmegen: Wolf Legal Publishers.

Valentine, J. C., Aloe, A. M., & Lau, T. S. (2015). Life After NHST: How to Describe Your Data Without "P-Ing" Everywhere. *Basic and Applied Social Psychology, 37*(5), 260–273.

van Spanje, J., & de Vreese, C. (2011). So What's Wrong with the EU? Motivations Underlying the Eurosceptic Vote in the 2009 European Elections. *European Union Politics, 12*(3), 405–429.

Van Wolleghem, P. G. (2017). Why Implement Without a Tangible Threat? The Effect of a Soft Instrument on National Migrant Integration Policies. *JCMS: Journal of Common Market Studies, 55*(5), 1127–1143.

Wren, A., & McElwain, K. M. (2009). Voters and Parties. In R. E. Goodin (Ed.), *The Oxford Handbook of Political Science*. New York: Oxford University

Press. Available at http://www.oxfordhandbooks.com/view/10.1093/oxfordhb/9780199604456.001.0001/oxfordhb–9780199604456–e–019. Last Consulted March 22, 2016.

EU Acts and Other Official Documents

C (2007) 3926 Final—European Commission. (2007). *Commission Decision of 21/VIII/2007 Implementing Council Decision 2007/435/EC as Regards the Adoption of Strategic Guidelines for 2007 to 2013.*

COM (2001) 387 Final—European Commission. (2001). *Communication from the Commission to the Council and the European Parliament on an Open Method of Coordination for the Community Immigration Policy.*

CHAPTER 6

Capacity or Preferences? Explaining the Implementation of the European Integration Fund

The adoption of the European Integration Fund (EIF) signalled the passage from the bottom-up Europeanization phase to its top-down equivalent (see Chapter 2). The results presented in Chapter 5 show that, when it comes to programming the spending of the fund, governments' preferences are the main implementation driver. This chapter proposes to look into another aspect of implementation, concerned with the actual use of the fund. Once programmes are drafted and adopted, what determines the actual use of the fund at national level?

Immigration to European countries has drastically increased during the last decade. More than one million immigrants come to the EU each year, more than to any other OECD country (OECD 2016). In an ageing Europe, migration has positive economic effects. By feeding the workforce, it alleviates the dependency ratio and the uncertainty over the European population's ability to sustain the economy.[1] Immigration also poses considerable socio-economic challenges to receiving societies. Firstly because migrants' contribution to the EU labour market and its economy in general is by no means immediate. Coming from different cultural but also linguistic backgrounds, migrants need to adapt to a reasonable extent to pre-existing structures. As a matter of fact, migrants are still overrepresented amongst the unemployed and are often

---

[1] See Testa (2014), but see also European Commission (2011).

© The Author(s) 2019
P. G. Van Wolleghem, *The EU's Policy on the Integration of Migrants*, Palgrave Studies in European Union Politics,
https://doi.org/10.1007/978-3-319-97682-2_6

overqualified for their job. The increasing diversity within societies also creates tensions between natives and new- (and old-) comers and thus threatens social cohesion. Resultantly, integrating migrants is key to making the most of the potential migration holds.[2]

Aware of the advantages of migration, but conscious of the challenges it poses, EU member states have seized the opportunity of the creation of an EU competence on immigration to call for a 'more vigorous integration policy'.[3] Accordingly, a EIF was created in 2007 in order to help member states in their integration efforts. Although such a fund was based on a common understanding of integration,[4] the absence of a clear EU mandate on the matter in primary law translated into rather flexible objectives. Even so, about 18% of the fund remained unused at the end of the implementation period in 2014, much more than is usually the case for structural funds (Tosun 2014). This chapter aims at explaining why. More formally, it answers the question: why do member states not use the money they have available for their integration policies?

Little attention has been paid to the EU integration policy as of yet,[5] and no study has looked into the EIF implementation gap. Yet, the adoption of the new Asylum, Migration and Integration Fund (AMIF) for the period 2014–2020 suggests that the EU's activity in this field is set to last. Therefore, it appears relevant to start digging into implementation gaps in this field. Since the question of unused EU funding has been primarily investigated in the literature on the absorption of structural funds, I draw therefrom a first set of hypotheses relating to member states' capacity to use such funds. Notwithstanding, this strand in the literature has neglected more political stakes behind the use of EU money. I thus examine the existing literature on compliance with EU outputs and posit the role of government preferences in implementing the EIF. Preferences are likely to matter because the use of EU funding has consequences for public budgets due to the co-financing principle. Committing EU funds implies that the member state supplements such funding. This chapter

---

[2] Realizing the potential of migration has been a recurring theme of the EU integration policy from 2003 onwards; see notably COM (2003) 336 final.

[3] European Council (1999).

[4] See notably the Common Basic Principles for immigrant integration policy (CBPs), Box 3.2.

[5] See Chapter 1 for a selective literature review.

therefore confronts capacity-based explanations to preference-based ones. In order to test my hypotheses, I apply time-series cross-section methods to an original dataset[6] with a view to account for country-to-country, but also year-to-year, variation. Previous quantitative studies have ignored variation over time in the implementation of EU funds with the consequence of overestimating the role of structural factors to the detriment of more situational explanations. The analysis I present tests hypotheses across member states and over the seven years of the programme. I find that the implementation of the EIF is a matter of capacity, not of preferences. The results, however, contradict recent research on absorption. More than administrative capacity, I find that financial capacity and decentralisation increase the use of the fund in the case at issue.

The first part of this chapter recalls the main features of the functioning of the EIF and introduces the puzzle at hand. The second part goes through the literature on the absorption of structural funds and through the literature on compliance with EU outputs; I state my hypotheses concurrently. I then present my empirical findings in a third part, report on post-estimation analyses in a fourth and conclude in a fifth.

THE EIF AND ITS USE BY MEMBER STATES

Whereas immigration fell within the scope of EU competences with the Treaty of Amsterdam, integration was never mentioned in primary law, until the Treaty of Lisbon came into force.[7] A number of policy instruments were adopted nevertheless; but given the sensitivity of matters linked to legal migration (as integration would appear to be) those instruments would be adopted with the unanimity of the member states and would mostly consist in soft law instruments. The EIF was adopted within this context in 2007.

The EIF is a rather small fund compared to the structural funds. It amounts to €825 million and aims at financing integration projects over the period 2007–2013 for the 26 participating countries (Croatia was not a member at the time and Denmark does not partake in the Area of Freedom, Security and Justice). Smaller but more flexible, it was

---

[6]This chapter uses the same type of models as that presented in the previous chapter. Note that the specifics and data used are detailed in the appendices.

[7]A first mention was made in the rejected constitutional treaty though.

originally modelled on the structural funds[8] but was gradually deprived of some of its most constraining provisions during the decision-making process[9]: implementation rules became simpler and placed member states' central administrations in control. Two elements are worth recalling. Firstly, the principle of additionality—whereby member states are prevented from substituting their national funding with EU funding—was removed. Resultantly, the EIF could be used as a way to finance member states' own integration policy, thus facilitating its absorption. Secondly, the principle of partnership—whereby a range of actors (notably sub-national authorities) are associated with the decision-making—was considerably weakened, rendering the participation of entities other than government optional. In fact, Carrera and Faure Atger (2011) show that the principle was applied with discretion, mostly in the initial programming phase, and in a consultative fashion. Unlike structural funds, which provide for a considerable involvement of sub-national bodies for the design of Regional Operational Programmes, nothing of the sort is in place for the EIF. Without the additionality principle and with a weak partnership principle, governments enjoy considerable leeway in the way they use the funding available. Limitations consist in the financial regulations established at EU level that provide for legal and sound financial management.

Another characteristic very similar to that of the structural funds is the co-financing principle; i.e., EU money is meant to finance a certain share of a project. As a rule, EU co-financing amounts to 50% of integration projects. This contribution may be increased to 75% where the state addresses specific indications. By way of derogation, the member states falling under the cohesion fund receive 75% of EU co-financing unconditionally (see Chapter 4). Member states are therefore required to co-finance 25–50% of the projects financed under the fund.[10]

Unlike structural funds, the principle underlying the EIF is not economic solidarity; it does not consider financial imbalances among member states. Whereas the distribution of structural funds is aimed at

---

[8]During the negotiation phase, the Commission declared having 'copied' the provisions regarding spending rules from the structural funds [see Council of the European Union 5578/06 (2006)].

[9]Chapter 4 goes through the policy-making process and describes this point in detail.

[10]Note that, in the absence of the additionality principle, co-financing conditions may be easily met where the member state presents a significant integration budget (see below).

reducing economic disparities, the EIF is distributed as a function of the number of migrants granted legal residence, irrespective of the differences in wealth between member states. Member states thus receive an allocation that is proportional to the number of newcomers they grant residence to. In theory, and because they have committed to the objectives of the fund, member states should have little trouble implementing it.

Figure 6.1 shows a starker reality. It reports the mean and standard deviation of the fund's implementation rates by country; i.e., the proportion of the money they actually engaged compared to the amount they were allocated. Only 82.3% of the money available was spent over the 7 years of the programme, less than what is usually engaged for the structural funds (with a grand mean at 92.4%; see Tosun 2014). This dry figure, however, covers a more chaotic reality: some member states have had a very low implementation rate with high variation from one year to another (such as Malta, Ireland or Slovenia) whereas others display a high and steady implementation rate (Poland, Italy or Germany

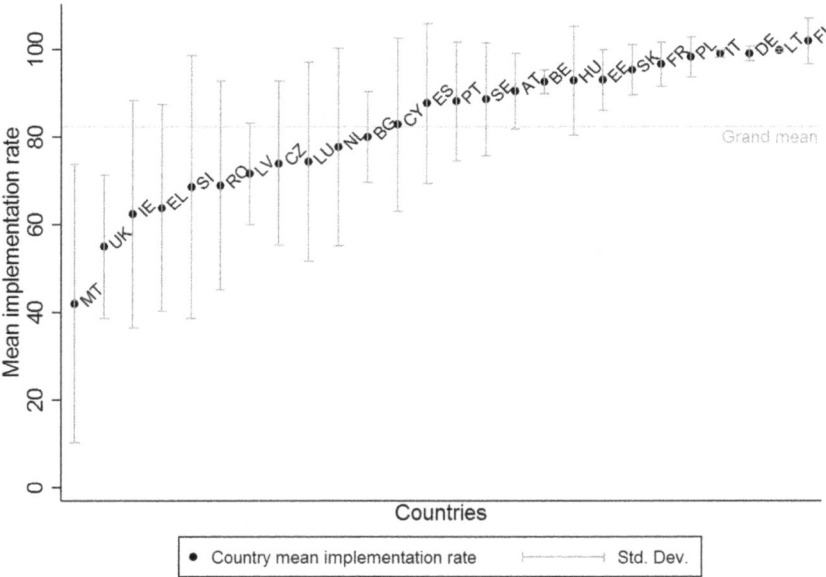

Fig. 6.1 Implementation rate means and standard deviation over the period 2007–2013, for 26 member states

Table 6.1 Difference in implementation rates between and within units

Implementation rate	Mean	Std.D	Min.	Max.
Variation	82.291	21.952	0	113.91
Within		15.665	41.98	101.951
Between		15.501	32.915	131.971

Note Total number of observations = 177; number of groups = 26; number of observations per group = 6.808

for instance). Some countries display surprising figures. The United Kingdom's implementation mean stalls at 55% for a policy it opted in for.[11] At the other end, Lithuania displays a steady 99.8% implementation rate. Interestingly, there is almost as much variation between countries as there is within: the average implementation rate may vary upward or downward by about 15 points between one country and another and by about 14 points for the same country from one year to another (see Table 6.1); thus confirming the need to account for variation of implementation rates over time.

Explaining the Implementation of the EIF

Integration of third country nationals has been on EU and national agendas for quite some time now. At national level, integration was already a matter of concern in the late 1980s, 1990s[12] and, as the European Commission reports,[13] almost all 15 EU member states already had integration policies in place by 2003. At EU level, the European Council, gathered in Tampere in 1999, called for "a more vigorous integration policy". Nevertheless, integration as an EU policy has been little studied by social scientists.[14] Likewise, the EIF has attracted

---

[11] The United Kingdom does not systematically take part in policies relating to the Area of Freedom, Security and Justice. It may, however, opt in for some policies; as it did for the EIF.

[12] For more on this point, see Schnapper (1994), Wischenbart (1994), Zincone et al. (2011) Mouritsen and Hovmark Jensen (2014), Mandin (2014), Fischler (2014); but see also Chapter 3.

[13] COM (2003) 336 final.

[14] Mulcahy (2011) is an exception; see Chapter 1 for more on this. More generally, law scholars have been more interested in the topic, notably because of potential conflicts

little attention, despite it being arguably the most significant policy instrument in this policy realm. Cited in most articles touching upon integration at EU level,[15] no study has explored its actual implementation, except perhaps for Carrera and Faure Atger (2011) who investigate the substantive aspects of the fund and the projects it finances.[16] Their study, published in 2011, covered the first three years of the EIF and concentrated on the programming phase (as opposed to the fund engagement phase or actual implementation). Understanding its actual implementation is nonetheless important, since the EU has taken further steps forward with the introduction of a new fund on Asylum, Migration, and Integration[17] for the period 2014–2020, and appears to be willing to develop this policy field at EU level.

More attention has been paid to the structural funds. However, most studies have concentrated on how to explain the allocation of the funds,[18] and only recently has the focus shifted to the actual implementation with attempts to answer the question why member states engage or not their respective allocations (Horvat 2005; Milio 2007; Bachtler et al. 2014; Hapenciuc et al. 2013; Tosun 2014). These studies have mostly considered the capacity member states show in absorbing structural funds. It is true that spending EU funds can be demanding since it requires a sound administrative and organizational structure on the one hand, and national budgetary capacity on the other.

Capacity therefore endorses different meanings that are dependent on the characteristics of the fund itself (NEI Regional and Urban Development 2002). One is administrative capacity; the ability of the administration to evaluate, contract, implement and monitor the projects

of competence between levels and consequences on legal frameworks (see *inter alia* Groenendijk 2004; Szyszczak 2006; Velluti 2007; Murphy 2009).

[15] See, for instance, Geddes and Achtnich (2015), Pratt (2015), Scholten and Penninx (2016); to name but a few. Note that Mulcahy did not mention the EIF in her *opus* on the EU integration policy.

[16] Several EU reports have looked into the implementation of the EIF (Ramboll 2011, 2013; European Court of Auditors 2012). They highlight the issues that arose in the process in a descriptive fashion without undertaking systematic or complete (most were written before the end of the programme) analysis of implementation.

[17] Regulation 516/2014/EU.

[18] On this point, see notably Barca et al. (2012), Mendez (2013), Kemmerling and Bodenstein (2006), Bouvet and Dall'Erba (2010), Dellmuth (2011).

covered by the fund (Milio 2007). In order to use the amounts it is allocated, the state must ensure it follows management and financial rules and foresees monitoring and control mechanisms; notably through the designation of a responsible authority (usually ministries of the interior for the EIF), a certifying authority (for the expenditure) and an audit authority. Accordingly, administrative capacity likely eases implementation; and the higher the administrative capacity, the swifter the adaptation to EU requirements (and hence the higher the implementation rate).

H1a: The higher the administrative capacity, the higher the implementation rate.

H1b: The higher the administrative capacity, the swifter a high implementation rate is reached.

Beside administrative capacity, budgetary capacity likely eases the absorption of the fund, especially so because of the co-financing principle (Horvat 2005; Tosun 2014). However, different aspects of budgetary capacity matter. Firstly, member states have different migration histories and they may therefore relate differently to integration policies. A member state that already had a sizable budget for integration in the past is more likely to be able to absorb the EIF than a member state that has to create a budget for integration *ex-nihilo*. The absence of the additionality principle (see above) reinforces the role of a previous integration budget in absorbing the funding. Secondly, global financial capacity is likely to matter (NEI Regional and Urban Development 2002; Horvat 2005), notably over a timespan characterised by the economic downturn of the late 2000s (Carrera and Faure Atger 2011; Collett 2011). Negative change in GDP is likely to go with a lower implementation rate.

H2a: The higher previous funding for integration policy, the higher the implementation rate.

H2b: The more GDP decreases, the lower the implementation rate

Another understanding of capacity ought to consider the capacity of co-implementers and the administrative organisation of the state. In ever slimmer states, out-sourcing government activities is often a favoured option to cut bureaucracies expenses (Majone 1999). Delivery of public services by the third sector has become increasingly common. In the case of the EIF, programming is the governments' remit but ground implementation often falls to third parties, be they sub-national bodies or third sector entities.[19]

Civil Society Organizations (CSOs) are primary targets for the implementation of the fund. Considered as direct co-implementers, they are likely to boost the implementation rate, provided they display the capacity to meet the accountability requirements set by EU rules in order to comply with the sound financial management principle.

H3: The higher CSO capacity, the higher the implementation rate.

Regional authorities are likely to play a significant role, too. The compliance literature has shown that implementation varies according to the level of decentralisation: compliance with EU law may be lower where competences are shared amongst different levels of decision making (Mbaye 2001; König and Luetgert 2009). The object of these studies, however, revolves around timely and correct transposition of EU Directives. Implementation therefore regards a constraint to comply with rules adopted from above, rather than taking advantage of financial opportunities to tackle local issues. In response, the literature on structural funds has posited the positive role of decentralisation in easing EU funds absorption (Milio 2007; Tosun 2014). In decentralised states, subnational authorities may possess the institutional structures and resources to better absorb the funds. They may also be more dependent on the generation of their own revenue in which case they would be incentivised to use the funds available. Whilst immigration is mostly a national competence, integration is often devolved to lower levels of government (Hepburn 2010; Thränhardt 2014), save in cases of strong centralist tradition (Scholten and Penninx 2016). In a decentralised state, the number of co-implementers consistently rises which increases the probability of a higher implementation rate.

H4: The more decentralized the state, the higher the implementation rate.

The literature on the absorption of structural funds has seldom looked into explanations that are more political.[20] Focusing on capacity, it has

---

[19]See Commission Decision C. (2008) 795 establishing the rules for implementation. It notably constrains the possibility for government to act as a direct implementer.

[20]See, for instance, Kemmerling and Bodenstein (2006), who consider the role of left-right cleavages.

overlooked member states' willingness to engage EU funding. Yet, preferences may very well matter for at least two reasons: on the one hand, immigration has been quite topical for public opinion over the past decade; on the other hand, engaging EU funds possibly entails national commitments via the co-financing principle. Whilst the literature on compliance with EU outputs has posited the role of capacity-based factors in facilitating or hampering implementation (Pridham 1994; Lampinen and Uusikylä 1998; Mbaye 2001; Falkner et al. 2007), it has also looked into the role of preferences (Thomson et al. 2007; König and Luetgert 2009).

Despite the fact that the literature on compliance has focused on Directives, and thus conferred a particular meaning to implementation (Börzel 2001; Treib 2014), similar explanatory mechanisms were put forth in other studies investigating the implementation of other policy instruments, amongst which were studies on the Open Method of Coordination (Saurugger and Terpan 2013). In the case at issue, I posit that preferences may explain the use of the EIF. Due to the particular design of the fund, notably the absence of the additionality principle and the weak partnership principle (see Chapter 4), preferences are to be considered at national level. That is, member states' central administrations are given the possibility to maintain a firm grip on the use of the EIF to pursue their preferences with little involvement of subnational authorities.[21] Considering the margins for manoeuvre member states have in defining the substantive content of their Annual Programmes (see Chapter 4), I posit that preferences are better operationalised with the salience of integration for government than with their substantive position on the matter. Integration may not be a priority of the government in office, and spending national resources may backfire in coming elections (Green-Pedersen and Mortensen 2013). Taking advantage of the fund may thus have consequences on national politics. All the more so since immigration-related issues tend to be salient for the public. Several EU barometers over the 2000s and 2010s show that immigration ranks amongst Europeans' most important concerns.[22] In Spring

---

[21]A particularly relevant example is that of France which used at least 90% of the first two years of allocations to finance its national integration strategy (see Carrera and Faure Atger 2011).

[22]See notably Eurobarometer 60 in 2004 and Eurobarometer 83 in 2015.

2015, it revealed that immigration was the foremost concern for EU citizens, before economics and unemployment (Les Echos 2015). Since policy-makers have limited attention available (Howlett and Giest 2013) salience in public opinion may contrast government's ability to take advantage of the money available (salience for public opinion will therefore be controlled for; see the appendices for its operationalisation).

H5: The more salient integration is for government, the higher the implementation rate.

The section that follows presents the results of the time-series cross-section regressions run (see appendices for the method). Model (1) only considers capacity-related independent variables. Model (2) tests the hypothesis relating to preferences. Model (3) introduces an interaction term to test H1b. All three models include the passage of time and salience of immigration in public opinion as controls (see the appendices for more on this).

EMPIRICAL ANALYSIS: PREFERENCES OR CAPACITY?

The empirical results reported in Table 6.2 show a prevalent effect of capacity over preferences. Even so, not all aspects of capacity matter. The effect of administrative capacity (H1a) is uncertain as it is sensitive to model specification and influential observations[23] (models 1 and 2). The ability of the administration to formulate and implement policies is therefore not the main obstacle to the use of the EIF, a result that contrasts recent research on the absorption of structural funds (Milio 2007; Tosun 2014). Since the EIF was moulded into the structural funds' design, the central administration was likely accustomed to spending rules. Financial capacity proves otherwise able to improve absorption. Variation in GDP has a significant and sizeable effect on the ability of governments to implement the fund (H2b; models 1–3), thereby contrasting with Tosun (2014). A 1% increase in GDP is associated with a change of one percentage point in the implementation rate. The economic crisis that hit

[23] Robustness checks (next section on post-estimation analyses) show that the variable is significant in model (2), provided that Greece, Finland or Romania be present in the model. In other words, these three countries are influential level-two units that mitigate the effect of the variable. See the appendices for more detail.

Table 6.2   Regression results: implementation of the EIF across member states, 2008–2013

	Model (1)	Model (2)	Model (3)
Administrative capacity	4.415	10.271**	6.764
	(5.259)	(4.677)	(6.144)
Previous funding	−0.037*	−0.031 *	−0.031*
	(0.020)	(0.016)	(0.016)
Δ GDP per capita	0.909**	1.022***	1.058***
	(0.360)	(0.373)	(0.375)
CSO capacity	0.992	−0.387	−0.464
	(2.686)	(2.110)	(2.113)
Decentralization	0.897***	0.865***	0.861***
	(0.318)	(0.260)	(0.261)
Salience for government		−1.042	−1.035
		(1.458)	(1.459)
Public opinion		−0.54	−0.552
		(0.346)	(0.347)
Time effect	0.453	−0.129	−1.448
	(0.780)	(0.782)	(1.691)
Adm. capacity * Time			1.126
			(1.278)
Constant	69.258***	76.867***	81.128***
	(6.958)	(7.508)	(8.934)
Random effects			
Country			
Std.D year	2.90E-08	0	0
	(1.09E-07)	(0.000)	(0.002)
Std.D constant	12.954	9.304	9.308
	(2.462)	(2.173)	(2.177)
Std.D residual	14.358	14.089	14.101
	(0.918)	(0.929)	(0.934)
Model fit			
Prob. > Wald χ^2	0.004	0.003	0.004
Multilevel vs. linear model; Prob. > χ^2	0.000	0.000	0.000

Number of obs 143; *Number of groups* 25; *Avg obs per group* 5.7
***$p < 0.01$; **$p < 0.05$; *$p < 0.1$; Std.error in parenthesis

Europe in the late 2000s has forced governments to cut public budgets across the board with dire consequences on integration policies (Carrera and Faure Atger 2011; Collett 2011). Figure 6.2 describes for instance the relationship between overall yearly implementation rate and overall yearly change in GDP. The fall in GDP is strongly associated with the fall

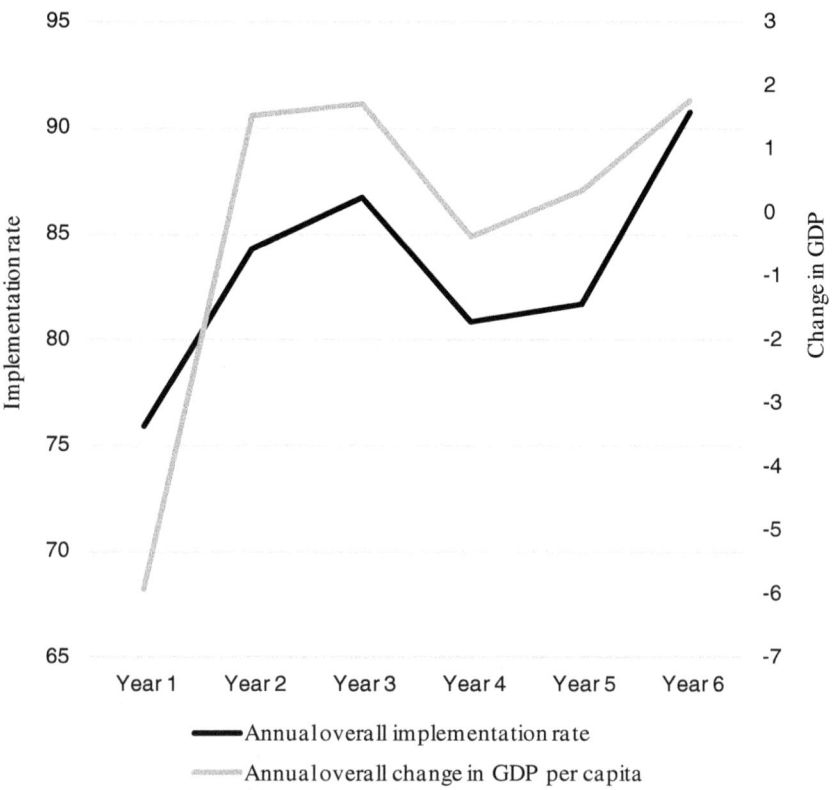

Fig. 6.2 Annual overall implementation rate and annual overall change in GDP per capita, for annual programmes 2007–2013, 26 member states

of implementation rates. Unexpectedly, the availability of previous funding at national level does not affect the use of the fund[24] (H2a; models 1–3), despite the absence of the principle of additionality (see above). The most likely explanation lies with the fact that, given the lengthy implementation rules compared to the size of the envelope, the amounts allocated represent little incentive to use them for countries with significant integration budgets. Differently, decentralisation (H4) appears to be

---

[24] Robustness checks show that the variable is sensitive to influential level-two units, notably to data points relating to the United Kingdom. See the next section for more detail.

a strong and statistically significant determinant of the actual use of the funding available so that the more decentralised the administration, the higher the implementation rate (models 1–3). This is an interesting result as it contradicts empirical evidence brought forward in both research on compliance (Mbaye 2001; König and Luetgert 2009) and research on absorption.[25] As hypothesised, the fund seems to represent an opportunity to finance local integration policies and tackle local integration challenges.

The passage of time has no effect whatsoever, even when considered together with administrative capacity (H1b; model 3). No evidence is found in support of a differentiated effect of administrative capacity with the passage of time. Looking at the average marginal effect of administrative capacity at different moments in time shows an effect that is positive and significant at 95% from year 2 onwards (Fig. 6.3). Nevertheless, I consider such a result as invalid given the sensitivity of administrative capacity to influential level-two observations.[26] Put differently, the effect of administrative capacity over time is not valid across member states.

CSO capacity does not seem to affect implementation (H3; models 1–3): its coefficient is always of little magnitude and never statistically significant. This is an interesting finding considering the widely acknowledged role of non-governmental organizations in facilitating migrant integration (Bücker-Gärtner 2011; CSES 2013). This finding does not question the role of CSOs in migrant integration but rather their capacity for being co-implementers of the EIF. The most probable explanations consist in the role of sub-national authorities in implementing the fund on the one hand; and on the capacity of government to compensate low CSO capacity on the other hand.[27]

Turning now to preferences, salience of the issue for government (H5; models 2 and 3) has no effect either, despite the fact that central governments control in large part spending on integration and that they are at the centre of the EIF implementation process. Eventually,

---

[25] Tosun (2014). Tosun hypothesised the positive role of decentralisation but did not find supporting evidence.

[26] Dropping any of the level-two influential observations dismisses the results displayed in Fig. 6.3 (see next section). They are therefore considered invalid.

[27] This explanation originates from midterm implementation reports summarized in Ramboll (2011: 45).

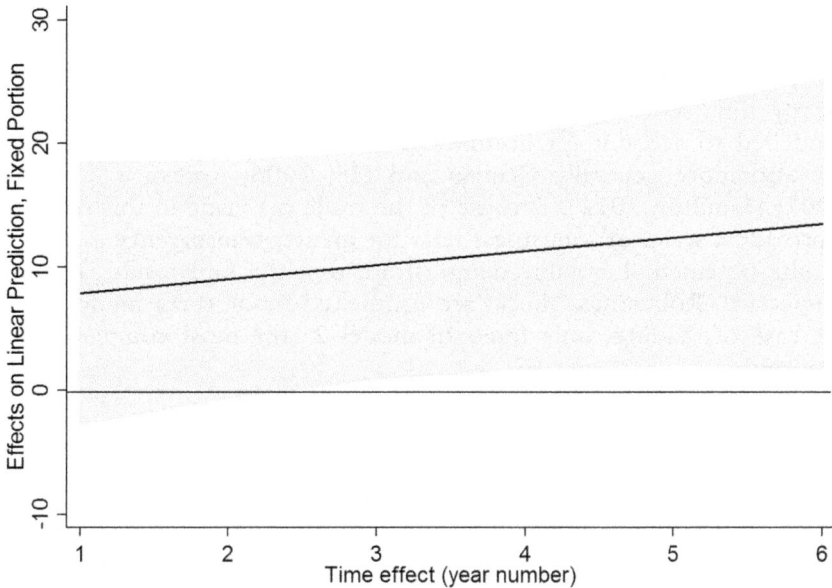

Fig. 6.3 Average marginal effect of administrative capacity at different years of implementation, with 95% confidence intervals

it is more member states' capacity to spend than their will to engage the funding that matters. A plausible reason for this lies in the fact that the purposes pursued by the fund are not highly ideologically marked (as are the debates on citizenship or voting rights for foreigners; see Poppelaars and Scholten 2008; Keating 2009) so that preferences of central governments are less likely to affect implementation outcomes.

ROBUSTNESS TESTS

This section is relatively technical but nonetheless useful to assess the soundness of the results obtained. The reader who is less interested in technicalities can skip to this chapter's conclusion.

Implementation rate is a variable bounded up and down, therefore violating some of the assumptions underlying the use of linear regressions. The most suitable models for this kind of data are beta and fractional regressions (Ferrari and Cribari-Neto 2004; Ospina and Ferrari 2012). Stata 14 introduced the possibility of running fractional regressions but not in a multilevel fashion. Yet, the data at hand is clearly time-series cross-section, and a multilevel structure must be modelled to account for non-independent observations (Beck 2006; see also more generally Gelman and Hill 2006; Agresti and Finlay 2007; Hamilton 2012). Because of the trade-off made in this respect, I provide a series of robustness tests for greater transparency as to the results obtained. I notably demonstrate that the said results are not artefactual. Robustness checks are conducted for all three models but, for ease of reading, only those of model 2 (the most complete) are reported.

Testing Influential Level-One Observations

Considering that the best model fit cannot be implemented, the residuals of my model are not normally distributed (Fig. 6.4); this because of the distribution of the dependent variable is inflated at the higher end of the

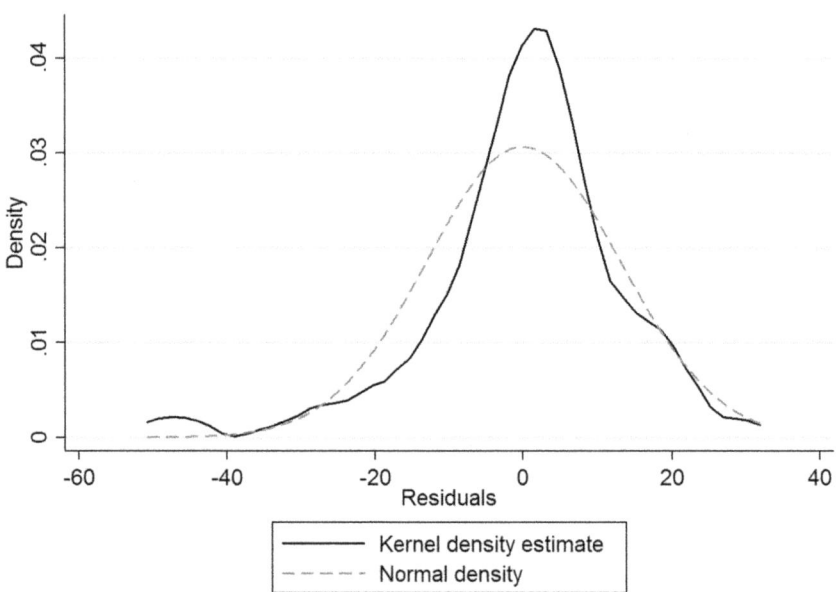

Fig. 6.4   Kernel density estimate of the residuals

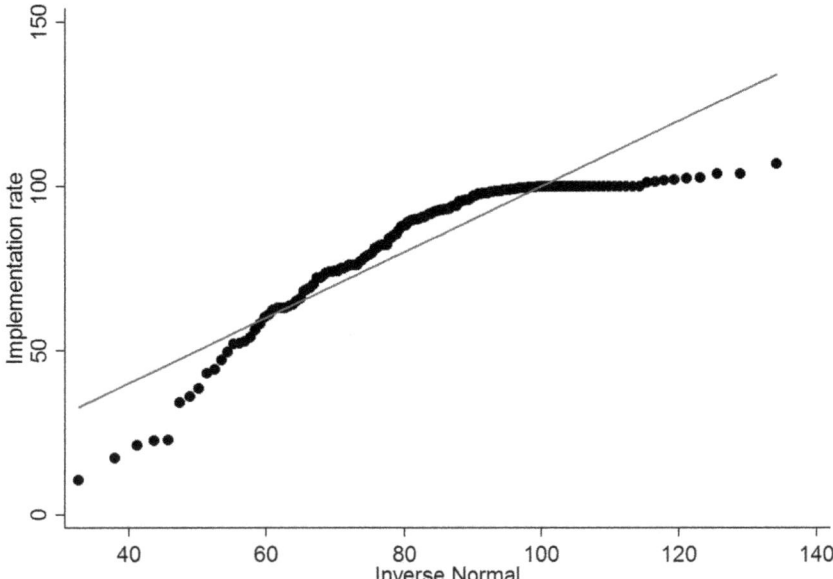

Fig. 6.5   Q-Q plot of the dependent variable

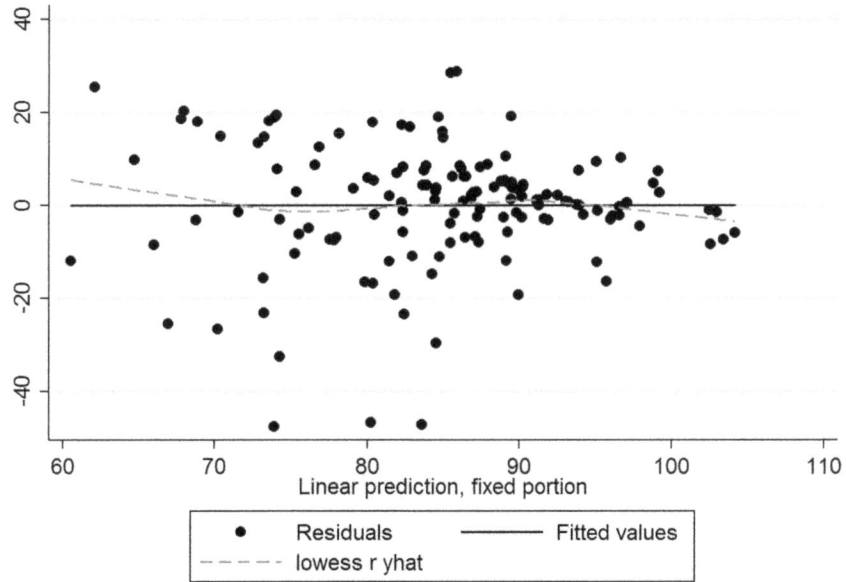

Fig. 6.6   Residuals vs. fitted values with linear prediction and LOWESS prediction

scale (Fig. 6.5). Plotting the residuals against fitted values (Fig. 6.6) nevertheless shows a rather homoscedastic distribution. That said, the locally weighted smoothing prediction (LOWESS) suggests some points may be influential; they regard the Annual Programmes (AP) of Ireland 2009, Slovenia 2011, Greece 2012 and the United Kingdom 2013. Dropping these four cases one by one slightly alters the coefficients but not their statistical significance or the conclusions reached and expressed above. The estimates are therefore unbiased by individual observations.

Testing Influential Level-Two Observations

In order to test for potential influential level-two units (country), I re-run the regressions, dropping them one by one. Note that, each time, six data points are dropped. Three countries prove problematic: Finland, Greece and Romania; although only the variable on administrative capacity changes when dropping them the one after the other (see Table 6.3). Its coefficient and statistical significance oscillate. Given the fact that there is no theoretical reason to justify these countries being abandoned for the analysis, I consider the results obtained regarding the variable administrative capacity as invalid. The other coefficients and confidence intervals prove stable across models and regardless of the influential level-two units. The conclusions reached in the previous section therefore hold.

Table 6.3 Partial regression results dropping potential influential level-two units

	Full model	Drop Finland	Drop Greece	Drop Romania
Administrative capacity	10.271**	8.224	6.791	7.833
CSO capacity	−0.387	−0.135	−0.391355	−0.138
Decentralization	0.865***	0.863***	0.815***	0.865***
Salience for government	−1.042	−0.842	−0.042	−1.137
Public opinion	−0.54	−0.514	−0.46	−0.48
Previous funding	−0.031*	−0.03*	−0.032*	−0.031*
Time effect	−0.129	−0.118	0.268	−0.209
Δ GDP per capita	1.022***	1.109***	1.02***	0.909***
Constant	76.867***	77.028***	75.039***	80.05***

Note ***$p < 0.01$; **$p < 0.05$; *$p < 0.1$; Std.error in parenthesis

CONCLUSION

If integration of third country nationals is deemed essential to realise the potential of immigration, little attention has been granted to the policies adopted at EU level in this respect. In 2007, the member states of the EU adopted the EIF by unanimity. At the end of the implementation period, the rate of use of the fund stalled at 82%, much lower a rate than that for structural funds. This summary figure, however, covers wide disparities in terms of use between member states and over the years, ranging on average (but with wide dispersion around the mean in some instances) from 42% for Malta to a little more than a 100% for Finland. This chapter sought to explain this variation across countries and over time. Namely, why is it that some countries in some years use the totality of the funding available whilst some others do not? Drawing from different trends in the current literature, I have put two main series of explanations to the test. On the one hand, I have tested the role of member states' capacity to engage EU funding, as suggested by the absorption scholarship. On the other hand, I have posited the effect of preferences on implementation, inspiring my hypotheses from the literature on compliance with EU outputs.

Through the analysis of yearly implementation rates throughout the member states involved in the programme, I show that capacity more than preferences matters in the implementation of the EIF. That said, the results I present contradict the findings set forth in the absorption scholarship in different ways. Whilst the absorption literature has underlined the role of administrative capacity (i.e. the capacity to formulate and implement policies), I find no support for it and show that it is financial capacity that makes the difference. In addition, I show that decentralisation plays a positive role in the use of the fund, thereby contradicting the literature on compliance and moderating some of the hypotheses advanced in the absorption literature. Overall, the actual use of the fund seems to be determined by macro-economic changes and the existence of a network of subnational bodies that act as co-implementers. Upstream, it appears that economic ups and downs had dire consequences on the ability to absorb the funding available; the economic crisis and ensuing public debt crisis of the late 2000s/early 2010s have strained public finances and forced budget cuts across the board. Downstream, decentralisation has eased the spending of the EIF. In decentralised states, the competence of integrating migrants likely falls to sub-national authorities which take advantage of the fund to tackle local integration challenges.

The absence of evidence in support of the role of government preferences suggests that greater implementation might not be attained by augmenting the acknowledgement of a policy issue on the part of governments but rather by relaxing co-financing requirements in order to alleviate the hindrance financial capacity may represent. However, such a measure inevitably accentuates the tension between effectiveness of the policy instrument at EU level and political accountability of the member states. Decreasing the co-financing share may translate into increased implementation but it may also have a counterproductive effect by reducing the incentive for efficient spending on the part of the public administration.

If this chapter is chiefly concerned with the EU integration policy, it also contributes, albeit in an indirect manner, to the literature on structural funds. Firstly, it proposes considering preferences to explain implementation gaps. Even though I do not find evidence supporting their role in the implementation of the EIF, the hypothesis still stands for structural funds (and future integration funds). Secondly, the absorption literature has tried to explain the implementation gap through quantitative methods whilst ignoring variation in implementation over time. Basing the analysis on mean values without accounting for year-to-year variation likely overstates the importance of structural factors to the detriment of more situational explanations. The use of time-series cross-section methods could remedy such a shortage.

Finally, it appears that climbing down the implementation ladder goes along with the decreasing importance of preferences over capacity factors. Whilst the programming phase emphasised the importance of how much governments care about the issue, the actual spending of the fund appears to depend more on whether they are capable of using the amounts allocated.

References

Scholarship and Expert References

Agresti, A., & Finlay, B. (2007). *Statistical Methods for the Social Sciences* (4th ed.). Upper Saddle River, NJ: Pearson Education Limited.

Bachtler, J., Mendez, C., & Oraže, H. (2014). From Conditionality to Europeanization in Central and Eastern Europe: Administrative Performance and Capacity in Cohesion Policy. *European Planning Studies, 22*(4), 735–757.

Barca, F., McCann, P., & Rodríguez-Pose, A. (2012). The Case for Regional Development Intervention: Place-Based Versus Place Neutral Approaches. *Journal of Regional Science, 52*(1), 134–152.

Beck, N. (2006). *Time-Series–Cross-Section Methods.* No. Draft as of June 5, 2006.

Börzel, T. A. (2001). Non-compliance in the European Union: Pathology or Statistical Artefact? *Journal of European Public Policy, 8*(5), 803–824.

Bouvet, F., & Dall'Erba, S. (2010). European Regional Structural Funds: How Large Is the Influence of Politics on the Allocation Process? *JCMS: Journal of Common Market Studies, 48*(3), 501–528.

Bücker-Gärtner, H. (2011). *Europe Needs Innovative Ideas to Integrate Immigrants and Ethnic Minorities—Challenges and Creative Activities in Education and Civil Society (A Comparison of Five European Countries).* Berlin: Berlin School of Economics and Law.

Carrera, S., & Faure Atger, A. (2011). *Integration as a Two-Way Process in the EU? Assessing the Relationship Between the European Integration Fund and the Common Basic Principles.* Brussels: Centre for European Policy Studies.

Collett, E. (2011). Immigrant Integration in Europe in a Time of Austerity. *Migration Policy Institute.* Available at http://www.migrationpolicy.org/research/TCM-immigrant-integration-europe-time-austerity. Last Consulted November 12, 2016.

CSES—Centre for Strategy and Evaluation Services. (2013). *Study on Practices of Integration of Third-Country Nationals at Local and Regional Level in the European Union.* Otford: Centre for Strategy and Evaluation Services.

Dellmuth, L. M. (2011). The Cash Divide: The Allocation of European Union Regional Grants. *Journal of European Public Policy, 18*(7), 1016–1033.

European Commission. (2011). *The 2012 Ageing Report: Underlying Assumptions and Projection Methodologies.* Brussels: European Commission.

Falkner, G., Hartlapp, M., & Treib, O. (2007). Worlds of Compliance: Why Leading Approaches to European Union Implementation Are Only "Sometimes-True Theories". *European Journal of Political Research, 46*(3), 395–416.

Ferrari, S., & Cribari-Neto, F. (2004). Beta Regression for Modelling Rates and Proportions. *Journal of Applied Statistics, 31*(7), 799–815.

Fischler, F. (2014). *Integration Policy Netherlands Country Report* (Interact Research Report 2014/15).

Geddes, A., & Achtnich, M. (2015). Research-Policy Dialogues in the European Union. In P. Scholten, H. Entzinger, R. Penninx, & S. Verbeek (Eds.), *Integrating Immigrants in Europe: Research-Policy Dialogues* (pp. 293–314). Amsterdam: IMISCOE Research Series.

Gelman, A., & Hill, J. (2006). *Data Analysis Using Regression and Multilevel/Hierarchical Models* (3rd ed.). Cambridge: Cambridge University Press.

Green-Pedersen, C., & Mortensen, P. B. (2013). Policy Agenda-Setting Studies: Attention, Politics and the Public. In E. Araral, S. Fritzen, & M. Howlett (Eds.), *Routledge Handbook of Public Policy* (pp. 167–174). New York: Taylor & Francis.

Groenendijk, K. (2004). Legal Concepts of Integration in EU Migration Law. *European Journal of Migration and Law, 6*(2), 111–126.

Hamilton, L. C. (2012). *Statistics with Stata: Updated for Version 12* (8th ed.). Boston: Brooks and Cole-Cengage Learning.

Hapenciuc, C. V., Moroşan, A. A., & Gaube, G. A. (2013). Absorption of Structural Funds—International Comparisons and Correlations. *Procedia Economics and Finance, 6*, 259–272.

Hepburn, E. (2010). "Citizens of the Region": Party Conceptions of Regional Citizenship and Immigrant Integration. *European Journal of Political Research, 50*(4), 504–529.

Horvat, A. (2005). *Why Does Nobody Care About the Absorption? Some Aspects Regarding Administrative Absorption Capacity for the EU Structural Funds in the Czech Republic, Estonia, Hungary, Slovakia and Slovenia before Accession* (WIFO Working Papers, No. 258).

Howlett, M., & Giest, S. (2013). *Routledge Handbook of Public Policy*. New York: Taylor & Francis.

Keating, M. (2009). Social Citizenship, Devolution and Policy Divergence. In S. L. Greer (Ed.), *Devolution and Social Citizenship in the UK* (pp. 97–116). Bristol: Policy Press.

Kemmerling, A., & Bodenstein, T. (2006). Partisan Politics in Regional Redistribution: Do Parties Affect the Distribution of EU Structural Funds across Regions? *European Union Politics, 7*(3), 373–392.

König, T., & Luetgert, B. (2009). Troubles with Transposition? Explaining Trends in Member-State Notification and the Delayed Transposition of EU Directives. *British Journal of Political Science, 39*(1), 163–194.

Lampinen, R., & Uusikylä, P. (1998). Implementation Deficit? Why Member States Do Not Comply with EU Directives?' *Scandinavian Political Studies, 21*(3), 231–251.

Les Echos. (2015, August 1). L'immigration, Principale Preoccupation Des Europeens. *Les Echos.*

Majone, G. (1999). The Regulatory State and Its Legitimacy Problems. *West European Politics, 22*(1), 1–24.

Mandin, J. (2014). *An Overview of Integration Policies in Belgium* (Interact Research Report 2014/20).

Mbaye, H. A. D. (2001). Why National States Comply with Supranational Law: Explaining Implementation Infringements in the European Union, 1972–1993. *European Union Politics, 2*(3), 259–281.

Mendez, C. (2013). The Post-2013 Reform of EU Cohesion Policy and the Place-Based Narrative. *Journal of European Public Policy, 20*(5), 639–659.

Milio, S. (2007). Can Administrative Capacity Explain Differences in Regional Performances? Evidence from Structural Funds Implementation in Southern Italy. *Regional Studies, 41*(4), 429–442.

Mouritsen, P., & Hovmark Jensen, C. (2014). *Integration Policies in Denmark* (INTERACT Research Report 2014/06).

Mulcahy, S. (2011). *Europe's Migrant Policies: Illusions of Integration*. Basingstoke: Palgrave Macmillan.

Murphy, C. (2009). Immigration, Integration and Citizenship in European Union Law: The Position of Third Country Nationals. *Hibernian Law Journal, 8,* 155–177.

NEI Regional and Urban Development. (2002). *Key Indicators for Candidate Countries to Effectively Manage the Structural Funds*. Rotterdam: NEI Regional and Urban Development.

OECD. (2016). *Recruiting Immigrant Workers: Europe*. Paris: OECD Publishing.

Ospina, R., & Ferrari, S. L. P. (2012). A General Class of Zero-or-One Inflated Beta Regression Models. *Computational Statistics & Data Analysis, 56*(6), 1609–1623.

Poppelaars, C., & Scholten, P. (2008). Two Worlds Apart: The Divergence of National and Local Immigrant Integration Policies in the Netherlands. *Administration & Society, 40*(4), 335–357.

Pratt, S. (2015). EU Policymaking and Research: Case Studies of the Communication on a Community Immigration Policy and the Common Basic Principles for Integration. In P. Scholten, H. Entzinger, R. Penninx, & S. Verbeek (Eds.), *Integrating Immigrants in Europe: Research-Policy Dialogues* (pp. 117–131). Amsterdam: IMISCOE Research Series.

Pridham, G. (1994). National Environmental Policy-making in the European Framework: Spain, Greece and Italy in Comparison. *Regional Politics and Policy, 4*(1), 80–101.

Ramboll. (2011). *Synthesis of the National Evaluation Reports on Implementation of Actions Co Financed by the European Fund for the Integration of Third-Country Nationals from 2007 to 2009 and Report at European Union Level Final Report*. Brussels: Ramboll.

Ramboll. (2013). *Synthesis of the National Evaluation Reports on the Results and Impacts of Actions Co-Financed by the European Fund for the Integration of Third-Country Nationals from 2007 to 2010*. Brussels: Ramboll.

Saurugger, S., & Terpan, F. (2013). Resisting EU Norms. A Framework for Analysis. *HAL Archives Ouvertes*.

Schnapper, D. (1994). The Debate on Immigration and the Crisis of National Identity. *West European Politics, 17*(2), 127–139.

Scholten, P., & Penninx, R. (2016). The Multilevel Governance of Migration and Integration. In *Integration Processes and Policies in Europe. Contexts, Levels and Actors* (pp. 91–108). Amsterdam: IMISCOE Research Series.

Szyszczak, E. (2006). Experimental Governance: The Open Method of Coordination. *European Law Journal, 12*(4), 486–502.

Testa, M. R. (2014). *The Contribution of Migration to the Demography of Europe Between 1991 and 2011—An Overview.* (Fondazione ISMU, KING Project, Desk Research, No. 19).

Thomson, R., Torenvlied, R., & Arregui, J. (2007). The Paradox of Compliance: Infringements and Delays in Transposing European Union Directives. *British Journal of Political Science, 37*(4), 685.

Thränhardt, D. (2014). *The State of European Integration Governance: A Comparative Evaluation* (Fondazione ISMU, KING Project, Desk Research Paper, No. 7).

Tosun, J. (2014). Absorption of Regional Funds: A Comparative Analysis. *JCMS. Journal of Common Market Studies, 52*(2), 371–387.

Treib, O. (2014). Implementing and Complying with EU Governance Outputs. *Living Reviews in European Governance, 9*(5), 1–47.

Velluti, S. (2007). What European Union Strategy for Integrating Migrants? The Role of OMC Soft Mechanisms in the Development of an EU Immigration Policy. *European Journal of Migration and Law, 9*(1), 53–82.

Wischenbart, R. (1994). National Identity and Immigration in Austria—Historical Framework and Political Dispute. *West European Politics, 17*(2), 72–90.

Zincone, G., Penninx, R., & Borkert, M. (2011). *Migration Policymaking in Europe: The Dynamics of Actors and Contexts in Past and Present.* Amsterdam: IMISCOE Research Series.

EU Acts and Other Official Documents

C. (2008). 795—European Commission (2008). *Commission Decision of 5 March 2008 laying down rules for the implementation of Council Decision 2007/435/EC establishing the European Fund for the Integration of third-country nationals for the period 2007 to 2013 as part of the General programme 'Solidarity and Management of Migration Flows' as regards Member States' management and control systems, the rules for administrative and financial management and the eligibility of expenditure on projects co-financed by the Fund.*

COM (2003) 336 Final—European Commission. (2003). *Communication from the Commission on Immigration, Integration and Employment.*

Council of the European Union 5578/06. (2006). *Note.*

European Council. (1999). *Tampere European Council 15 and 16 October 1999, Presidency Conclusions.*

European Court of Auditors. (2012). Do the European Integration Fund and European Refugee Fund Contribute Effectively to the Integration of Third-Country.

CHAPTER 7

Conclusion: EU Integration Policy or EU Policy on Integration?

I started this book with a question that can be summarised as follows: is there soft-Europeanization of integration policies? I also proposed an immediate answer: it depends. Now that we reach the end of this research, the answer has not budged significantly. There does exist a policy on integration at EU level, but has it become an EU integration policy?

Taking Stock: A Summary of the Findings

As an international organization, although more integrated and with farther-reaching effects, the European Union does not have the capacity to define its own competence. Relying on the principle of conferral, it is the member states that delegate or not some or all of their competence to it. The construction of an immigration policy has been a long and winding road. Member states were quite reluctant to abandon some of their competence over such a sovereign feature. The completion of the common market, however, entailed the creation of an area within which one could move without obstacles at internal borders. The Area of Freedom, Security and Justice (AFSJ)—as this area happened to be called—necessarily pushed the borders of the EU at its outer ends.

Vested with transnational stakes, the integration of migrants, also a subset of the wider immigration policy, would follow a similar path. Diverging interests, despite common commitments, would place the

© The Author(s) 2019

P. G. Van Wolleghem, *The EU's Policy on the Integration of Migrants*, Palgrave Studies in European Union Politics, https://doi.org/10.1007/978-3-319-97682-2_7

integration policy at EU level on a fragile equilibrium. Despite their commitment to a more vigorous integration policy, member states disagreements emerged when it came to giving it effect. The relative failure of the first couple of Directives on legal migration and the failure of the Open Method of Coordination (OMC) on the matter taught the Commission a decisive lesson: if member states agree in principle, the way in which it is approached is important (Chapter 2). If an integration policy was to unfold, it had to be through soft instruments.

In quite a hostile context, a policy for the integration of migrants emerged nonetheless. Already on the agenda of most member states since the late 1980s/early 1990s, integration was the object of national policies, although not always systematic ones. At EU level, migration was mainly looked at through a security lens, a prevalent take reinforced by the terrorist attacks on the Twin Towers in the USA. But at the same time, the social inclusion paradigm was gaining momentum. Launched in the 1980s, it was to encompass, to a limited extent, the inclusion of migrants, recognized as a vulnerable category. With a policy space available and a window of opportunity swinging open, a stronger commitment on the part of some member states was enough to have the policy emerging at EU level. This phenomenon is attributable to the combination of three conditions: a necessary condition, a sufficient condition and a facilitating factor. Firstly, whatever its content, a policy instrument to be proposed for adoption could only be of a soft law nature (the necessary condition). This eased member states' agreement insofar as it was potentially more costly for them to block the adoption of a text under the unanimity rule than to adopt a policy instrument that they would not necessarily have to implement in the end. On this basis, the succession within a reasonable timeframe of three Presidencies of the Council of the EU with similar preferences and their readiness to place these preferences on the EU agenda allowed for integration to emerge and stay on the EU agenda (the sufficient condition). Since any initiative in the domain had to be soft, member states could adopt the proposals put forth by the Presidencies. An intervening (or facilitating) factor lies with the European Commission which, drawing lessons from the shaky start of the policy, kept its proposals within the margins of acceptability of the member states. At the same time though, the Commission gradually occupied the policy space thereby opened to carve out a role for itself on integration matters, gradually developing the idea (and the acceptability) of a fund for integration. Starting small with the INTI programme—a funding scheme under its direct management—the Commission proposed a systematic and, therefore, more significant fund be put in place: the European Integration Fund (EIF) (Chapter 3). Such a proposal opened a policy cycle that held the potential for sounder Europeanization through soft law.

Without a strong foothold on integration matters and with a voting rule providing for unanimity decision-making, the adoption of a fund at EU level that would consistently enforce a European view of integration was unlikely. The absence of a clear legal basis would necessarily imply a limited role for the Commission in the definition of substantive directions and limited control mechanisms. The unanimity rule would almost automatically result in considerable discretion left to the member states in the programming and implementation of the fund. These two aspects governed the fund's negotiation process and determined the end-result. On the substantive front, the proposal from the Commission set a series of objectives that would be endorsed by the member states without much discussion. Casting a wide net, these objectives allowed member states to use the fund according to their own priorities. On the procedural front, the negotiation of the Commission's proposal guaranteed member states' grip on the spending of the fund. Some of the most constraining provisions were considerably weakened or simply removed; i.e. the principles of partnership and additionality, established with the reform of the cohesion policy in 1988. Most of the contention revolved around the distribution of the amounts amongst member states. Disputes in this regard also ended up rendering the use of the fund more flexible. Overall, the end of the negotiation came to a successful conclusion: the fund was adopted (Chapter 4).

The adoption of the fund, however, came at a price: flexible, it would be up to the state to address one issue or the other. In the programming phase; i.e. when member states planned, year after year, the use of their allocations, attention to the indications provided by the EU proved moderately successful, despite the financial incentives. Only 28.4% of the total funding planned to tackle EU indications. Evidence shows that the financial incentive provided by the EU did not have any effect. What seemed to matter most is how much governments cared about the issue on the one hand, and how much public opinion and Civil Society Organisation capacity could mitigate governments' interest in the matter on the other hand. Because the EIF was basically a soft law instrument, the influential actors were necessarily national actors, playing within national games. Therefore, the EU had little leverage to push member states' preferences towards its own (Chapter 5).

Despite the importance of national allocations under the EIF in the negotiation process, the flexibility member states enjoyed in the definition of their priorities in the programming phase and the recognised importance of integration at EU level, the actual engagement of EU amounts at national level over the entire period covered by the fund resulted in a consistent implementation gap. Only 82% of the money available was actually spent, a surprisingly low figure considering the salience migration-related issues have acquired over the past 10 years. Evidence shows however, that how much governments care about the issue is not relevant when it comes to actual implementation. Rather, it is governments' financial capacity and their capacity to rely on a network of sub-national authorities that count (Chapter 6).

ANSWERING THE QUESTION: EU POLICY OR POLICY AT EU LEVEL?

In order to conclude this book, this section goes back to the two questions delineated above and proposes elements of answer. Is there an EU integration policy? Is there (or has there been) soft-Europeanization of integration policies?

The answer to the first question is rather straightforward. From the evidence gathered and processed throughout the four empirical chapters, I conclude that there is no EU integration policy. There is a consistent set of policy instruments that together form a policy relating to integration, but talking of an EU integration policy as of yet is hardly valid. Confirming the conclusions reached by Mulcahy (2011) regarding the very marginal effect of the Common Basic Principles on member states, I show that, overall, the European Integration Fund has had little effect on member states' integration policy; if not that of reinforcing national approaches to integration, substantiating them with EU funding.

That said, can we speak of a Europeanization of integration policies? The answer to this question is more nuanced. If one understands Europeanization as a process, there may well be a Europeanization process under way. If member states remain in control of their integration policy to a large extent, if they may use the EIF for their own purposes or not use it at all, they have to report it to the Commission. As one of my interviewees recalled, the principles on which the fund was based were necessarily wide, "We couldn't afford to have them more stringent", but the EIF offered the opportunity of "get[ting] the member states to report back on what they were doing". One must consider that the policy started from scratch and blossomed into a consistent set of instruments that would lead member states to report to the Commission on a policy for which the EU had little competence over.

The end of the EIF (covering the period 2007–2013) and the adoption of its sequel, the Asylum, Migration and Integration Fund (AMIF; for the period 2014–2020), send ambiguous signals as to whether Europeanization is progressing or stalling. Between the EIF and the AMIF, there was the adoption of the Lisbon Treaty, which brought the legal migration special regime to an end. The adoption of the ordinary legislative procedure in this domain meant the end of unanimity voting and an actual role for the European Parliament. If this could, in some ways, be looked at as a further step in the Europeanization process, the provisions contained in the AMIF Regulations[1] may be regarded as a step back for a series of reasons. First of all, the AMIF merges a number of previous funds into one, providing that a sheer 20% of the total at least be dedicated to integration. Consequently, the minimum share of the AMIF dedicated to integration is lower than the EIF provided for.[2] Going over this minimum is then up to the state and how it intends to distribute its allocation between integration, asylum, solidarity and return. Secondly, references to the Common Basic Principles are less prevalent in the AMIF than they were in the EIF. Whereas the EIF was explicitly designed to implement the CBPs, the AMIF only includes loose references to it.[3] Thirdly, taking into account the complexity felt for the EIF expenditure, the objective of the AMIF was not so much the enforcement of a European view of integration but rather a simplification of its spending rules to guarantee the engagement of the amounts allocated.[4]

---

[1] Regulation 514/2014/EU, so-called horizontal Regulation, lays down general provisions for Home affairs funds. Regulation 516/2014/EU establishes the Asylum, Migration and Integration Fund.

[2] Whilst the EIF granted about €767 million for member states' integration policies, 20% of the amount placed at their disposal under the AMIF equals to about €478 million.

[3] The only direct reference is Recital (20), Regulation 516/2014/EU. Indirect references can be seen in the reading of article 9 that specifies the kind of integration measures that the fund supports.

[4] The reader interested in knowing more on this aspect may refer to Malmström (2014) and European Parliamentary Research Service (2014).

Everything considered, we may well be witnessing a stammering process of Europeanization, the hesitant construction of a policy at EU level. The National Contact Points on Integration, the Common Basic Principles and the European Integration Fund are indeed unprecedented achievements. Although the AMIF may be regarded as a setback, it is clear that the EU has secured a say on integration, for want of a sound competence.[5] Recalling the definition of Europeanization endorsed in this book; i.e. a definition which encompasses both bottom-up and top-down phases,[6] there is little doubt that a bottom-up Europeanization process has taken place. Differently, whether there has been top-down Europeanization is harder to ascertain. Because bottom-up Europeanization occurred via *soft* law, the implementation of EU outputs allows for wide discretion, thus undermining the effect of these outputs on member states' policies. Arguably, it would take a sounder EU competence on integration—that is, further bottom-up Europeanization—before one may indisputably demonstrate that top-down Europeanization has taken place, too.

CONTRIBUTION AND AGENDA FOR FURTHER RESEARCH

This book intends to contribute to several strands in the existing literature. In doing so, it may have unveiled areas for further research, despite its limitations.

Contribution to the Existing Literature

Academic research has not looked significantly into the development of an integration policy at EU level, or into soft-Europeanization instances, or indeed, into the effects, more simply, of soft-steering policy instruments. This book is placed at the crossroads of different research agendas; namely, the EU's integration policy, Europeanization, policy instruments and soft mechanisms, bargaining in the Council, implementation of EU outputs and EU funds' absorption capacity.

---

[5] As already mentioned, article 79.4 TFEU provides an explicit legal basis for.

[6] More precisely, the bottom-up phase consists in the process by which the policy emerges as an EU policy whereas the top-down phase looks into member states' response to EU soft outputs, or else their effects on member states via implementation (see Chapter 1 and notably Fig. 1.1).

The development of an integration policy at EU level is under-investigated. Of course, the pressing issues that need to be addressed in the present and very near future revolve around asylum and international protection. But integration will inevitably be the next step, for those who are granted refugee status, for those who are granted subsidiary protection statuses, for those over-staying their visa and who will eventually obtain a residence permit and for those who see their protection claims rejected but who end up stuck in a legal limbo in the EU. For this reason, integration policies are of the utmost importance and a certain level of homogeneity amongst EU member states is desirable so that we avoid the "postcode lottery" (Phillimore 2014: 13) of nationally defined policies. Imbalances between member states' integration efforts may entail negative effects for other EU member states and may result in a difference in treatment and opportunities for migrants themselves. It is thus important that the integration policy at EU level be studied. To date, very few studies have examined the development of this policy field at EU level. Almost none have looked into the effects of its outputs on member states. The main contribution of this book is to attempt to remedy such a shortage. It complements the legal and sociological scholarship by adding a missing piece to the puzzle; that of a policy analysis approach. Its focus on the European Integration Fund may be considered an important contribution. Despite being the most significant policy output in this realm, it has largely been ignored, whilst much more attention was paid to the Common Basic Principles. It is true that these principles form together a first conceptualisation of what integration means at EU level. It is also true that this conceptualisation is of decisive importance as it defines the cognitive approach that further EU instruments are to implement. But because they are mere principles, they lend themselves to analytical approaches, much less to empirical studies. Their effect therefore remains hard to fathom. The focus on the EIF, the 'hardest'; so to speak, of the soft instruments ever adopted in this realm, is justified in that it was likely to have more effects and those effects were likely to be better appraised. In this study, I have chosen a comparative approach through inferential statistics. But other approaches are possible and much is yet to be uncovered about the EIF (see the limitations and paths for further research below).

This study is also part of the wider body of studies relating to Europeanization. The concept of Europeanization has acquired compelling relevance over the years, with numerous articles and books referenced with this keyword. Soft-Europeanization on the other hand has been mentioned only sporadically, without having been significantly conceptualized or empirically analysed. But soft law is not no law; soft law may be not binding, but this does not mean it cannot affect member states' policies. More empirical studies of EU soft law outputs and their implementation could flesh out new research perspectives, whether relating to the integration of migrants or not. If the study of Europeanization has touched upon a wide range of policies and instruments (notably the OMC), the compliance literature has seldom gone beyond the study of Directives, which, consequently, gave a peculiar meaning to implementation: that of transposition. A lot has been said on implementation already. Soft-law scholars have focused on the processes that lead actors to take account of soft provisions, whereas those concerned with compliance have concentrated on the factors that determine implementation. To put it differently, the former have aimed to answer *how* questions when it comes to soft law, whilst the latter have striven to answer *why* questions when it comes to hard law, thereby leaving a gap in the literature relating to the *why* question when it comes to soft law. In this respect, the contribution of this book is twofold. On the one hand, it looks at a soft (some would say odd) instance of Europeanization in a comprehensive manner; on the other hand, it contributes to filling the gap in the implementation literature outlined above.

Limitations

Even though it contributes to the existing literature in several respects, this book also features limitations that constitute many paths for further research. As with any book, the choice to study certain elements implies the neglect of others. For the purpose of this book, the emphasis was placed on the EU policy from an EU perspective, be it in the bottom-up or top-down Europeanization phase, rather than from a member state perspective. Both options are legitimate but the results achieved endorsing the one or the other perspective may vary to a significant extent. The choice for emphasising the EU perspective translates into two main limitations to my work that, once again, reflect the two phases of Europeanization.

On the bottom-up phase, the focus on the EU policy has stressed the importance of the processes that: led the policy onto the EU agenda;

and led to the adoption of the EIF. As a consequence, the relevant evidence was limited to those elements that directly contributed to the outcome observed: upward Europeanization. The attentive reader will have noticed that it is mostly a question of three member states in Chapter 3, and a handful of states in Chapter 4. This does not mean that the other member states did not matter or did not attempt to have their interest prevail. They may very well have tried to influence the outcomes of the negotiations. Their exclusion from the analysis is due to their marginal role in explaining the outcome: the EU policy on integration in Chapter 3; the adoption of the EIF in Chapter 4. Other studies taking member states' perspectives as a starting point may well reach different conclusions.

In the same vein, the choices made for the study of the top-down phase entail other exclusions. If the empirical choice to focus on the European Integration Fund instead of, for example, the Common Basic Principles, is justified, there are many angles to look at it from. Resorting to quantitative methods to compare a medium number of cases necessarily implies a trade-off between depth and coverage. Comparing a smaller number of cases allows a more detailed analysis but ignores other cases that may be as important as the ones under scrutiny. Conversely, covering all the cases possible implies we reason at a higher level of abstraction. In resorting to quantitative methods, the analysis necessarily disregards the particularities of a given national context at a given point in time, or the specificities that may lay behind single implementation instances. Highlighting macro tendencies in a comparative fashion is indeed a relevant exercise as it allows the understanding of what is going on *throughout the EU*. The analysis could, however, gain from the understanding of micro or meso phenomena through the identification of relevant cases (be they peculiar or representative) and the use of qualitative methods in order to confirm or disconfirm the results obtained at a higher level of abstraction. This is mostly because implementation occurs at several levels. There are at least three levels one can think of: (i) the implementation of an EU instrument at EU level, considering the fund in its entirety (as this book did); (ii) the implementation at national level, considering the fund in parts to be implemented within the frontiers of each member state; and (iii) the implementation at the level of the single project as it concretely takes shape on the ground once it lies with its end-beneficiaries. Those are three different levels of aggregation possible and I have opted for the first one to answer my research question, thus ignoring other dynamics at play at other levels.

Further Research

Some of the ways in which to build upon this research have already been outlined in the two previous sections. Nevertheless, some more inputs on what is needed regarding research on this policy field may be useful to students willing to investigate it.

First of all, more research in general on the EU policy for the integration of third country nationals is necessary. Immigration is unlikely to recede and the EU will need new citizens to sustain its economy and social policies. Newcomers need to be given the same opportunities as natives, and less discrepancy between national integration policies is the condition to the permanence of the free circulation of EU citizens and to the yet-to-come free circulation of legally residing migrants. In this regard, The EU's role in promoting integration shall prove of decisive relevance in the years to come. But if the EU is to bring about more homogeneity between member states' policies, a deeper understanding of what has been done thus far is necessary.

As of now, some four years after the closure of the EIF, there is still very little on its implementation at meso- and micro-levels, no case studies[7] on the shape the fund has taken at national level, no small-N qualitative comparative analysis of national programmes, no in-depth studies on project-level integration successes or failures, and very little on the effect of the fund at its different levels of implementation, to cite but a few examples. In this context, EU policy-making in this domain seems to face things as they occur, without much foresight. But considering the EU's activity in this realm is set to last, notably with the adoption of the Asylum Migration and Integration Fund, more research on the implementation of the EIF is needed. As already mentioned, the analysis conducted here on the EIF regards its EU-wide implementation. Implementation at meso- and micro-levels should be carried out in order to inform further policy making.

---

[7]At least in the English language.

REFERENCES

SCHOLARSHIP AND EXPERT REFERENCES

Malmström. (2014, March 13). Commissioner Malmström Welcomes the Parliament's Vote on the New EU Home Affairs' Funds 2014–2020. *European Commission Press Release.*

Mulcahy, S. (2011). *Europe's Migrant Policies: Illusions of Integration.* Basingstoke: Palgrave Macmillan.

Phillimore, J. (2014). *Local and Experiential Aspects of Migrant Integration: An Overview* (Fondazione ISMU, KING Project, Overview Paper, No. 7).

EU ACTS AND OTHER OFFICIAL DOCUMENTS

European Parliamentary Research Service. (2014). EU Funds for Asylum, Migration and Borders (European Parliament).

APPENDICES

A.1. DATA AND METHOD FOR QUALITATIVE ANALYSES

As already mentioned in the main text, the method used in Chapters 3 and 4 borrows from case studies and process tracing. As Vennesson (2008: 229) argues, case studies comprise three different acts that cannot be analysed separately. Taking on Bachelard's theory of science, he argues that the scientific fact must be conquered, constructed and observed (*conquis, construit, constaté*). It is conquered when a break with the immediate experience is consumed; when the question "what is it a case of?" is answered. It is constructed with the effort of theory construction. And it is observed when the researcher departs from assumptions to find evidence. The first two acts appear evidently in the two chapters' premises. The third one; relating to finding evidence, relies on process tracing methods (see this book's introduction).

To evidence causal chains, I relied on multiple streams of data (Checkel 2005; Bowen 2009). I first went through a considerable amount of official documents ranging from unpublicised minutes of expert committees, dealing with immigration and integration before any proposal be made, to more official pieces of documentation (the most important documents are cited in the main text's footnotes). In order to get a better feel of the issue, and flesh out my findings, I conducted interviews with key actors. Semi-structured interviews were carried out, considering the literature on élite interviews (Harvey 2011).

© The Editor(s) (if applicable) and The Author(s) 2019
P. G. Van Wolleghem, *The EU's Policy on the Integration of Migrants*, Palgrave Studies in European Union Politics,
https://doi.org/10.1007/978-3-319-97682-2

Official Documents

I obtained data resorting mainly to two sorts of documents. Firstly, I relied on official documents available online, and that can be systematically searched in various EU databases using specific identifiers (therefore avoiding leaving any document aside). Such documents are Communications from the Commission, European Council Conclusions, Council meeting documents, documents from other EU institutions, Commission officials' speeches and so forth. Secondly, I launched a series of requests to the European Commission websites to obtain the documents which were not accessible online. These requests notably concerned documents linked to Commission committees and expert groups and consisted mostly in meeting minutes as well as documents classified as "Limited access"; i.e. that may be accessed upon request to the competent authority. The documents that are fundamental for the understanding of the empirical evidence presented are cited in the footnotes of the chapters concerned.

Élite Interviews with Key Actors

The fact that the policy unfolded about 15 years ago comprises both advantages and disadvantages. On the advantage side, after-the-facts discourse reduces the stakes of the interview for the interviewees, all the more so when they have changed professional positions over the years. Similarly, lower stakes also reduce the reticence towards recorded interview. The main drawback though lies in the fact that memory is fallible and 15 years after the facts decrease the quality of the data that can be collected. Accordingly, I limited the scope of interviews to key-actors, those most likely to remember the steps of the process. Peripheral actors or those for whom the issue was not salient are less reliable sources. Another inconvenience lies in the difficulty in finding the people in charge back in the day. Some retired, or changed positions, or could not be found.

Four interviews were conducted on the phone or via video conference (interviewees were disseminated across Europe). For the respect of the interviewees' privacy, no mention of their names and surnames is made in the text. Where it is explicitly referred to one interviewee in particular, she or he is referred to as female, irrespective of her/his actual gender. In addition to my interviews, I was also able to retrieve interviews conducted in 2010 for another study.[1] Note that the interviews were used as a complement to documents, in order to check some facts or substantiate connections, and not as an autonomous source of information.

Two interviews were conducted with Commission officials from the DG for Justice, Freedom and Security. They were working as high-ranking officials in the Unit on Immigration and Asylum over the period of time considered in this study. They both played a key role in designing the first initiatives in this policy field.

Two other interviews were conducted with high-ranking national government officers who worked on the EU policy for integration in one way or another. One of them worked for the German Ministry of the Interior and took part in the elaboration of a European policy for the integration of third country nationals from the very beginning. She also participated in the coordination of the EIF's implementation later on. The other one worked for the Finnish Ministry of the Interior when the EIF was decided upon, under the Finnish Presidency of the Council of the European Union. If the text was eventually adopted in April 2007, negotiation ended in November 2006, under the Finnish presidency.

Finally, I could retrieve the material of another study, which Bourdrez (2010) kindly placed at my disposal: the discourse of a Dutch permanent representative to the EU working on integration at the time.

A.2. Data and Method for Quantitative Analyses

Data and Operationalisation

The data covers the whole period of the fund (2007–2013). It considers the 26 member states that took part in the EIF. Due to missing values and the EIF's inception specificities, the datasets used count fewer data-points than the 182 expected (26 countries times 7 years). There are 156 data-points for Chapter 5; and 152 for Chapter 6. This is because considerable delay characterized the launch of the programme. Accordingly, in most cases, Annual Programmes (AP) for the year 2007 and for the year 2008 were submitted to the Commission at the same time and were

---

[1] I thank Mr. Lucas Bourdrez for kindly putting his research material at my disposal.

Table A.1 Descriptive statistics of the variable introduced in the models, Chapter 5

	Nb. of Obs.	Mean	St. Dev.	Min	Max
Dependent variable					
EU indications	156	28.29288	33.29182	0	95.31
Independent variables					
Public opinion	156	8.132532	7.936963	0.175	38.5
CSO capacity	156	1.296154	1.343797	0.2	6.6
Financial Incentive	156	5.672111	13.92771	0	73.91305
Position on multiculturalism	156	5.860975	1.447003	2.6	8.77778
Muliculturalism salience	147	5.111583	1.714265	1.8144	7.875
Corporatism	156	0.0842566	0.730095	−1.32022	1.485859
Administrative capacity	156	1.10635	0.594096	−0.36	2.26

Table A.2 Descriptive statistics of the variables introduced in the models, Chapter 6

	Nb. of Obs.	Mean	St. Dev.	Min	Max
Dependent variable					
Implementation rate	152	83.343	20.444	10.5	106.82
Independent variables					
Administrative capacity	156	1.12	0.59	−0.7	2.26
CSO capacity	156	1.296	1.344	0.2	6.6
Decentralization	156	11.247	11.054	0	35.848
Salience for government	147	5.14	1.706	1.814	7.875
Public opinion	156	7.796	7.896	0.175	45.9
Previous funding (modified)	156	99.912	189.771	0	750
Previous funding (original)	*156*	*9,99,00,000*	*19,00,00,000*	*0*	*75,00,00,000*
Δ GDP per capita	155	−0.17	3.878	−14.56	8.467

validated by the latter at the same time, too.[2] I have therefore averaged the values for the two years, thus eliminating 26 data-points in each of the two datasets.

---

[2]See Ramboll (2011, 2013); see also all the Commission Decisions validating the 52 Annual Programmes for 2007 and 2008, and the national midterm implementation reports.

Missing data was treated according to list-wise deletion (see descriptive statistics Tables A.1 and A.2). I was able to contain missing values and only 9 data points out of 156 were deleted for Chapter 5: the whole of Malta (so the analysis actually considers 25 countries) and Latvia's data for 2008, 2009 and 2010. There are therefore 147 data points considered in total. For Chapter 6, the remaining missing data-points originate from the fact that Belgium failed to produce implementation figures for the AP 2008 through 2010 and Bulgaria failed to do so for the AP 2013.

Dependent Variables

In Chapter 5, I use as a dependent variable the percentage of total funding designated for tackling the five *specific priorities*[3] ("EU indications"), per year and per country. This percentage is drawn from member states' Annual Programmes[4] (see Table A.1 for its descriptive statistics).

For Chapter 6, I use as a dependent variable the implementation rate of EU funding; i.e., the share of EIF money actually spent compared to the amount available, per year and per country (see Table A.2 for its descriptive statistics). This percentage is drawn from member states' final evaluation reports.[5]

Independent Variables for Chapter 5

The models used in Chapter 5 seek to explain the share of funding *intended* for tackling EU indications, not their *actual* implementation. Consequently, independent variables values are taken a year ahead of the programming period.

Salience of immigration in public opinion is measured thanks to Eurobarometer 67–78, item 'What do you think are the most important issues facing your country at the moment' (two answers possible; TNS Opinion and Social 2007). For a given year, Eurobarometer's values for its spring and autumn editions were averaged.

---

[3]See C (2007) 3926 final for the *specific priorities*.

[4]Note that Annual Programmes are not available to the public but may be requested from the European Commission.

[5]Note that such reports are not available to the public but may be requested from the European Commission.

For CSO capacity, I use as a proxy the percentage of the working population working for NGO/non-profit sector as in the European Survey on Working Conditions 2010 (Eurofound 2010). Such data captures the capacity of CSOs to act as co-implementers, hence the "CSO capacity" formulation. In order to be co-implementers, CSOs need to have a sound administrative capacity in order to be, first, selected in the process of national calls for project proposals, and, second, able to absorb EU funding. This means organisations that are properly staffed, that present a year to year balanced budget and that can contract workers, etc. The advantage of such data is that it covers all member states, it is considered as one of the components of many indicators of civil society's size (Global Civil Society Index, CIVICUS, CSO Sustainability Index, Third Sector Impact Project[6]), it does not present other indexes' drawbacks (low coverage, low cross-indices comparability, lack of interpretability, and endogeneity issues), and does not count volunteering, but professionals within organizations likely competing for funding. In a different manner, it is true that this indicator does not account for CSOs' sector of activity, so that the variable does not specifically consider CSOs concerned with migration. This is in part because such data does not exist. Beyond that, it is also because integration is a multifaceted phenomenon (Penninx 2013) that touches on different domains such as literacy, language, social inclusion, social housing, cultural and religious matters, family rights and so forth.[7] Consequently, the CSOs likely to be consulted for the programming of the EIF or to receive funding in the spending phase need not be directly concerned with migrant integration but may be *de facto* dealing with it.

The position of governments on multiculturalism and its salience is measured thanks to the Chapel Hill Expert Survey 2010 (Bakker et al. 2012). CHES measures the positions of parties on a range of issues and not the position of governments. However, in many instances governments consist of a coalition of parties. Using CHES data, I traced back

---

[6]See inter alia (Salamon et al. 1999; Heinrich 2004; Anheier 2004; Lyons 2009).

[7]A look at the list of final beneficiaries of the EIF at national level confirms such tendency. At the time of writing, such lists are notably available for France (in French) and Ireland, respectively at http://www.immigration.interieur.gouv.fr/Info-ressources/ Fonds-europeens/Le-Fonds-europeen-d-integration-FEI/Les-beneficiaires-du-Fonds-europeen-d-integration-FEI and https://www.pobal.ie/FundingProgrammes/ EuropeanIntegrationFund/Pages/EIF-Projects.aspx.

the parties in government at the time of programming and I aggregated their preferences following Gamson's law (Browne and Franklin 1973). I have done the same for salience of multiculturalism.

In order to test my hypotheses, I control for a series of other explanations. First, given that the EIF is an incentive-based instrument, the incentive itself must be controlled for. I consider that in order for the incentive to play the intended role, it has to represent substantial financial bait. As said before, there is no incentive for member states falling under the cohesion fund, since they receive 75% co-financing right away. For other member states, the incentive is measured by comparing the yearly amount they are entitled to with the amount they planned to spend before the EIF existed (2006 if available, 2007 otherwise). Information is drawn from member states' multiannual programmes. Second, the weight that CSO capacity is likely to have on a government's choice is likely to depend on how much a government involves organized interests in policy-making (Saurugger 2007). I therefore introduce an index of corporatism to control for it. Jahn (2014) provides up-to-date data on corporatism[8] from 1960 to 2010. I averaged the data 2005–2010 and applied a single value over the period 2007–2012. Third, I control for member states administrative capacity as proposed by the literature on compliance and OMC. I use for that the worldwide governance indicators of effectiveness (Kaufman and Kraay 2015).

Independent Variables for Chapter 6

In order to test my hypotheses, values for the independent variables correspond to the period of eligibility of expenses as per Commission Decision; that is, the year following the programming period.

Administrative capacity is measured with the Worldwide Governance Indicator on government effectiveness (Kaufman and Kraay 2015). Established by the World Bank, this indicator summarizes the quality of the administration as to policy formulation and implementation and quality of public services.

Financial capacity is twofold; specific and global capacity. Specific financial capacity for integration policy is measured through the budget member states allocated to integration prior to the inception of the fund (in 2006 if available, in 2007 otherwise). Information is drawn from

---

[8]Based on Siaroff's conceptualisation (1999).

member states' multiannual programmes.[9] In order to ease the reading of the regression table produced in Chapter 6, the variable regarding previous funding has been slightly modified, without changing its distribution (see Table A.2). As for global financial capacity, I consider the annual percentage change in GDP per capita.[10] This allows a more dynamic conception of financial capacity that accounts for the economic downturn of the late 2000s. This data is taken from the World Bank's world development indicators.

CSO capacity is operationalised in the same manner as in Chapter 5, as the proxy used also captures the idea of CSOs that may weigh in on implementation as they likely meet EU fund management requirements.

I then use the Regional Authority Index (RAI; Hooghe et al. 2016) as a measure of decentralization within member states. Covering a wide range of dimensions (notably fiscal and political), it is deemed to be the most comprehensive indicator of decentralization (Ezcurra and Rodriguez-Pose 2013). Since the data available covers the period 1950–2010, four years are missing (2011–2014). I therefore average the values over the period 2006–2010 in order to fill the gap. This can be done for at least three reasons. Firstly, the literature on regionalism dates the decentralization process across Europe with the reform of the Cohesion policy in the late 1980s. For new member states, the same phenomenon can be observed as an effect of conditionality to their accession to the EU (Bachtler and McMaster 2008). Resultantly, little change in decentralization is expected for the period 2006–2014. Secondly, a look at the RAI trend over the 1950–2010 period confirms the devolution process occurred mostly from the 1980s to the early 2000s. Thirdly, no significant change is observable from 2006 to 2010, confirming the possibility to average the values and apply them over the period considered.

Government preferences are measured through the salience of integration for government, as in Chapter 5. Given the loose rules of the fund regarding its substantive aspects, the position of government on the issue matters less than how much the government cares about it (see Chapter 5).

To test my hypotheses, some controls are in order. First of all, as mentioned in H5, public opinion may shrink the impact of government preferences insofar as an attentive public may blame government for the action

---

[9]Note that what is considered is the funding allocated precisely to integration and not to asylum, as refugees fall out of the scope of the EIF (see European Refugee Fund).

[10]Based on constant local currency.

it takes and therefore weigh on government's will to implement. Salience of immigration in public opinion is measured thanks to Eurobarometers 67–82 (TNS Opinion and Social 2007) with the question 'what do you think are the most important issues facing your country at the moment?' (two answers possible). Since Eurobarometer is conducted twice a year, I averaged the two to obtain a yearly value. Secondly, the passage of time is controlled for. Since the policy instrument is new, its inception may have strained the administration which may in turn have delayed effective implementation at the outset. With the passage of time, the administration is likely to learn and adapt to the fund's requirements. Since learning cannot be appropriately measured, time is controlled for.

Method of Analysis

The data at hand is time-series cross-section (Beck 2006) and strongly balanced. Assuming that repeated observations over time, within a country, are more similar than observations across countries, I implement mixed effect multilevel models to account for the violation of the i.i.d. assumption (Gelman and Hill 2006; Agresti and Finlay 2007). More specifically, I include random effects for countries and years of implementation in order to reduce the problem of correlated error (Kohler and Kreuter 2012; Beck 2006). As for the estimation technique, I used residual maximum likelihood (REML) (see Oehlert 2012; Kreft and de Leeuw 1998; Patterson and Thomson 1971; Corbeil and Searle 1976).

The main issue arising concerns the dependent variable that is bounded up and down. Resultantly, the best model fit would be a beta regression model (Ferrari and Cribari-Neto 2004; Ospina and Ferrari 2012). Unfortunately, there do not exist routine techniques to implement multilevel beta regression. As a consequence of the relative misfit, the residuals are not normally distributed. That said, plotting residuals against fitted values for the different models shows rather homoscedastic pictures, hinting at properly modelled correlated errors (see post-estimation tests in Chapters 5 and 6).

Equation (A.1) consists in a general specification for multilevel models. Equation (A.2) corresponds to those models where an interaction term was introduced. Equation (A.3) regards the one model with a three-way interaction term, used in Chapter 5.

$$Y_{it} = \alpha_0 + \beta_1 X 1_{it} + \beta_2 X 2_{it} + \beta_3 X 3_{it} + u_{0i} + u_{1t} + e_{it} \qquad \text{(A.1)}$$

$$Y_{it} = \alpha_0 + \beta_1 X1_{it} + \beta_2 X2_{it} + \beta_3 X3_{it} + \beta_7 (X1_{it} * X2_{it}) + u_{0i} + u_{1t} + e_{it} \qquad \text{(A.2)}$$

$$Y_{it} = \alpha_0 + \beta_1 X1_{it} + \beta_2 X2_{it} + \beta_3 X3_{it} + \beta_7 (X1_{it} * X2_{it}) + \beta_8 (X1_{it} * X3_{it})$$
$$+ \beta_9 (X2_{it} * X3_{it}) + \beta_7 (X1_{it} * X2_{it} * X3_{it}) + u_{0i} + u_{1t} + e_{it} \qquad \text{(A.3)}$$

where Y_{it} is the value taken by the dependent variable in annual programme i for year t. XN_{it} are the values taken by the different independent variables. I account for auto-correlation within country (u_{0i}) and year (u_{1t}).

For Chapter 5, H2, and Chapter 6, H1b, further investigation is done through the calculation and graphing of average marginal effects. As for Chapter 5, H4, I introduce a three-way interaction term (Equation (3)), which considers the effect of salience for government onto the dependent variable at high and low values (mean $+/-$ one standard deviation) of both CSO capacity and public opinion (see Dawson 2013 for more on three-way interaction terms).

REFERENCES

Agresti, A., & Finlay, B. (2007). *Statistical Methods for the Social Sciences* (4th ed.). Upper Saddle River, NJ: Pearson Education Limited.

Anheier, H. K. (2004). *Civil Society. Measurement, Evaluation, Policy.* London: Earthscan.

Bachtler, J., & McMaster, I. (2008). EU Cohesion Policy and the Role of the Regions: Investigating the Influence of Structural Funds in the New Member States. *Environment and Planning C: Government and Policy, 26*(2), 398–427.

Bakker, R., de Vries, C., Edwards, E., Hooghe, L., Jolly, S., Marks, G., et al. (2012). Measuring Party Positions in Europe: The Chapel Hill Expert Survey Trend File, 1999–2010. *Party Politics, 21*(1), 143–152.

Beck, N. (2006). *Time-Series–Cross-Section Methods.* No. draft as of June 5.

Bourdrez, L. (2010). *The EU Policy on the Integration of Third-Country Nationals. "A Two-way Process?"* (Master's thesis). University of Amsterdam.

Bowen, G. A. (2009). Document Analysis as a Qualitative Research Method. *Qualitative Research Journal, 9*(2), 27–40.

Browne, E. C., & Franklin, M. N. (1973). Aspects of Coalition Payoffs in European Parliamentary Democracies. *The American Political Science Review, 67*(2), 453–469.

Checkel, J. T. (2005). *It's the Process Stupid! Process Tracing in the Study of European and International Politics* (ARENA Centre for European Studies Working Papers No. 26). University of Oslo.

Corbeil, R. R., & Searle, S. R. (1976). Restricted Maximum Likelihood (REML) Estimation of Variance Components in the Mixed Model. *Technometrics, 18*(1), 31–38.

Dawson, J. F. (2013). Moderation in Management Research: What, Why, When, and How. *Journal of Business and Psychology, 29*(1), 1–19.

EuroFound. (2010). European Survey on Working Condition 2010.

Ezcurra, R., & Rodríguez-Pose, A. (2013). Political Decentralization, Economic Growth and Regional Disparities in the OECD. *Regional Studies, 47*(3), 388–401.

Ferrari, S., & Cribari-Neto, F. (2004). Beta Regression for Modelling Rates and Proportions. *Journal of Applied Statistics, 31*(7), 799–815.

Gelman, A., & Hill, J. (2006). *Data Analysis Using Regression and Multilevel/ Hierarchical Models* (3rd ed.). Cambridge: Cambridge University Press.

Harvey, W. S. (2011). Strategies for Conducting Elite Interviews. *Qualitative Research, 11*(4), 431–441.

Heinrich, V. F. (2004). Assessing and Strengthening Civil Society Worldwide. *CIVICUS Civil Society Index Paper Series, 2*(1), 45–48.

Hooghe, L., Marks, G., Schakel, A., Chapman, S., Niedzwiecki, S., &Shair-Rosenfield, S. (2016). *Measuring Regional Authority. A Postfunctionalist Theory of Governance. Volume I: Measuring Regional Authority*. Oxford: Oxford University Press.

Jahn, D. (2014). Changing of the Guard: Trends in Corporatist Arrangements in 42 Highly Industrialized Societies from 1960 to 2010. *Socio-Economic Review, 14*(1), 47–71.

Kaufman, D., & Kraay, A. (2015). *Worldwide Governance Indicators*. The World Bank.

Kohler, U., & Kreuter, F. (2012). *Data Analysis Using Stata* (3rd ed.). College Station: Stata Press.

Kreft, I. G. G., & de Leeuw, J. (1998). *Introducing Multilevel Modeling*. London: Sage.

Lyons M. (2009). Measuring and Comparing Civil Societies. *Cosmopolitan Civil Societies Journal, 1*(1), 71–84.

Oehlert, G. W. (2012). A Few Words About REML. *Stat 5303, University of Minesota.*

Ospina, R., & Ferrari, S. L. P. (2012). A General Class of Zero-or-One Inflated Beta Regression Models. *Computational Statistics & Data Analysis, 56*(6), 1609–1623.

Patterson, H. D., & Thomson, R. (1971). Recovery of Inter-Block Information When Block Sizes Are Unequal. *Biometrika, 58*(3), 545–554.

Penninx, R. (2013). *Research on Migration and Integration in Europe: Achievements and Lessons*. Amsterdam, Netherlands: Vossiuspers UvA.

Ramboll. (2011). *Synthesis of the National Evaluation Reports on Implementation of Actions Co Financed by the European Fund for the Integration of*

Third-Country Nationals from 2007 to 2009 and Report at European Union Level Final Report. Brussels: Ramboll.

Ramboll. (2013). *Synthesis of the National Evaluation Reports on the Results and Impacts of Actions Co-financed by the European Fund for the Integration of Third-Country Nationals from 2007 to 2010.* Brussels: Ramboll.

Salamon L. M., Anheier H. K., List R., Toepler S., Sokolowski S. W., & Associates. (1999). *Global Civil Society: Dimensions of the Non-profit Sector.* Baltimore: Johns Hopkins Center for Civil Society Studies.

TNS Opinion and Social. (2007). Eurobarometer 67.2 to 78.1.

Vennesson, P. (2008). Case Studies and Process Tracing Theories and Practices. In D. Della Porta & M. Keating (Eds.), *Approaches and Methodologies in the Social Sciences: A Pluralist Perspective* (4th ed., pp. 223–239). Cambridge, NY: Cambridge University Press.

REFERENCES

SCHOLARSHIP AND EXPERT REFERENCES

Acosta Arcarazo, D. (2014). *EU Integration Policy: Between Soft Law and Hard Law* (Fondazione ISMU, KING project, Desk Research Paper No. 1).

Agresti, A., & Finlay, B. (2007). *Statistical Methods for the Social Sciences* (4th ed.). Upper Saddle River, NJ: Pearson Education Limited.

Albaek, E., Green-Pedersen, C., & Nielsen, L. B. (2007). Making Tobacco Consumption a Political Issue in the United States and Denmark: The Dynamics of Issue Expansion in Comparative Perspective. *Journal of Comparative Policy Analysis: Research and Practice, 9*(1), 1–20.

Alonso, S., & Fonseca, S. C. d. (2011). Immigration, Left and Right. *Party Politics, 18*(6), 865–884.

Anderson, B., & Blinder, S. (2015). Who Counts as a Migrant? Definitions and Their Consequences. *The Migration Observatory*. Available at http://www.migrationobservatory.ox.ac.uk/resources/briefings/who-counts-as-a-migrant-definitions-and-their-consequences/. Last Consulted November 12, 2016.

Anheier, H. K. (2004). *Civil Society. Measurement, Evaluation, Policy*. London: Earthscan.

Aus, J. P. (2008). The Mechanisms of Consensus: Coming to Agreement on Community Asylum Policy. In D. Naurin & H. Wallace (Eds.), *Unveiling the Council of the European Union: Games Governments Play in Brussels* (pp. 99–120). Basingstoke: Palgrave Macmillan.

© The Editor(s) (if applicable) and The Author(s) 2019   211
P. G. Van Wolleghem, *The EU's Policy on the Integration of Migrants*, Palgrave Studies in European Union Politics,
https://doi.org/10.1007/978-3-319-97682-2

Bache, I. (2005). *Europeanization and Britain: Towards Multi-level Governance?* Paper Prepared for the EUSA 9th Biennial Conference in Austin, Austin, TX, March 31–April 2.

Bache, I. (2010). Partnership as an EU Policy Instrument: A Political History. *West European Politics, 33*(1), 58–74.

Bachtler, J., & McMaster, I. (2008). EU Cohesion Policy and the Role of the Regions: Investigating the Influence of Structural Funds in the New Member States. *Environment and Planning C: Government and Policy, 26*(2), 398–427.

Bachtler, J., & Mendez, C. (2007). Who Governs EU Cohesion Policy? Deconstructing the Reforms of the Structural Funds. *JCMS: Journal of Common Market Studies, 45*(3), 535–564.

Bachtler, J., Mendez, C., & Oraže, H. (2014). From Conditionality to Europeanization in Central and Eastern Europe: Administrative Performance and Capacity in Cohesion Policy. *European Planning Studies, 22*(4), 735–757.

Bakker, R., de Vries, C., Edwards, E., Hooghe, L., Jolly, S., Marks, G., et al. (2012). Measuring Party Positions in Europe: The Chapel Hill Expert Survey Trend File, 1999–2010. *Party Politics, 21*(1), 143–152.

Barca, F., McCann, P., & Rodríguez-Pose, A. (2012). The Case for Regional Development Intervention: Place-Based Versus Place Neutral Approaches. *Journal of Regional Science, 52*(1), 134–152.

Baubock, R. (2005). Expansive Citizenship: Voting Beyond Territory and Membership. *Political Science and Politics, 38*(4), 683–687.

Beck, N. (2006). *Time-Series–Cross-Section Methods.* No. draft as of June 5.

Bercusson, B. (2009). *European Labour Law* (2nd ed.). Cambridge: Cambridge University Press.

Bigo, D. (1996). *Polices En Réseaux: L'éxpérience Européenne.* Paris: Presses de la Fondation nationale des sciences politiques.

Blom, S. (2014). *Local Migration and Integration Policies in Amsterdam* (Fondazione ISMU, KING Project, In-Depth Study No. 16).

Borràs, S., & Jacobsson, K. (2004). The Open Method of Co-ordination and New Governance Patterns in the EU. *Journal of European Puölic Policy, 11*(2), 185–208.

Börzel, T. A. (2000). Why There Is No "Southern Problem". On Environmental Leaders and Laggards in the European Union. *Journal of European Public Policy, 7*(1), 141–162.

Börzel, T. A. (2001). Non-compliance in the European Union: Pathology or Statistical Artefact? *Journal of European Public Policy, 8*(5), 803–824.

Börzel, T. A. (2002). Pace-Setting, Foot-Dragging, and Fence-Sitting: Member State Responses to Europeanization. *JCMS. Journal of Common Market Studies, 40*(2), 193–214.

Börzel, T. A., & Risse, T. (2003). Conceptualising the Domestic Impact of Europe. In K. Featherstone & C. Radaelli (Eds.), *The Politics of Europeanization* (pp. 57–82). Oxford: Oxford University Press.

Bourdrez, L. (2010). *The EU Policy on the Integration of Third-Country Nationals. "A Two-Way Process?"* (Master's thesis). University of Amsterdam.

Bouvet, F., & Dall'Erba, S. (2010). European Regional Structural Funds: How Large Is the Influence of Politics on the Allocation Process? *JCMS: Journal of Common Market Studies, 48*(3), 501–528.

Bowen, G. A. (2009). Document Analysis as a Qualitative Research Method. *Qualitative Research Journal, 9*(2), 27–40.

Brams, S. J., & Affuso, P. J. (1985). New Paradoxes of Voting Power on the EC Council of Ministers. *Electoral Studies, 4*(2), 135–139.

Bribosia, E. (2012). Les Politiques D'intégration de l'Union Européenne et Des Etats Membres à L'épreuve Du Principe de Non-discrimination. In Y. Pascouau & T. Strik (Eds.), *Which Integration Policies for Migrants? Interaction Between the EU and Its Member States* (pp. 51–82). Nijmegen: Wolf Legal Publishers.

Browne, E. C., & Franklin, M. N. (1973). Aspects of Coalition Payoffs in European Parliamentary Democracies. *The American Political Science Review, 67*(2), 453–469.

Brubaker, R. (2001). The Return of Assimilation? Changing Perspectives on Immigration and Its Sequels in France, Germany, and the United States. *Ethnic and Racial Studies, 24*(4), 531–548.

Bruquetas-Callejo, M., Garcés-Mascareñas, B., Penninx, R., & Scholten, P. (2011). The Case of the Netherlands. In G. Zincone, R. Penninx, & M. Borkert (Eds.), *Migration Policymaking in Europe: The Dynamics of Actors and Contexts in Past and Present* (pp. 129–165). Amsterdam: Amsterdam University Press.

Buchanan, J. M., & Tullock, G. (1958). *The Calculus of Consent: The Foundations of Constitutional Democracy.* Carmel, IN: Liberty Fund. Available at http://www.econlib.org/library/Buchanan/buchCv3c7.html. Last Consulted November 12, 2016.

Büchs, M. (2007). *New Governance in European Social Policy: The Open Method of Coordination.* Southampton: Palgrave Macmillan.

Bücker-Gärtner, H. (2011). *Europe Needs Innovative Ideas to Integrate Immigrants and Ethnic Minorities. Challenges and Creative Activities in Education and Civil Society (A Comparison of Five European Countries).* Berlin: Berlin School of Economics and Law.

Cantle, T. (2001). *Community Cohesion: A Report of the Independent Review Team.* London: Home Office.

Caporaso, J. (2007). The Three Worlds of Integration Theory. In P. R. Graziano (Ed.), *Europeanization: New Research Agendas* (pp. 23–34). Basingstoke: Palgrave Macmillan.

Carens, J. H. (2000). *Culture, Citizenship, and Community a Contextual Exploration of Justice as Evenhandedness.* Oxford: Oxford University Press.

Carrera, S. (2006). *A Comparison of Integration Programmes in the EU. Trends and Weaknesses* (Centre for European Policy Studies, Challenge No. 1).

Carrera, S. (2008). *Benchmarking Integration in the EU. Analyzing the Debate on Integration Indicators and Moving It Forward.* Gütersloh: Bertelsmann Foundation.

Carrera, S. (2009). *In Search of the Perfect Citizen? The Intersection Between Integration, Immigration and Nationality in the EU.* Leiden: Martinus Nijhoff Publishers.

Carrera, S., & Faure Atger, A. (2011). *Integration as a Two-Way Process in the EU? Assessing the Relationship Between the European Integration Fund and the Common Basic Principles.* Brussels: Centre for European Policy Studies.

Carrera, S., & Wiesbrock, A. (2009). *Civic Integration of Third-Country Nationals Nationalism Versus Europeanization in the Common EU Immigration Policy.* Brussels: Centre for European Policy Studies.

Castles, S. (1995). How Nation-States Respond to Immigration and Ethnic Diversity. *Journal of Ethnic and Migration Studies, 21*(3), 293–308.

Castles, S., de Haas, H., & Miller, M. J. (2013). *The Age of Migration. International Population Movements in the Modern World* (5th ed.). Basingstoke: Palgrave Macmillan.

Caviedes, A. (2004). The Open Method of Co-ordination in Immigration Policy: A Tool for Prying Open Fortress Europe? *Journal of European Public Policy, 11*(2), 289–310.

Checkel, J. T. (2005). *It's the Process Stupid! Process Tracing in the Study of European and International Politics* (ARENA Centre for European Studies Working Papers No. 26). University of Oslo.

Christiansen, T. (2006). The Council of Ministers: Facilitating Interaction and Developing Actorness in the EU. In J. Richardson (Ed.), *European Union: Power and Policy-Making* (3rd ed.). New York: Routledge.

Collett, E. (2011). Immigrant Integration in Europe in a Time of Austerity. *Migration Policy Institute.* Available at http://www.migrationpolicy.org/research/TCM-immigrant-integration-europe-time-austerity. Last Consulted November 12, 2016.

Collier, D. (2011). Understanding Process Tracing. *PS: Political Science & Politics, 44*(4), 823–830.

Corbeil, R. R., & Searle, S. R. (1976). Restricted Maximum Likelihood (REML) Estimation of Variance Components in the Mixed Model. *Technometrics, 18*(1), 31–38.

Cram, L. (1997). *Policy-Making in the European Union: Conceptual Lenses and the Integration Process*. New York: Taylor & Francis.

Cremona, M. (2012). Introduction. In M. Cremona (Ed.), *Compliance and the Enforcement of EU Law*. Oxford: Oxford University Press.

Cross, J. P. (2012). Everyone's a Winner (Almost): Bargaining Success in the Council of Ministers of the European Union. *European Union Politics, 14*(1), 70–94.

CSES—Centre for Strategy and Evaluation Services. (2013). *Study on Practices of Integration of Third-Country Nationals at Local and Regional Level in the European Union*. Brussels: Centre for Strategy and Evaluation Services.

Dai, X. (2005). Why Comply? The Domestic Constituency Mechanism. *International Organization, 59*(2), 363–398.

Dawson, J. F. (2013). Moderation in Management Research: What, Why, When, and How. *Journal of Business and Psychology, 29*(1), 1–19.

de Bruycker, P. (2005). Le Niveau D'harmonisation Legislative de La Politique Européenne D'immigration et D'asile. In Julien-Laferriere and Labayle (Eds.), *La politique européenne d'immigration et d'asile: bilan critique 5 ans après le traité d'Amsterdam*. Brussels: Bruylant.

de Haas, H., & Czaika, M. (2013). Measuring Migration Policies: Some Conceptual and Methodological Reflections. *Migration and Citizenship, 1*(2), 40–47.

de la Porte, C. (2002). Is the Open Method of Coordination Appropriate for Organising Activities at European Level in Sensitive Policy Areas? *European Law Journal, 8*(1), 38–58.

de la Porte, C., & Pochet, P. (2012). Why and How (Still) Study the Open Method of Co-ordination (OMC)? *Journal of European Social Policy, 22*(3), 336–349.

Dehousse, R. (2005). La Méthode Ouverte de Coordination. Quand L'instrument Tient Lieu de Politique. In P. Lascoumes & P. Le Galès (Eds.), *Gouverner par les Instruments* (pp. 331–356). Paris: Presses de Sciences Po «Académique».

Dellmuth, L. M. (2011). The Cash Divide: The Allocation of European Union Regional Grants. *Journal of European Public Policy, 18*(7), 1016–1033.

Delors, J. (1985). *Intervention de Jacques Delors, Luxembourg, 9 septembre 1985*. Bulletin des Communautés européennes, Luxembourg: Office des publications officielles des Communautés européennes Septembre 1985, n° 9.

Di Quirico, R. (2003). Italy, Europe and the European Presidency of 2003. *Notre Europe, Research and European Issues, 27*.

Duez, D. (2008). *L' Union Europeenne et L'immigration Clandestine: De La Securite Interieure a La Construction de La Communaute Politique*. Bruxelles: Editions de l'Universite de Bruxelles.

Dür, A., & Mateo, G. (2010). Bargaining Power and Negotiation Tactics: The Negotiations on the EU's Financial Perspective, 2007–13. *JCMS: Journal of Common Market Studies, 48*(3), 557–578.

Elgström, O. (2000). Norm Negotiations. The Construction of New Norms Regarding Gender and Development in EU Foreign Aid Policy. *Journal of European Public Policy, 7*(3), 457–476.

ELIAMEP. (2014). *Migration in Greece Recent Developments in 2014.* Athens: Hellenic Foundation for European and Foreign Policy.

Eurofound. (2010). European Survey on Working Condition 2010.

European Commission. (2011). *The 2012 Ageing Report: Underlying Assumptions and Projection Methodologies.* Brussels: European Commission.

Eurostat. (1996). Asylum-Seekers in Europe 1985–1995. *Statistics in Focus.*

Eurostat. (2014). Standard Eurobarometer 82 Autumn 2014.

Exadaktylos, T., & Radaelli, C. M. (2012). Looking for Causality in the Literature on Europeanization. In T. Exadaktylos & C. M. Radaelli (Eds.), *Research Design in European Studies: Establishing Causality in Europeanization.* Basingstoke: Palgrave Macmillan.

Ezcurra, R., & Rodríguez-Pose, A. (2013). Political Decentralization, Economic Growth and Regional Disparities in the OECD. *Regional Studies, 47*(3), 388–401.

Faist, T., & Ette, A. (2007). The Europeanization of National Policies and Politics of Immigration: Research, Questions and Concepts. In T. Faist & A. Ette (Eds.), *The Europeanization of National Policies and Politics of Immigration: Between Autonomy and the European Union* (pp. 3–31). New York: Palgrave Macmillan.

Falkner, G., Hartlapp, M., & Treib, O. (2007). Worlds of Compliance: Why Leading Approaches to European Union Implementation Are Only "Sometimes-True Theories". *European Journal of Political Research, 46*(3), 395–416.

Falkner, G., & Treib, O. (2008). Three Worlds of Compliance or Four? The EU-15 Compared to New Member States. *JCMS: Journal of Common Market Studies, 46*(2), 293–313.

Falkner, G., Treib, O., & Hartlapp, M. (2005). *Complying with Europe: EU Harmonisation and Soft Law in the Member States.* Cambridge: Cambridge University Press.

Favell, A. (2001). *Philosophies of Integration: Immigration and the Idea of Citizenship in France and Britain* (2nd ed.). New York: Palgrave Macmillan in association with Centre for Research in Ethnic Relations, University of Warwick.

Featherstone, K. (2003). Introduction: In the Name of "Europe". In K. Featherstone & C. M. Radaelli (Eds.), *The Politics of Europeanization* (pp. 3–26). New York: Oxford University Press.

Featherstone, K. (2005). "Soft" Co-ordination Meets "Hard" Politics: The European Union and Pension Reform in Greece. *Journal of European Public Policy, 12*(4), 733–750.

Ferrari, S., & Cribari-Neto, F. (2004). Beta Regression for Modelling Rates and Proportions. *Journal of Applied Statistics, 31*(7), 799–815.

Fischler, F. (2014). *Integration Policy Netherlands Country Report* (Interact Research Report 2014/15).

Franchino, F. (2004). Delegating Powers in the European Community. *British Journal of Political Science, 34*(2), 269–293.

Franchino, F. (2007). *The Powers of the Union: Delegation in the EU.* Cambridge: Cambridge University Press.

Geddes, A. (2000). Lobbying for Migrant Inclusion in the European Union: New Opportunities for Transnational Advocacy? *Journal of European Public Policy, 7*(4), 632–649.

Geddes, A. (2003). *The Politics of Migration and Immigration in Europe.* London: Sage.

Geddes, A. (2004). Britain, France, and EU Anti-discrimination Policy: The Emergence of an EU Policy Paradigm. *West European Politics, 27*(2), 334–353.

Geddes, A., & Achtnich, M. (2015). Research-Policy Dialogues in the European Union. In P. Scholten, H. Entzinger, R. Penninx, S. Verbeek (Eds.), *Integrating Immigrants in Europe. Research-Policy Dialogues* (pp. 293–314). Amsterdam: IMISCOE Research Series.

Gelman, A., & Hill, J. (2006). *Data Analysis Using Regression and Multilevel/ Hierarchical Models* (3rd ed.). Cambridge: Cambridge University Press.

Gilardoni, G., D'odorico, M., & Carrillo, D. (2015). *KING Knowledge for INtegration Governance Evidence on Migrants' Integration in Europe.* Milan: Fondazione ISMU.

Giuliani, M. (2003). Europeanization in Comparative Perspective: Institutional Fit and National Adaptation. In K. Featherstone & C. M. Radaelli (Eds.), *The politics of Europeanization.* New York: Oxford University Press.

Grabosky, P. N. (1995). Counterproductive Regulation. *International Journal of the Sociology of Law, 23*(4), 347–369.

Green-Pedersen, C., & Mortensen, P. B. (2013). Policy Agenda-Setting Studies: Attention, Politics and the Public. In E. Araral, S. Fritzen, & M. Howlett (Eds.), *Routledge Handbook of Public Policy* (pp. 167–174). New York: Taylor & Francis.

Groenendijk, K. (2004). Legal Concepts of Integration in EU Migration Law. *European Journal of Migration and Law, 6*(2), 111–126.

Groenendijk, K., Fernhout, R., van Dam, D., van Oers, R., & Strik, T. (2007). *The Family Reunification Directive in EU Member States: The First Year of Implementation.* Nijmegen: Centre for Migration Law.

Guild, E. (1998). Competence, Discretion and Third Country Nationals: The European Union's Legal Struggle with Migration. *Journal of Ethnic and Migration Studies, 24*(4), 613–625.

Guild, E. (2001). *Immigration Law in the European Community.* The Hague: Kluwer Law International.

Guiraudon, V. (2003). The Constitution of a European Immigration Policy Domain: A Political Sociology Approach. *Journal of European Public Policy, 10*(2), 263–282.

Gunningham, N., & Sinclair, D. (1998). *Designing Smart Regulation.* Paris: OECD/International Energy Agency.

Hailbronner, K. (2010). *Implications of the EU Lisbon Treaty on EU Immigration Law.* Paper Prepared for the Transatlantic Exchange for Academics in Migration Studies, San Diego.

Halleskov, L. (2005). The Long-Term Residents Directive: A Fulfilment of the Tampere Objective of Near-Equality? *European Journal of Migration and Law, 7*(2), 181–202.

Hamilton, L. C. (2012). *Statistics with Stata: Updated for Version 12* (8th ed.). Boston: Brooks/Cole-Cengage Learning.

Hammar, T. (1990). *Democracy and the Nation State: Aliens, Denizens and Citizens in a World of International Migration.* Aldershot: Ashgate Publishing.

Handoll, J. (2012). Integration Policy in the European Union: The Question of Competence. In Y. Pascouau & T. Strik (Eds.), *Which Integration Policies for Migrants? Interaction Between the EU and Its Member States* (pp. 15–50). Nijmegen: Wolf Legal Publishers.

Hapenciuc, C. V., Moroşan, A. A., & Gaube, G. A. (2013). Absorption of Structural Funds—International Comparisons and Correlations. *Procedia Economics and Finance, 6,* 259–272.

Harvey, W. S. (2011). Strategies for Conducting Elite Interviews. *Qualitative Research, 11*(4), 431–441.

Hauschild, C. (2008). Die Integration von Zuwanderern. Ein Neues Politikfeld Für Die Europäische Union. In S. Magiera, K.-P. Sommermann, & J. Ziller (Eds.), *Verwaltungswissenschaft und Verwaltungspraxis in nationaler und transnationaler Perspektive* (pp. 59–74). Berlin: Duncker & Humbliot.

Haverland, M. (2000). National Adaptation to European Integration: The Importance of Institutional Veto Points. *Journal of Public Policy, 20*(1), 83–103.

Heidbreder, E. (2014). *When Multiple Levels Meet Migration: The Specific Challenges of a EU Immigration Regime* (Fondazione ISMU, KING Project, Desk Research Paper No. 3).

Heinrich, V. F. (2004). Assessing and Strengthening Civil Society Worldwide. *CIVICUS Civil Society Index Paper Series, 2*(1), 1–64.

Helbling, M. (2013). Validating Integration and Citizenship Policy Indices. *Comparative European Politics, 11*(5), 555–576.

Helbling, M., Bjerre, L., Römer, F., & Zobel, M. (2013). The Immigration Policies in Comparison (IMPIC) Index: The Importance of a Sound Conceptualization. *Migration and Citizenship, 1*(2), 8–14.

Hepburn, E. (2010). "Citizens of the Region": Party Conceptions of Regional Citizenship and Immigrant Integration. *European Journal of Political Research, 50*(4), 504–529.

Hinich, H. J., & Munger, M. C. (1997). *Analytical Politics*. Cambridge: Cambridge University Press.

Hix, S. (2005). *The Political System of the European Union* (2nd ed.). Basingstoke: Palgrave Macmillan.

Hix, S., & Niessen, J. (1996). *Reconsidering European Migration Policies: The 1996 Intergovernmental Conference and the Reform of the Maastricht Treaty*. Brussels: Migration Policy Group.

Hollifield, J. F. F. (1992). *Immigrants, Markets, and States: The Political Economy of Postwar Europe*. Cambridge: Harvard University Press.

Hooghe, L. (1996). Building a Europe with the Regions: The Changing Role of the European Commission. In L. Hooghe (Ed.), *Cohesion Policy and European Integration: Building Multi-level Governance*. Oxford: Oxford University Press.

Hooghe, L., & Marks, G. (2001). *Multi-level Governance and European Integration*. Lanham: Rowman & Littlefield.

Hooghe, L., Marks, G., Schakel, A., Chapman, S., Niedzwiecki, S., & Shair-Rosenfield, S. (2016). *Measuring Regional Authority. A Postfunctionalist Theory of Governance. Volume I: Measuring Regional Authority*. Oxford: Oxford University Press.

Horvat, A. (2005). *Why Does Nobody Care About the Absorption? Some Aspects Regarding Administrative Absorption Capacity for the EU Structural Funds in the Czech Republic, Estonia, Hungary, Slovakia and Slovenia before Accession* (WIFO Working Papers No. 258).

Hosli, M. O. (1995). The Balance Between Small and Large: Effects of a Double-Majority System on Voting Power in the European Union. *International Studies Quarterly, 39*(3), 351.

Howlett, M., & Giest, S. (2013). *Routledge Handbook of Public Policy*. New York: Taylor & Francis.

Huysmans, J. (2000). The European Union and the Securitization of Migration. *JCMS: Journal of Common Market Studies, 38*(5), 751–777.

Jacobs, D., & Rea, A. (2008). *The End of National Models? Integration Courses and Citizenship Trajectories in Europe*. Paper Presented at the European Union Studies Association, 17–19 May.

Jahn, D. (2014). Changing of the Guard: Trends in Corporatist Arrangements in 42 Highly Industrialized Societies from 1960 to 2010. *Socio-Economic Review, 14*(1), 47–71.

Kantor Management Consultants. (2009). *The Evaluation of the INTI Program Framework Contract for Evaluation and Evaluation Related Services.* Kantor Management Consultants.

Kasimis, C. (2012) *Greece: Illegal Immigration in the Midst of Crisis.* Migration Policy Institute. Available at http://www.migrationpolicy.org/article/greece-illegal-immigration-midst-crisis. Last Consulted November 16, 2016.

Kassim, H., & Le Galès, P. (2010). Exploring Governance in a Multi-level Polity: A Policy Instruments Approach. *West European Politics, 33*(1), 1–21.

Kassim, H., & Menon, A. (2003). The Principal-Agent Approach and the Study of the European Union: Promise Unfulfilled? *Journal of European Public Policy, 10*(1), 121–139.

Kate, M.-A., & Niessen, J. (2007). *Locating Immigrant Integration Policy Measures in the Machinery of the European Commission.* Brussels: European Programme for Integration and Migration.

Kaufman, D., & Kraay, A. (2015). *Worldwide Governance Indicators.* The World Bank.

Keating, M. (2009). Social Citizenship, Devolution and Policy Divergence. In S. L. Greer (Ed.), *Devolution and Social Citizenship in the UK* (pp. 97–116). Bristol: Policy Press.

Keman, H. (2011). Comparative Research Methods. In D. Caramani (Ed.), *Comparative Politics* (2nd ed., pp. 50–64). Oxford: Oxford University Press.

Kemmerling, A., & Bodenstein, T. (2006). Partisan Politics in Regional Redistribution: Do Parties Affect the Distribution of EU Structural Funds Across Regions? *European Union Politics, 7*(3), 373–392.

Knill, C., & Lehmkuhl, D. (2002). The National Impact of European Union Regulatory Policy: Three Europeanization Mechanisms. *European Journal of Political Research, 41*(2), 255–280.

Knill, C., & Lenschow, A. (2005). Compliance, Competition and Communication: Different Approaches of European Governance and Their Impact on National Institutions. *JCMS: Journal of Common Market Studies, 43*(3), 583–606.

Kohler, U., & Kreuter, F. (2012). *Data Analysis Using Stata* (3rd ed.). College Station: Stata Press.

König, T., & Luetgert, B. (2009). Troubles with Transposition? Explaining Trends in Member-State Notification and the Delayed Transposition of EU Directives. *British Journal of Political Science, 39*(1), 163–194.

König, T., & Mäder, L. (2014). The Strategic Nature of Compliance: An Empirical Evaluation of Law Implementation in the Central Monitoring System of the European Union. *American Journal of Political Science, 58*(1), 246–263.

Kostakopoulou, T. (2002a). "Integrating" Non-EU Migrants in the European Union: Ambivalent Legacies and Mutating Paradigms. *Columbia Journal of European Law, 8*(2), 181–201.

Kostakopoulou, T. (2002b). Long-Term Resident Third-Country Nationals in the European Union: Normative Expectations and Institutional Openings. *Journal of Ethnic and Migration Studies, 28*(3), 443–462.

Kraler, A. (2011). The Case of Austria. In G. Zincone, R. Penninx, & M. Borkert (Eds.), *Migration Policymaking in Europe. The Dynamics of Actors and Contexts in Past and Present* (pp. 21–60). Amsterdam: IMISCOE Research Series.

Kreft, I. G. G., & de Leeuw, J. (1998). *Introducing Multilevel Modeling.* London: Sage.

Kröger, S. (2009). The Open Method of Coordination: Underconceptualisation, Overdetermination, De-Politicisation and Beyond. *European Integration Online Papers, 13*(1).

Kundnani, A. (2012). Multiculturalism and Its Discontents: Left, Right and Liberal. *European Journal of Cultural Studies, 15*(2), 155–166.

Kymlicka, W. (1995). *Multicultural Citizenship: A Liberal Theory of Minority Rights.* New York: Oxford University Press.

Laffan, B., & Lindner, J. (2005). The Budget. In H. Wallace, W. Wallace, & M. A. Pollack (Eds.), *Policy-Making in the European Union* (5th ed., pp. 191–212). Oxford: Oxford University Press.

Lampinen, R., & Uusikylä, P. (1998). Implementation Deficit? Why Member States Do Not Comply with EU Directives? *Scandinavian Political Studies, 21*(3), 231–251.

Lanzieri, G. (2010). *Fewer, Older and Multicultural? A Projection of the Populations of the European Union Member States by Foreign/national Background.* Eurostat Statistical Working Paper.

Lasswell, H. D. (1936). *Politics; Who Gets What, When, How.* New York: Whittlesey House, McGraw-Hill Book.

Les Echos. (2015, August 1). L'immigration, Principale Preoccupation Des Europeens. *Les Echos.*

López-Santana, M. (2007). *Soft Europeanization? How the Soft Pressure from Above Affects the Bottom (Differently): The Belgian, Spanish and Swedish Experiences* (EUI Working Papers, 10).

Lowi, T. J. (1964). American Business, Public Policy, Case-Studies, and Political Theory. *World Politics, 16*(4), 677–715.

Luedtke, A. (2005). European Integration, Public Opinion and Immigration Policy: Testing the Impact of National Identity. *European Union Politics, 6*(1), 83–112.

Luedtke, A. (2011). Uncovering European Union Immigration Legislation: Policy Dynamics and Outcomes. *International Migration, 49*(2), 1–27.

Lupia, A. (2003). Delegation and Its Perils. In K. Strom, W. C. Muller, & T. Bergman (Eds.), *Delegation and Accountability in Parliamentary Democracies*. New York: Oxford University Press.

Lyons M. (2009). Measuring and Comparing Civil Societies. *Cosmopolitan Civil Societies Journal, 1*(1), 71–84.

Mahoney, J. (2010). After KKV: The New Methodology of Qualitative Research. *World Politics, 62*(1), 120–147.

Majone, G. (1999). The Regulatory State and Its Legitimacy Problems. *West European Politics, 22*(1), 1–24.

Malmström. (2014, March 13). Commissioner Malmström Welcomes the Parliament's Vote on the New EU Home Affairs' Funds 2014–2020. *European Commission Press Release*.

Mandin, J. (2014). *An Overview of Integration Policies in Belgium* (Interact Research Report 2014/20).

Marks, G. (1993). Structural Policy and Multilevel Governance in the EC. In A. W. Cafruny & G. G. Rosenthal (Eds.), *The State of the European Community*. Boulder: Lynne Rienner.

Mathieson, J., Popay, J., Enoch, E., Escorel, S., Hernandez, M., Johnston, H., & Rispel, L. (2008) *Social Exclusion. Meaning, Measurement and Experience and Links to Health Inequalities*. A Review of Literature. WHO Social Exclusion Knowledge Network Background Paper, 1.

Mazeron, F. (2008). Le Droit Communautaire de L'immigration et de L'asile à L'épreuve Du Droit International. In C. Bertrand (Ed.), *L'immigration dans l'Union Européenne : aspects actuels de droit interne et de droit européen*. Paris: L'Harmattan.

Mbaye, H. A. D. (2001). Why National States Comply with Supranational Law: Explaining Implementation Infringements in the European Union, 1972–1993. *European Union Politics, 2*(3), 259–281.

McCubbins, M. D., & Schwartz, T. (1984). Congressional Oversight Overlooked: Police Patrols Versus Fire Alarms. *American Journal of Political Science, 28*(1), 165–179.

Mendez, C. (2013). The Post-2013 Reform of EU Cohesion Policy and the Place-Based Narrative. *Journal of European Public Policy, 20*(5), 639–659.

Milio, S. (2007). Can Administrative Capacity Explain Differences in Regional Performances? Evidence from Structural Funds Implementation in Southern Italy. *Regional Studies, 41*(4), 429–442.

Miller, D. (2008). Immigrants, Nations, and Citizenship. *Journal of Political Philosophy, 16*(4), 371–390.

Moravcsik, A. (1998). *The Choice for Europe: Social Purpose and State Power from Messina to Maastricht*. Ithaca: Cornell University Press.

Morjé Howard, M. (2008). The Causes and Consequences of Germany's New Citizenship Law. *German Politics, 17*(1), 41–62.

Mouritsen, P., & Hovmark Jensen, C. (2014). *Integration Policies in Denmark* (INTERACT Research Report 2014/06).

MPI. (2003). *Press Release: Top Migration Experts to Meet in Athens Under the Leadership of the Migration Policy Institute and the Auspices of the Greek Presidency of the EU to Discuss Migration Issues of Concern to Europe.* Migration Policy Institute. Available at http://www.migrationpolicy.org/ news/top-migration-experts-meet-in-athens. Last Consulted October 21, 2016.

Mügge, L., & van der Haar, M. (2016). Who Is an Immigrant and Who Requires Integration? Categorizing in European Policies. In B. Garcés-Mascareñas & R. Penninx (Eds.), *Integration Processes and Policies in Europe. Contexts, Levels and Actors* (pp. 77–90). Amsterdam: IMISCOE Research Series.

Mulcahy, S. (2011). *Europe's Migrant Policies: Illusions of Integration.* Basingstoke: Palgrave Macmillan.

Murard, N. (2002). Guilty Victims: Social Exclusion in Contemporary France. In P. Chamberlayne, M. Rustin, & T. Wengraf (Eds.), *Biography and Social Exclusion in Europe: Experiences and Life Journeys.* Bristol: Policy Press.

Murphy, C. (2009). Immigration, Integration and Citizenship in European Union Law: The Position of Third Country Nationals. *Hibernian Law Journal, 8,* 155–177.

Nardo, M., Saisana, M., Saltelli, A., Tarantola, S., Hoffman, A., & Giovannini, E. (2005). *Handbook on Constructing Composite Indicators: Methodology and User Guide.* Paris: Organization for Economic Co-operation and Development (OECD).

NEI Regional and Urban Development. (2002). *Key Indicators for Candidate Countries to Effectively Manage the Structural Funds.* Rotterdam.

Noiriel, G. (2006). *Le Creuset Francais: Histoire de L'immigration, XIXe–XXe Siecles.* Paris: Seuil.

North, D. C. (1990). *Institutions, Institutional Change, and Economic Performance.* Cambridge: Cambridge University Press.

OECD. (2016). *Recruiting Immigrant Workers: Europe.* Paris: OECD.

Oehlert, G. W. (2012). A Few Words About REML. *Stat 5303, University of Minesota.*

Oosterom-Staples, H. (2007). The Family Reunification Directive: A Tool Preserving Member State Interest or Conducive to Family Unity? In A. Baldaccini, H. Toner, & P. E. Guild (Eds.), *Whose Freedom, Security and Justice? EU Immigration and Asylum Law and Policy* (pp. 451–488). Oxford: Hart Publishing.

Ospina, R., & Ferrari, S. L. P. (2012). A General Class of Zero-or-One Inflated Beta Regression Models. *Computational Statistics & Data Analysis, 56*(6), 1609–1623.

Ostrom, E. (2007). Institutional Rational Choice: An Assessment of the Institutional Analysis and Development Framework. In P. A. Sabatier (Ed.), *Theories of the Policy Process* (2nd ed., pp. 21–34). Boulder, CO: Westview Press.

Patterson, H. D., & Thomson, R. (1971). Recovery of Inter-Block Information When Block Sizes Are Unequal. *Biometrika, 58*(3), 545–554.

Penninx, R. (2005). Integration of Migrants. Economic, Social, Cultural and Political Dimensions. In M. Macura, A. L. MacDonald, & W. Haug (Eds.), *The New Demographic Regime. Population Challenges and Policy Responses* (pp. 137–152). Geneva: United Nations.

Penninx, R. (2009). *Decentralising Integration Policies. Managing Integration in Cities, Regions and Localities.* Policy Network Paper.

Penninx, R. (2013). *Research on Migration and Integration in Europe: Achievements and Lessons.* Amsterdam, Netherlands: Vossiuspers UvA.

Penninx, M., Garcés-Mascareñas, B., Protasiewicz, P. M., Schwarz, H., & Caponio, T. (2014). *European Cities and Their Migrant Integration Policies A State of the Art Study for the Knowledge for Integration Governance (KING) Project* (Fondazione ISMU, KING Project, Overview Paper No. 5).

Petrovic, M. (2012). *Belgium: A Country of Pemanent Immigration.* Migration Policy Institute. Available at http://www.migrationpolicy.org/article/belgium-country-permanent-immigration. Last Consulted October 21, 2016.

Phillimore, J. (2014). *Local and Experiential Aspects of Migrant Integration. An Overview* (Fondazione ISMU, KING Project, Overview Paper No. 7).

Pollack, M. A. (1997). Delegation, Agency, and Agenda Setting in the European Community. *International Organization, 51*(1), 99–134.

Poppelaars, C., & Scholten, P. (2008). Two Worlds Apart: The Divergence of National and Local Immigrant Integration Policies in the Netherlands. *Administration & Society, 40*(4), 335–357.

Pratt, S. (2015). EU Policymaking and Research: Case Studies of the Communication on a Community Immigration Policy and the Common Basic Principles for Integration. In P. Scholten, H. Entzinger, R. Penninx, & S. Verbeek (Eds.), *Integrating Immigrants in Europe: Research-Policy Dialogues* (pp. 117–131). Amsterdam: IMISCOE Research Series.

Pridham, G. (1994). National Environmental Policy-Making in the European Framework: Spain, Greece and Italy in Comparison. *Regional Politics and Policy, 4*(1), 80–101.

Princen, S. (2007). Agenda-Setting in the European Union: A Theoretical Exploration and Agenda for Research. *Journal of European Public Policy, 14*(1), 21–38.

Radaelli, C. (2003a). *The Open Method of Coordination: A New Governance Architecture for the European Union?* (Swedish Institute for European Policy Studies No. 1).

Radaelli, C. (2003b). The Europeanization of Public Policy. In K. Featherstone & C. M. Radaelli (Eds.), *The Politics of Europeanization* (pp. 27–56). New York: Oxford University Press.

Radaelli, C. M. (2008). Europeanization, Policy Learning, and New Modes of Governance. *Journal of Comparative Policy Analysis: Research and Practice, 10*(3), 239–254.

Ramboll. (2011). *Synthesis of the National Evaluation Reports on Implementation of Actions Co Financed by the European Fund for the Integration of Third-Country Nationals from 2007 to 2009 and Report at European Union Level Final Report*. Brussels: Ramboll.

Ramboll. (2013). *Synthesis of the National Evaluation Reports on the Results and Impacts of Actions Co-financed by the European Fund for the Integration of Third-Country Nationals from 2007 to 2010*. Brussels: Ramboll.

Rant, V., & Mrak, M. (2010). The 2007–13 Financial Perspective: Domination of National Interests. *JCMS: Journal of Common Market Studies, 48*(2), 347–372.

Rasmussen, A., Carroll, B. J., & Lowery, D. (2013). Representatives of the Public? Public Opinion and Interest Group Activity. *European Journal of Political Research, 53*(2), 250–268.

Regonini, G. (2001). *Capire le politiche pubbliche*. Bologna: Il Mulino.

Richardson, J. (2012). Supranational State Building in the European Union. In J. Richardson (Ed.), *Constructing a Policy-Making State? Policy Dynamics in the EU*. Oxford: Oxford University Press.

Rosenow, K. (2009). The Europeanization of Integration Policies. *International Migration, 47*(1), 133–159.

Rubio-Marín, R. (2004). *Immigration as a Democratic Challenge: Citizenship and Inclusion in Germany and the United States*. Cambridge: Cambridge University Press.

Salamon, L. M. (2000). The New Governance and the Tools of Public Action: An Introduction. *Fordham Urban Law Journal, 28*(5), 1611–1674.

Salamon L. M., Anheier H. K., List R., Toepler S., Sokolowski S. W., & Associates. (1999). *Global Civil Society: Dimensions of the Non-profit Sector*. Baltimore: Johns Hopkins Center for Civil Society Studies.

Saurugger, S. (2007). Democratic Misfit? Conceptions of Civil Society Participation in France and the European Union. *Political Studies, 55*(2), 384–404.

Saurugger, S. (2012). Beyond Non-compliance with Legal Norms. In T. Exadaktylos & C. M. Radaelli (Eds.), *Research Design in European Studies: Establishing Causality in Europeanization*. Basingstoke: Palgrave Macmillan.

Saurugger, S., & Terpan, F. (2013). Resisting EU Norms. A Framework for Analysis. *HAL Archives Ouvertes*.

Schain, M. (2010). Managing Difference: Immigrant Integration Policy in France, Britain, and the United States. *Social Research: An International Quarterly, 77*(1), 205–236.

Scharpf, F. W. (1990). Games Real Actors Could Play: The Problem of Mutual Predictability. *Rationality and Society, 2*(4), 471–494.

Scharpf, F. W. (1997). *Games Real Actors Play: Actor-Centered Institutionalism in Policy Research.* Boulder: Westview Press.

Scharpf, F. W. (2003). *Problem-Solving Effectiveness and Democratic Accountability in the EU* (MPifG Working Papers, 3(1)).

Schild, J. (2008). How to Shift the EU's Spending Priorities? The Multi-Annual Financial Framework 2007–13 in Perspective. *Journal of European Public Policy, 15*(4), 531–549.

Schnapper, D. (1994). The Debate on Immigration and the Crisis of National Identity. *West European Politics, 17*(2), 127–139.

Scholten, P., & Penninx, R. (2016). The Multilevel Governance of Migration and Integration'. In *Integration Processes and Policies in Europe. Contexts, Levels and Actors* (pp. 91–108). Amsterdam: IMISCOE Research Series.

Schuyler House, R., & Araral, E. (2013). The Institutional Analysis and Development Framework. In E. Araral, S. Fritzen, M. Howlett, M. Ramesh, & X. Wu (Eds.), *Routledge Handbook of Public Policy* (pp. 115–125). New York: Taylor & Francis.

Scott, J., & Trubek, D. M. (2002). Mind the Gap: Law and New Approaches to Governance in the European Union. *European Law Journal, 8*(1), 1–18.

Shachar, A., & Hirschl, R. (2007). Citizenship as Inherited Property. *Political Theory, 35*(3), 253–287.

Siaroff, A. (1999). Corporatism in 24 Industrial Democracies: Meaning and Measurement. *European Journal of Political Research, 36*(2), 175–205.

Snyder, F. (1993). Soft Law and Institutional Practice in the European Community. In S. Martin (Ed.), *The Construction of Europe: Essays in Honour of Emile Noel* (pp. 197–225). Boston: Kluwer Academic Publishers.

Spendzharova, A., & Versluis, E. (2013). Issue Salience in the European Policy Process: What Impact on Transposition? *Journal of European Public Policy, 20*(10), 1499–1516.

Steunenberg, B. (2007). A Policy Solution to the European Union's Transposition Puzzle: Interaction of Interests in Different Domestic Arenas. *West European Politics, 30*(1), 23–49.

Steunenberg, B., & Rhinard, M. (2010). The Transposition of European Law in EU Member States: Between Process and Politics. *European Political Science Review, 2*(03), 495–520.

Susskind, L. (2006). Arguing, Bargaining, and Getting Agreement. In M. Moran, M. Rein, & R. E. Goodin (Eds.), *The Oxford Handbook of Public Policy* (pp. 269–295). New York: Oxford University Press.

Sussmuth, R. (2009). *The Future of Migration and Integration Policy in Germany.* Migration Policy Institute. Available at http://www.migration-policy.org/research/future-migration-and-integration-policy-germany. Last Consulted January 15, 2017.

Szyszczak, E. (2006). Experimental Governance: The Open Method of Coordination. *European Law Journal, 12*(4), 486–502.

Taagepera, R. (2008). *Making Social Sciences More Scientific: The Need for Predictive Models.* Oxford: Oxford University Press.

Tallberg, J. (2003). The Agenda-Shaping Powers of the EU Council Presidency. *Journal of European Public Policy, 10*(1), 1–19.

Testa, M. R. (2014). *The Contribution of Migration to the Demography of Europe between 1991 and 2011—An Overview* (Fondazione ISMU, KING Project, Desk Research No. 19).

The Economist. (2001, September 27). Charlemagne; Antonio Vitorino. *The Economist.*

Thielemann, E. (2001). *The "Soft" Europeanization of Migration Policy: European Integration and Domestic Policy Change.* Paper Presented at the ECSA Seventh Biennial International Conference.

Thiesse, A.-M. (2001). *La Création Des Identités Nationales: Europe XVIIIe–XXe Siècle.* Paris: Éditions du Seuil.

Tholoniat, L. (2010). The Career of the Open Method of Coordination: Lessons from a "Soft" EU Instrument. *West European Politics, 33*(1), 93–117.

Thomson, R., Torenvlied, R., & Arregui, J. (2007). The Paradox of Compliance: Infringements and Delays in Transposing European Union Directives. *British Journal of Political Science, 37*(4), 685–709.

Thränhardt, D. (2014). *The State of European Integration Governance: A Comparative Evaluation* (Fondazione ISMU, KING Project, Desk Research Paper No. 7).

Tilly, C., & Goodin, R. E. (2011). Overview of Contextual Political Analysis It Depends. In R. E. Goodin (Ed.), *The Oxford Handbook of Political Science.* Oxford: Oxford University Press.

TNS Opinion and Social. (2007). Eurobarometer 67.2 to 78.1.

TNS Qual+. (2011). Migrant Integration. Qualitative Eurobarometer. *European Commission.*

Tosun, J. (2014). Absorption of Regional Funds: A Comparative Analysis. *JCMS: Journal of Common Market Studies, 52*(2), 371–387.

Treib, O. (2014) Implementing and Complying with EU Governance Outputs. *Living Reviews in European Governance, 9*(1), 1–47.

Trimikliniotis, N. (2012). The Instrumentalisation of EU Integration Policy: Reflecting on the Dignified Efficient and Undeclared Policy Aspects. In Y. Pascouau & T. Strik (Eds.), *Which Integration Policies for Migrants?*

Interaction Between the EU and Its Member States (pp. 109–128). Nijmegen: W.L.P. (Wolf Legal Publishers).

Tsebelis, G. (2001). *Veto Players: How Political Institutions Work.* Princeton: Princeton University Press.

Tsebelis, G. (2013). Bridging Qualified Majority and Unanimity Decisionmaking in the EU. *Journal of European Public Policy, 20*(8), 1083–1103.

Urth, H. (2005). Building a Momentum for the Integration of Third-Country Nationals in the European Union. *European Journal of Migration and Law, 7*(2), 163–180.

Valentine, J. C., Aloe, A. M., & Lau, T. S. (2015). Life After NHST: How to Describe Your Data Without "p-ing" Everywhere. *Basic and Applied Social Psychology, 37*(5), 260–273.

van Spanje, J., & de Vreese, C. (2011). So What's Wrong with the EU? Motivations Underlying the Eurosceptic Vote in the 2009 European Elections. *European Union Politics, 12*(3), 405–429.

Van Wolleghem, P. G. (2014). Inclusive Political Community: The Challenge of Liberal Polities. In E. Codini & M. D'Odorico (Eds.), *Democracy and Citizenship in the 21st Century: Critical Issues and Perspectives* (pp. 23–38). Milan: McGraw-Hill Education.

Van Wolleghem, P. G. (2016). *Migrations and Policy Cycle in the UK: Overview of Recent Trends.* Fondazione ISMU, Working Paper series.

Van Wolleghem, P. G. (2017). Why Implement Without a Tangible Threat? The Effect of a Soft Instrument on National Migrant Integration Policies. *JCMS: Journal of Common Market Studies, 55*(5), 1127–1143.

Vanhercke, B. (2012). Social Policy at EU Level: From the Anti-poverty Programmes to Europe 2020. *European Social Observatory,* VC/2012/0658.

Velluti, S. (2007). What European Union Strategy for Integrating Migrants? The Role of OMC Soft Mechanisms in the Development of an EU Immigration Policy. *European Journal of Migration and Law, 9*(1), 53–82.

Vennesson, P. (2008). Case Studies and Process Tracing Theories and Practices. In D. Della Porta & M. Keating (Eds.), *Approaches and Methodologies in the Social Sciences: A Pluralist Perspective* (4th ed., pp. 223–239). Cambridge, NY: Cambridge University Press.

Vitorino, A. (2002a). *Closing Speech at the Conference on the Role of Civil Society in Promoting Integration, SPEECH/02/371.* Paper Presented, Brussels, 2002.

Vitorino, A. (2002b). Interview with Mr António Vitorino, European Commissioner for Justice and Home Affairs. *Immigration, Asylum and Social Integration, European Communities.*

Wallace, H. (1985). The Presidency of the Council of Ministers of the European Community: Tasks and Evolution. In C. O. Nuallain (Ed.), *The Presidency of the European Council of Ministers.* London: Routledge.

Wallace, W. (1983). Less than a Federation. More Than a Regime. The Community as a Political System. In H. Wallace & W. Wallace (Eds.), *Policy-Making in the European Community* (pp. 403–436). Oxford: Oxford University Press.

Walzer, M. (1983). *Spheres of Justice: A Defense of Pluralism and Equality.* New York: Basic Books.

Wischenbart, R. (1994). National Identity and Immigration in Austria— Historical Framework and Political Dispute. *West European Politics, 17*(2), 72–90.

Wren, A., & McElwain, K. M. (2009). Voters and Parties. In R. E. Goodin (Ed.), *The Oxford Handbook of Political Science.* New York: Oxford University Press. Available at http://www.oxfordhandbooks.com/view/10.1093/oxfordhb/9780199604456.001.0001/oxfordhb-9780199604456-e-019. Last Consulted March 22, 2016.

Ziller, J. (2009). Le Droit Au Séjour et à La Libre Circulation Dans l'Union Européenne, à La Lumière de La Jurisprudence et Du Traité de Lisbonne. In H. Bauer, P. Cruz Villalòn, and J. Iliopoulos-Strangas (Eds.), *The New Europeans—Migration and Integration in Europe.* Nomos Verlagsgesellschaft.

Zincone, G., Penninx, R., & Borkert, M. (2011). *Migration Policymaking in Europe: The Dynamics of Actors and Contexts in Past and Present.* Amsterdam: IMISCOE Research Series.

EU ACTS AND OTHER OFFICIAL DOCUMENTS

C. (2007). 3926 Final—European Commission (2007). *Commission Decision of 21/VIII/2007 Implementing Council Decision 2007/435/EC as Regards the Adoption of Strategic Guidelines for 2007 to 2013.*

C. (2008). 795—European Commission (2008). *Commission Decision of 5 March 2008 laying down rules for the implementation of Council Decision 2007/435/ EC establishing the European Fund for the Integration of third-country nationals for the period 2007 to 2013 as part of the General programme 'Solidarity and Management of Migration Flows' as regards Member States' management and control systems, the rules for administrative and financial management and the eligibility of expenditure on projects co-financed by the Fund.*

COM. (2000). 757 Final—European Commission (2000). *Communication from the Commission to the Council and the European Parliament on a Community Immigration Policy.*

COM. (2001). 387 Final—European Commission (2001). *Communication from the Commission to the Council and the European Parliament on an Open Method of Coordination for the Community Immigration Policy.*

COM. (2003). 336 Final—European Commission (2003). *Communication from the Commission on Immigration, Integration and Employment.*

COM. (2004). 101 Final/2—European Commission (2004). *Communication from the Commission to the Council and the European Parliament. Building our Common Future Policy Challenges and Budgetary Means of the Enlarged Union 2007–2013.*

COM. (2004). 487 Final—European Commission (2004). *Communication from the Commission to the Council and the European Parliament. Financial Perspectives 2007–2013.*

COM. (2004). 508 Final—European Commission (2004). *Communication from the Commission to the Council, the European Parliament, the European Economic and Social Committee and the Committee of the Regions. First Annual Report on Migration and Integration.*

COM. (2005). 123 Final—European Commission (2005). *Communication from the Commission to the Council and the European Parliament Establishing a Framework Programme on Solidarity and the Management of Migration Flows for the Period 2007–2013.*

COM. (2005). 389 Final—European Commission (2005). *Communication from the Commission to the Council, the European Parliament, the European Economic and Social Committee and the Committee of the Regions. A Common Agenda for Integration—Framework for the Integration of Third-Country Nationals.*

Council Decision 2004/927/EC. (2004). *Providing for Certain Areas Covered by Title IV of Part Three of the Treaty Establishing the European Community to Be Governed by the Procedure Laid down in Article 251 of That Treaty.*

Council Decision 2007/435/EC. (2007). *Establishing the European Fund for the Integration of Third-Country Nationals for the Period 2007 to 2013 as Part of the General Programme 'Solidarity and Management of Migration Flows.*

Council of the European Union 5578/06. (2006). *Note.*

Council of the European Union 6166/2/99. (1999). *Responsibilities of Council Bodies in the Field of Justice and Home Affairs Following Entry into Force of the Treaty of Amsterdam.*

Council of the European Union 6735/06 (2006). *Note.*

Council of the European Union 7214/06. (2006). *Note.*

Council of the European Union 8091/06. (2006). *Note.*

Council of the European Union 8373/1/06. (2006). *Note.*

Council of the European Union 8983/06. (2006). *Note.*

Council of the European Union 9028/06. (2006). *Note.*

Council of the European Union 9385/06. (2006). *Note.*

Council of the European Union 10432/06. (2006). *Revised Note.*

Council of the European Union 10865/06. (2006). *Outcome of Proceedings.*

Council of the European Union 12258/04. (2004). *Common Basic Principles for Immigrant Integration Policy in the European Union.*

Council of the European Union 12524/06. (2006) *Note.*

Council of the European Union 12802/05. (2005). *Outcome of Proceedings.*
Council of the European Union 12999/06. (2006). *Introductory Note.*
Council of the European Union 13407/06. (2006). *Note.*
Council of the European Union 14776/04. (2004). *Note.*
Council of the European Union 15434/04. (2004). *Information on the Ministerial Conferences of Groningen (9–11 November 2004) and of Rotterdam (6–7 July 2004).*
Danish EU Presidency. (2002). *Press Release: Informal Meeting of the Ministers in the Area of Justice and Home Affairs.*
European Commission. (1998). *Action Plan of the Council and the Commission on How Best to Implement the Provisions of the Treaty of Amsterdam on an Area of Freedom, Security and Justice.*
European Council. (1999). *Tampere European Council 15 and 16 October 1999, Presidency Conclusions.*
European Council. (2001). *European Council Meeting in Laeken 14 and 15 December 2001, Presidency Conclusions.*
European Council. (2002). *Seville European Council 21 and 22 June 2002, Presidency Conclusions.*
European Council. (2005). *The Hague Programme.*
European Council 11638/03. (2003). *Thessaloniki European Council 19 and 20 June 2003, Presidency Conclusions.*
European Council 15915/05. (2005). *Financial Perspective 2007–2013.*
European Court of Auditors. (2012). Do the European Integration Fund and European Refugee Fund Contribute Effectively to the Integration of Third-Country Nationals? (Luxembourg).
European Parliamentary Research Service. (2014). EU Funds for Asylum, Migration and Borders (European Parliament).
Irish EU Presidency. (2004). *Programme of the Irish Presidency.*
JHA Council. (1999). *Action Plan Of The Council And The Commission on How Best to Implement the Provisions of the Treaty of Amsterdam on an Area of Freedom, Security and Justice, 1999/C 19/01.*
JHA Council. (2002). *2455th Council Meeting, Luxembourg, 14/15 October 2002.*
JHA Council. (2004). *2618th Council Meeting, 19 November 2004, Brussels.*
Migrapol-Integration 4—European Commission. (2003). *Draft Summery Record of the 1st Meeting of the National Contact Points 24 March 2003.*
Migrapol-Integration 11—European Commission. (2003). *Draft Summery Record of the 2nd Meeting of the National Contact Points 18 July 2003.*
Migrapol-Integration 27—European Commission. (2004). *Draft Summary Record of the 6th Meeting of the National Contact Points 28 April 2004.*
Migrapol-Integration 33—European Commission. (2004). *Draft Summary Record of the 7th Meeting of the National Contact Points 7 July 2004.*
Migrapol-Integration 40—European Commission. (2004). *Draft Summary Record of the 9th Meeting of the National Contact Points October 2004.*

Migrapol-Integration 42—European Commission. (2004). *Discussion Paper on an Integration Fund (2007–2013)*.

Migrapol-Integration 43rev—European. Commission. (2004). *Draft Summary Record of the 10th Meeting of the National Contact Points on Integration, 14 December 2004.*

Migrapol-Integration 48—European Commission. (2005). *Discussion Paper on Assessing the Impact of the Integration Fund under the 2007–2013 Financial Perspectives.*

Migrapol-Integration 52—European Commission. (2005). *Draft Summary Record of the Extraordinary Meeting of the National Contact Points, 28 January 2005.*

SEC. (2005). 435 Final—European Commission (2005). *Commission Staff Working Document Annex to the General Programme Solidarity and Management of Migration Flows Extended Impact Assessment.*

SEC. (2005). 494 Final—European Commission (2005). *Commission Working Document Technical Adjustments to the Commission Proposal for the Multiannual Financial Framework 2007–2013.*

Index

© The Editor(s) (if applicable) and The Author(s) 2019
P. G. Van Wolleghem, *The EU's Policy on the Integration of Migrants*, Palgrave Studies in European Union Politics,
https://doi.org/10.1007/978-3-319-97682-2

Lightning Source UK Ltd.
Milton Keynes UK
UKHW01n0719101018
330306UK00010B/444/P